THE EVOLUTION OF IRISH NATIONALIST POLITICS

TOM GARVIN

Gill & Macmillan

Published by Gill & Macmillan Ltd
Hume Avenue, Park West, Dublin 12, Ireland
with associated companies throughout the world
www.gillmacmillan.ie

© Tom Garvin 1981
First published 1981
This edition published 2005

0 7171 3967 0
Index updated by Cover to Cover
Type design: Make Communication
Typesetting and print origination by Carrigboy Typesetting Services, Co. Cork
Printed and bound by Cox and Wyman, Reading, Berks

The paper used in this book is made from the wood pulp
of managed forests. For every tree felled, at least one tree
is planted, thereby renewing natural resources.

A catalogue record is available for this book from the
British Library.

5 4 3 2 1

CONTENTS

TABLES

FIGURES

IRELAND

**POLITICAL
and
ADMINISTRATIVE**

DONEGAL

Londonderry
(Derry)

ANTRIM

LONDONDERRY
(DERRY)

ULSTER

Belfast

TYRONE

DOWN

FERMANAGH

ARMAGH

Sligo

MONAGHAN

SLIGO

CAVAN

LEITRIM

LOUTH

MAYO

ROSCOMMON

MEATH

LONG-
FORD

CONNACHT

LEINSTER

GALWAY

WESTMEATH

DUB-
LIN

Galway

OFFALY (KING'S)

Dublin
Dun Laoghaire
(Kingstown)

KILDARE

LAOIS
(QUEEN'S)

CLARE

WICKLOW

KILKENNY

CAR-
LOW

Limerick

LIMERICK

TIPPERARY

WEXFORD

Waterford

MUNSTER

WATERFORD

KERRY

CORK

Cork

| 0 | | | | 50 |

miles

.... County boundaries

‒ ‒ ‒ ‒ ‒ ‒ Province boundaries

▬▬▬▬▬ Northern Ireland frontier

PREFACE

The structure of political action in the Irish Republic has fascinated me for many years, and my interest was further stimulated by the elementary observation that Irish political parties and ideological tendencies did not fit very comfortably into the stock categories of either ordinary political discourse or of comparative political science. This observation was scarcely original, but the usual reaction to it has been to classify Irish political affairs and habits as being hopelessly idiosyncratic, 'unique' and generally unlike such affairs and habits anywhere else. The literature on political development, on anti-colonial political movements and on quasi-religious political traditions convinced me that Ireland, far from being an oddity, was in many ways a classic example of the development of popular anti-colonial nationalism in a conquered country. Its peculiarities mainly derive from the fact that it was one of the first such cases, much as the oddities of the English Constitution derive in great part from the fact that England was the first true nation-state. Ireland was perhaps the first true colony of England, and therefore its tradition of anti-colonial nationalism may be one of the oldest in the world. I have therefore regarded the development of popular political culture prior to the mobilisation of the electorate in the early nineteenth century as a major explanatory factor in accounting for the structure of Irish political party systems since O'Connell. Essentially, I argue that the genealogy of modern Irish political culture and structures is far longer than some recent commentators have led us to believe, and that Irish nationalism has been a popular, as distinct from an elite, ideology for a very long time.

My intellectual debts are many, but the conclusions in this book are my responsibility. I would like to thank John Coakley, Art Cosgrove, Ronan Fanning, Brian Farrell, Michael Laffan, Bruce Logan, Art Mac Aonghusa, Peter Mair, Maurice Manning, the late

Conor Martin, Cormac Ó Grada, Diarmuid Ó Muirithe, Richard Sinnott and Breffni Tomlin, who have encouraged and otherwise helped me over the past few years in University College, Dublin. Eddie Buckmaster did the diagrams. John Baldock in London, Basil Chubb and Michael Gallagher in Trinity College, Dublin have been of considerable assistance, as has Colm McCarthy. I have benefited greatly from conversations and correspondence with R.K. Carty of the University of British Columbia, A.S. Cohan of the University of Lancaster and Andrew Orridge of the University of Birmingham. I owe much to the staffs of the Public Record Offices of London and Dublin, the State Paper Office, Dublin, the National Library of Ireland, the Archives Department, University College, Dublin and the Library, Trinity College, Dublin. Professors T.W. Moody and R.D. Edwards were helpful, as was Fintan Drury. Imelda Slattery typed an early draft. My father, John Garvin, read the text and gave me the benefit of his knowledge of Irish political, administrative and social lore. Hubert Mahony and Fergal Tobin of Gill & Macmillan prepared the text for publication. Lastly, I would like to thank my wife, Máire, who has helped me in innumerable ways and is certainly relieved that it is now finished before it finished us.

DUBLIN, AUGUST 1980
T.G.

These sentiments are imbibed, from Irish History, their own approved authors, and from their family traditions, which they rely on, more than all the writings, that could be produced . . . it is not Religion all together, that could be able to reconsile them, for the most ignorant of them, knows well, that it was the Pope of Rome, that encouraged Henry the second, to invade Ireland . . . and if it were not for Catholic Clergy they would keep no allegiance . . . anything contrary, is only dissimulation, and hypocrisy, or necessity, and Policy.

—INFORMER, 1821

'O mercy, sir!' the goat replied,
'And let me tell my story O
I am no rogue, no Ribbonman,
No Croppy, Whig or Tory O;
I'm guilty not of any crime
Of petty or high treason O,
And our tribe is wanted at this time,
For it is the milking season O.'

—THE PEELER AND THE GOAT, 1830s

It may, moreover, be observed that the Whiteboys have very retentive memories; that their *odia in longum recondita*, their ancient spites, are sometimes felt when their victims had for years lived in a false security. There seems to be no statute of limitation against Whiteboy vengeance; no prescription seems to give a title where the party has taken lands in contravention of the Whiteboy rules; and people are sometimes almost unable to find a motive for the punishment inflicted on them, so completely had the ground for complaint passed from their minds.

—GEORGE CORNEWALL LEWIS, 1836

Blackfeet and Whitefeet are said to have originated in a dispute between the owners of two horses—one of which had white, the other black feet. Each collected his own friends, who at length expanded into two political parties. They have private symbols, and their committees are sworn to secrecy. Both concur in their opposition to law and tithe; but disagreeing on some matters not generally known, variance continues to be perpetuated between them. These parties have faction-fights at fairs; and young men, such as respectable farmers, are their secret leaders.

—JONATHAN BINNS, 1837

Curse all Secret Societies!

—ATTRIB. EAMON DE VALERA, 1922

Fianna Fáil is a slightly constitutional party.

—SEÁN LEMASS, 1927

In Ireland there is one condition that is decidedly more frowned upon than being a bad Catholic, and that is the condition of being *anti-national*.

—CONOR CRUISE O'BRIEN, 1972

01 | IRISH PARTIES AND IRISH POLITICS

THE IRISH REPUBLIC: POST-COLONIAL POLITICS IN A WESTERN EUROPEAN STATE

The political parties of the Irish Republic are somewhat exotic entities. The country's party system, and its style of popular politics in general, are untypical of Western liberal democracies in many ways. The Republic is a Catholic country, but has no Communist Party of any size; it uses proportional representation, but has only three major political parties and has avoided the disintegrative effects associated with PR elsewhere; it is historically a poor country but has succeeded in achieving stable democratic political life; it is the inheritor of a long revolutionary tradition, but its parties defy attempts to arrange them in the usual left-to-right order.[1]

Not only do Irish parties defy conventional typologies, but the stability and peacefulness of the Irish state since 1923 contrast oddly with the incessant turmoil of the country's pre-independence history. The probable reasons for this anomaly are complex and need not be gone into here in any detail; obviously, the internal stability of the Republic is partly due to the country's exceptional ethnic and religious uniformity, to the role of the Catholic Church in social and political life, to the country's exceptional isolation and to economic stagnation coupled with emigration.

Democracy's survival in Ireland also owes much to certain institutional factors, however. In the first place, the new state inherited a well-developed administrative apparatus from the

British and started life with a large and well-trained corps of professional administrators. Secondly, the Catholic Church in Ireland was unusually fortunate in that it was a popular church with relatively few aristocratic allies and therefore had relatively little of an anti-democratic past to live down. Lastly, Irish political parties have succeeded in organising public opinion in support of the new state, thus heading off any large-scale hostility to that state and its institutions. The unusual ability of the post-independence politicians and party activists to build large and coherent cross-class political parties was crucial to the development of an ordered popular politics after 1922; it was possibly the main reason why democratic politics in Ireland did not disintegrate into instability and confusion, as happened in so many other new states. This organisational ability was, I shall argue, the product of an unusually long experience in building highly disciplined popular political organisations.

A general theme of this book, then, is the traditional character of mass politics in Ireland. Unlike many new states, the custom of electing leaders and the habit of mobilising everybody in the community for political action were deeply ingrained in the political culture. Another general theme of the book is the anti-colonial character of Irish popular politics, a feature which also makes the country unusual in Western Europe. An important source of confusion in interpreting the politics of the Republic is the habit of either treating the country as hopelessly unique or, at best, as a rather peculiar Western European country. The Republic is only a fringe member of the European group, as few of these countries have had extensive experience of external rule. Unlike most Western European countries, Ireland is, in a sense, a new country, and its state institutions are also unusually recent in origin by European standards. Other superficially comparable secession states in Europe such as Finland, Iceland or, perhaps, Norway were never submerged institutionally and culturally to the same extent.[2] Ireland cannot be easily slotted into the group of 'post-British' countries represented by the United States and the 'old' dominions any more than it can be included among the Western European group.[3] In these settler states, the aboriginal

populations had become insignificant, whereas in Ireland, outside
Ulster, the 'aboriginals' won, at the price of extensive assimilation
with the colonial invaders; modern Ireland is culturally hybrid
and represents a successful, if not totally harmonious, synthesis of
native and British cultural themes.

The rhetorical anti-imperialism of Irish politics after independence tended to obscure the fact that the institutions of the new
state were themselves in large part the product of the imperialists;
the Irish state machine is new, and its origins are colonial, not
native. The present-day Irish state is the direct descendant of the
British state in Ireland and, more distantly, it is the descendant
of the medieval kingdom of Ireland. It owes nothing to Gaelic
antecedents, an historical irony which is compounded by the
official myth of the Republic, which has asserted the state's
historical legitimacy as the successor state to a half-imaginary
Gaelic polity of the pre-conquest period.[4] The spuriousness of
this claim to continuity points to two central characteristics of
the Irish state: its newness and its need for legitimation. A joint
product of an emergent peasant people and of colonial administrators, its combination of traditional nationalist symbolism with
underlying newness is typical of many post-colonial states.

The party system is similarly post-colonial. The principal cleavage
does not divide right from left, as in most Western countries, nor
does it divide secular and confessionalist tendencies, although these
themes exist in subordinated and fragmented forms. Irish parties
are divided from each other over issues of national and cultural
identity, over relationships with the ex-imperial power and over
what might best be described as different strategies toward
national development. All of these divisions are softened by a
fundamental nationalist consensus from which few dissociate
themselves. All parties in the system are extremely pragmatic, a
pragmatism forced upon them by half a century of electoral
competition, and their organisational ancestry was a long one
even at the time of independence. All parties are the beneficiaries
of long traditions of quasi-military popular political organisation,
traditions which can be traced back to the middle of the
nineteenth century and even to the eighteenth.

Despite the system's resemblances to post-colonial systems else-where, there are, of course, important differences. In the first place, Irish experience of colonial rule came very early; if England was the first national state, then Ireland was the first colony of such a state. Also, the Irish experience of colonial rule was particularly long and, perhaps, particularly intense, dating as it did from the intrusion of the Tudor state into Gaelic and Old English tribal and feudal society in the sixteenth century. Thirdly, because it developed so early, ethnic identity in Ireland, whether Protestant or Catholic, became identified with religious affiliation rather than with the kinds of linguistic or racial distinction which were made popular by nationalist ideologues in the nineteenth century. These religion-based identities came to be guarded and perpetuated by well-organised Reformation and Counter-Reformation churches. Fourthly, the emergence of aggressive and large-scale political movements based on the lower classes occurred while the country was still pre-industrial and, in part, pre-commercial. Fifthly, the Irish case was unusual because the country was physically close to the empire's centre, a fact which prompted the attempt to convert it from a colony with a separate administrative and political identity to an integrated periphery of the imperial state itself. Lastly, the nationalist political leaders—and also the anti-nationalist political leaders—were permitted a foothold inside the imperial parliament itself instead of being either suppressed or isolated in a separate colonial assembly; Ireland became part of British domestic politics after 1800.

Despite these idiosyncracies, it is appropriate to view Irish political development as an evolution from colonial to independent status. In the twentieth century, the internal politics of countries which have undergone such an evolution are usually characterised by large-scale mobilisation of the public through parties or through substitutes for parties such as churches, conspiracies, armies or even sporting associations. Where elections are allowed and offer some prospect of a share in political power, a common outcome is the entry into the political arena of the middle and poorer sections and the breaking of the political monopoly of the traditional aristocracy. This development is often accompanied by the penetration of political organisation into the countryside and the mobilisation of the rural classes. The typical popular electoral movement unites urban middle- or working-class leaders with an increasingly humble and rural following. The typical ideology is nationalist, usually with a heavy admixture of traditional religious sentiment, populism and, in more recent cases, socialism.[5]

This mobilisation of the countryside for politics is often sudden and dramatic. The 'Green Uprising', as Huntington calls it, has usually been more important in countries which developed popular politics in the twentieth century and which achieved independence since 1945 than in those European and European-settled countries which received independence before 1918. In these older political systems, industrialisation and commercialisation had usually proceeded far enough to ensure the social and political dominance of the city over the countryside and popular radicalism was usually channelled into socialist and trade union-based parties. In underdeveloped countries of the mid-twentieth century, however, the mobilisation of the countryside has been important and often decisive, the form it took shaping the form of subsequent popular politics; typically, urban politicians became the leaders of rural-based political parties. If popular government was established, it tended to be supported by rural groups, and radical opposition tended to be centred in the towns. Even if political and property relations in the countryside are relatively egalitarian, it is a long time before government feels constrained to make concessions to town groups; in political systems which have experienced a 'Green Uprising', the countryside dominates national politics for a long time.[6] The United States was unusual among 'early modernisers' in experiencing a significant 'Green Uprising' in the nineteenth century, and this was the underlying reason for the absence of socialist politics on a mass scale there. The same explanation for a similar absence could be used for nationalist Ireland.

This summary calls to mind much of the development of popular politics in nationalist Ireland after 1790. In Ireland, the 'Green Uprising' had several phases and was preceded by a long period in which urban-based radicalism filtered out into the countryside and by an even longer period of endemic agrarian unrest. The first phase of the 'Green Uprising' was represented by the series of mass movements led by Daniel O'Connell between 1823 and 1847. During this period, the farmers and peasantry were mobilised under clerical and middle-class leadership against the Anglo-Irish aristocracy for the first time. The decisive phase of the 'Green Uprising' was the series of great agrarian-nationalist campaigns which began in 1879. O'Connell's campaigns and the later ones all benefited from and were heavily influenced by a tradition of militant proto-political organisation, popular and conspiratorial in character, which was already old in 1823. The effect of the open political campaigns was to spread a traditional form of political organisation over the country and through all social classes. Before 1790, popular political organisations had been secretive and small scale, and generally confined to the towns of the eastern littoral, while peasant organisation in inland areas was pre-political; by 1890, popular political organisation dominated the entire countryside. After independence in 1922, this pattern was re-echoed. Acceptance of the Anglo-Irish Treaty was more immediate in the long-mobilised east than in the more recently mobilised west and in the towns than in the countryside. Between 1922 and 1933 a final phase of the 'Green Uprising' occurred and was marked by the ascent to power of the nationalist-populist party of Eamon de Valera, Fianna Fáil, a party which was, classically, led by urban nationalists but supported most fervently by poorer rural and small-town voters.

This mobilisation of rural and humble support behind the anti-colonial movement also has the effect of strengthening some traditionalist forces and social values associated with rural society, often to the chagrin of the more advanced nationalist or socialist ideologues. A general, if usually partial, retreat from secular to sacred values occurs and is reflected in the rhetoric and policies of the political leaders. The popular acceptability of the post-independence regime itself comes to depend to an important extent on the degree to which it can be seen as being loyal to traditional values. Typically, there are attempts to create a continuity with traditional religious values or with the symbols of pre-conquest society.[7] Loyalty to a real or mythical past and respect for religion and tradition become politically important after independence, particularly in the electorally crucial areas; rural disaffection is more dangerous to the regime than urban unrest, and to be surrounded by a hostile countryside is the most dangerous circumstance any government can be in.[8]

POLITICAL CULTURE AND POLITICAL ORGANISATION

Four aspects of Irish political development receive particular attention in this book. These aspects are the origins of Irish political culture, the development of popular political organisation, the growth of 'public opinion' and lastly, the development of the machinery of the state. As the organisation of the argument is essentially chronological, these aspects are treated together for each period, only the development of the state apparatus receiving a separate chapter to itself.

Political culture is the psychological dimension of the political system and consists of the 'attitudes, beliefs, values and skills' which are current in a political community.[9] It is learned, either informally through parents and peers or through formal secondary institutions such as schools and churches. In rural societies, and in pre-literate societies in particular, political culture can be expected to 'breed true' over the generations, given the perennial character of many of the problems of such societies and the continuing validity of traditional solutions. Political culture can also be recreated by the individual as he acquires direct experience of the political life of his community. It is perhaps most usefully thought of as the 'memory' of the political system.[10]

The standard sketches of Irish political culture suggest that it is 'village' if not still 'peasant' in character, conformist, pragmatic, loyal and authoritarian.[11] These descriptions are not inaccurate, but do not sufficiently emphasise a wider cultural trait, that of *communal solidarity*. This tradition of solidarity generates pragmatism within a conformist consensus and has made possible the extraordinary discipline and monolithism of the major Irish political parties during their most successful phases. This cultural reflex of deferring to symbols and values thought to be connected

with the community's well-being and preservation has its roots
in a tradition of militant cultural and community defence which
goes back to the eighteenth century. Irish popular nationalism also
derives much of its extraordinary endurance, imperviousness to
outside criticism and dislike of internal disagreement from this
tradition; it is not for nothing that the 'split' is the original sin of
Irish politics, and it is also no coincidence that splits, when they
do occur, tend to become incurable as two or more rival solidarities are erected, each side pronouncing anathemas on the other.

A second general theme is the development of the militant,
pragmatic, disciplined mass *political party* as the characteristic
Irish political institution. Irish people have shown considerable
aptitude for the construction of large and flexible political
organisations involving large numbers of people. I suggest in later
chapters that the connections between the development of political
parties in nationalist Ireland and pre-existing 'paramilitary'
organisations of local defence are very strong.

A third and closely related theme is that *of public opinion*, in
particular the development of nationalism as the dominant
ideology of Irish Catholics in the nineteenth century. I will argue
that Irish nationalism has older roots than is sometimes suggested
and that it is a blend of religious communalism, a particularism
due to the traditional geographical and political separateness of
the country, class discontents and certain residual but vigorous
tribal and feudal traditions dating back to the seventeenth century
or even earlier. These older sources of a sense of separateness
harmonised well with the growth of class-based separatisms in the
towns in the late eighteenth century.

Lastly, I deal with the growth of the *state machine*. This
apparatus, a product of nineteenth-century modernisers, was
centralised and efficient by the standards of the period and
contrasted strangely with the ramshackle governmental apparatus
of eighteenth-century Ireland. Prior to 1800, the country was
scarcely governed at all; there was no true police force, no
equivalent of the English parochial welfare system, no recognised
educational system for Catholics, no security of tenure and, most
importantly, no physical means, such as a well-developed military

force, by which the government could perform its most primitive Hobbesian task of guaranteeing the physical safety of all groups. The absence of an army meant social peace in England; in Ireland it meant that no community was free from fear. By way of contrast, after the extraordinary state-building efforts of the nineteenth century, Ireland was governed by a centralised, 'rational-bureaucratic' state apparatus which was a distinctly modern political institution. Resented by the declining aristocracy because it took power from its hands and by the rising populist nationalists because it was unresponsive to their wishes, the Victorian Irish state was of doubtful popularity but of enormous political and social importance.

GEOGRAPHY, ECONOMICS AND METHOD

My concern is with the development of popular political organisations in nationalist Ireland, that is, the mainly Catholic Ireland which claims to be the inheritor of the pre-Reformation tradition. The internal dynamics of Ulster unionism are treated only in so far as they have a direct impact on the politics of nationalist Ireland. Nationalist leaders rarely faced up to the mutual fear that existed between Catholic and Protestant and tended to define the problem out of existence. Many of them, perhaps because they subconsciously knew that there was little they could do about popular unionism, simply ignored it. In 1825, O'Connell admitted that he had never been in seven of the nine counties of Ulster and had visited two fringe counties of the province on exactly one occasion.[12] From the time of Tone on, advanced nationalists tended to dismiss Ulster Protestant hostility to Catholics and to any Catholic-dominated separatism; less advanced, or more hard-headed, nationalists took up a frankly anti-Protestant stance, in line with the traditional popular sectarianism of previous centuries. Long before partition was mooted, nationalist politicians seem to have been subconsciously or covertly partitionist in their behaviour if not in their rhetoric. At local level the sectarianism was sometimes quite straightforward; 1798 was really the only genuine attempt at inter-confessional nationalist radicalism, and its collapse had been complete.

The book focuses on institutions and culture rather than on economics or property relations. Social class and the memory of previous class systems are, of course, assumed to be important determinants of political action. However, the shaping and conditioning effects of property relations and the indirect but profound impact of the physical environment are seen as being refracted through the cultural system and the social institutions of the society. Geography and economics are, however, seen as being very important. Geographically, Ireland, like ancient Gaul, can be divided into three regions: the north, the east and south, and the west. The northern province of Ulster, and in particular its eastern half, is the only part of Ireland where a large and unassimilable Protestant colony of British origin survived and prospered. In Ulster, a relative security of tenure existed and there was a relatively easy relationship between landlord and tenant. Ulster tenantry engaged in small-scale industrial production in the late eighteenth century, and Ulster participated in the British industrial revolution.

Outside Ulster, a different land system existed. Estates were larger, in many cases gigantic, society was in large part pre-commercial and the main response to the industrial revolution was the development of a commercialised pastoral agriculture geared to the British market. The tenantry were separated from their lords by religion and language and the legal system attempted to enforce a caste-like system of sectarian subordination. While these laws were not completely enforced, they were effective enough to prevent the building up of property in Catholic hands and to distort the growth of a Catholic middle class. It also silenced the expression of Catholic political sentiment in the public arena for a century. Catholic political sentiment appears to have consisted of a clinging to the old religion and to Jacobite loyalties, mingled with millenarian notions of eventually reversing the relationships between the religious communities. Gaelic peasant culture in particular preserved such sentiments, or at least their rhetoric, intact into the nineteenth century.

The landholding system in what was to become nationalist Ireland prevented the development of any considerable non-agricultural petty commodity production in the eighteenth century; land remained the sole source of wealth for most and social hierarchy was based almost totally on title to land, such title being dependent on religion. Catholic and Protestant middle classes did develop in the towns of the east and south but there was virtually no industrial bourgeoisie unconnected with agricultural production. In eastern and southern areas, where land was superior and more accessible, extensive stock-rearing farms developed in the eighteenth century. Attempts were made by the new commercial cattle farmers, often Catholic by religion, to clear the mainly Catholic peasantry from the land. In many areas, these attempts were resisted with considerable success and with considerable violence. In many places, clearances never took place.[13] Subsistence agriculture, extreme subdivision of holdings and increasing population pressure on the soil developed, and by 1800 a large proportion of the population, particularly in the uncleared western regions, was completely dependent on the potato. Even before then, 'a grim pattern was established, lasting until the twentieth century, whereby the density of the Irish rural population was in inverse proportion to the quality of the land on which it was settled'.[14] In the more fertile east and south, cattle-ranching, involving the employment of a rural proletariat, developed, whereas elsewhere a poverty-stricken subsistence tenantry farmed in primitive conditions. The 'east-west gradient' of Erhard Rumpf was the main conditioning factor, distance from the eastern littoral corresponding to increased rurality, poverty and inaccessibility, decreased access to urban or anglicised culture, stronger survival of Gaelic, clan or feudal loyalties and of other characteristics associated with pre-Cromwellian Ireland.

Besides these three large regions, several other subdivisions should be mentioned. Belfast, the centre of Protestant Ulster, developed in the nineteenth century as the island's only industrial city. Dublin, the cultural and administrative centre of the island, became the centre of an extensive communications network as early as the 1780s. Dublin's east coast position was the natural site for any would-be ruler of the island. Even the Gaelic polity had acknowledged the primacy of the area; Tara, symbolic centre of pre-conquest Ireland, is only twenty-five miles from Dublin and the medieval Pale of Dublin coincided substantially with the pre-conquest royal province of Meath (*Midhe* = middle, centre). Another important region was the borderland between Catholic Ireland and Protestant Ulster. The 'shatterbelt' is, or was historically, more extensive than the present-day Northern Ireland frontier would indicate. It included those areas on the fringe of Ulster where both religious groups had significant demographic strength, together with those areas on either side which saw themselves as being vulnerable to attack or colonisation. The early Catholic political society known as the Defenders, and its successor organisation the Ribbonmen, were strongest in this wide belt of territory.

In this book, the following regional divisions are used: *centre*, consisting of Dublin City, County and the present-day Dún Laoghaire County Borough; *heartland*, or the great agrarian provinces of Leinster and Munster, exclusive of Dublin and Louth in Leinster and Kerry and Clare in western Munster; *western periphery*, or the western province of Connacht together with Clare and Kerry; *border periphery*, consisting of the frontier counties of the post-1922 Irish state in Ulster plus Louth and, of course, *Unionist Ulster*, or the six counties which successfully resisted independence and which have had, historically, Protestant majorities or near-majorities. The term *Nationalist Ireland* shall be used to refer to the southern, western and eastern areas which became independent in 1922 and which coincide with the first four of the five regions stipulated above. The scheme is, of course, a simplification; the real pattern is one of physical, religious, economic and cultural gradients rather than one of neatly defined regions. For example, since the seventeenth century the religious gradient in Ireland has run from north-east to south-west, Protestants becoming fewer as the south-west is approached. Again, the linguistic gradient has run more or less due east and west, the Irish language surviving longer in the west. Agriculturally, the gradient runs from south-east to north-west, the latter quadrant of the island being less fertile. The line between the two periphery regions and the heartland corresponds closely to that between the big-farm and small-farm regions.

There is no doubt that the failure of the Irish rural economy outside Ulster to respond to the industrial revolution had much to do with the emergence of nationalist feeling. However, the economic changes of the late eighteenth century did not create a new identity; rather, they revitalised an old sense of identity which was shared by most Catholics. Another major problem with economistic arguments is the fact that although the economic exploitation of Ireland was indeed an important motivation for the seventeenth-century conquest, the British government's real concern with Ireland was political and strategic rather than economic; both the economic development of Ireland and the appeasement of the general population were subordinated to the security concerns of the British government. Ireland's importance as a potential bridgehead for an invasion of Britain by a continental power was paramount; having achieved a secure Ireland after 1690, London forgot about it. Despite the undoubted—and inefficient—exploitation of the local population and despite some confused legislation in restraint of Irish trade, the primacy of political over economic considerations appears evident. Even the emphasis on religious issues apparent in British policy drew much of its force from a fear of Catholicism as an international political organisation actually or potentially hostile to the English post-revolutionary political settlement. It is evident that religion was central to Anglo-Irish relations because religion was the basis of *English* national political integration in the seventeenth century: Catholics in seventeenth-century Britain or Ireland were politically unassimilable because the British Constitution was profoundly sectarian. Ironically, this fact ensured that religion became the basis of the political integration of the Irish nationalist community as well; religious passions were laid on top of an older sense of difference. The confessional basis of Irish ethnic identity was unwittingly derived from the religious basis of the English national revolution of the sixteenth and seventeenth centuries.[15]

The modernisation of the Irish Catholic community in the nineteenth century took place to a great extent under the sometimes reluctant tutelage of the Catholic Church. The Church's role was only too likely to be seen as counter-revolutionary, as indeed it was seen in terms of the English revolution. In terms of the Irish revolution, its role was interpreted in more ambiguous terms; the real irony of Irish political development was that the Church found itself forced to provide the social leadership for the pursuit of economic and political objectives not generically different from those of the English and French revolutions.[16] Simple economic interest underlay some nationalist sentiment, but sentiments such as the wish for land reform or for protection against British imports were consistently used by political leaders as fuel for the furtherance of a general nationalist cause. The community was integrated at quite an early date around a confessional and nationalist consensus, and particular economic sections found themselves constrained by the same culture of communal solidarity that constrained all other potential dissenters.

The plan of this book is quite simple. A series of chapters gives an account of the development of popular political organisations from the 1760s onward. Where possible, the local structure of these organisations is analysed and an effort is made to assess the social backgrounds of the activists. It is suggested that these 'primitive rebels' or 'primitive politicians' encountered a peasant culture with strong traditions of dislike of outsiders and of the Ascendancy and which also had strong traditions of local defence against landlord, clerical or state exaction. A well-developed prim- itive nationalist consciousness based on cultural and religious differences also existed. From this point of view, I argue that what constitutional politicians like O'Connell or Parnell were trying to do was not really all that different from what non-constitutional leaders like Tone or James Stephens were trying to do, as both types of leader were trying to blend local ideological traditions with modern political ideas, whether constitutional or revolu- tionary. Eventually, under Davitt and Parnell an extraordinary synthesis was achieved: the missionary efforts of activists and the growth of popular literacy combined to generate an explosive popular mobilisation which combined constitutional and revo- lutionary traditions in one mass movement, the Land League of 1879. This popular desire for radical reform was not new; as early as the 1790s, the leaders of the revolutionary United Irish Society had perceived that the peasantry were ripe for politicisation.[17] By 1900, this process of missionary conversion was complete and a blending of traditional sentiment with modern forms of political organisation had occurred, forming an unmistakably modern political culture. The last chapters of the book deal with the achievement of independence and with the structure of popular politics after 1922. In particular, an attempt is made to link the new political organisations of the post-1922 period with those which had gone before and to assess the relationship between the new political parties and state machine, a relationship which had no real precedent. A final chapter offers some comparative perspectives.

02 | THE ORIGINS OF IRISH POPULAR POLITICS

ROOTS OF IRISH POPULAR NATIONALISM

Irish separatist nationalism as a popular political creed originated in the towns in the late eighteenth century and it penetrated the popular consciousness rather slowly during the nineteenth century. However, an Irish nationalist consciousness of some sort is possibly primordial, and certainly dates back to the seventeenth century. Furthermore, modern Irish nationalism of the nineteenth and twentieth centuries bears clear traces of this pre-modern ancestry. It is necessary to make these perhaps elementary points because so much of recent writing has tended to present this popular ideology solely as a nineteenth-century product. Our particular concern is with the development of separatist nationalism among Catholics, but it should be remembered that a nationalism grew up among the Anglican and Dissenter communities in the eighteenth century, becoming stronger as these groups perceived the Catholic threat to be receding and shrinking as that threat was perceived to be growing again. The contributions made by Anglican parliamentary nationalism and Presbyterian radicalism to the mainly Catholic nationalism of the nineteenth century were important, but the real emotional taproot of Catholic nationalism was not in either of these traditions but in the political and social defeat of the Catholic landed aristocracy in the seventeenth century and the subsequent subordination of the Catholic community after 1690.

As early as 1593 a Kildare man had had his ears cut off for prophesying that an O'Donnell would one day be king of Ireland. The Catholic rebels of 1641 were similarly informed in their actions by popular political prophecies of this kind; the rebels' popular political ideology was a mixture of loyalty to the Stuart dynasty, hostility to the British settlers, religious hatred and a confused incipient separatism.[1] Common themes in Irish-language political poetry were rage at the invaders, the older glories of Ireland, contempt for the new English and expressions of feudal and Stuart loyalties. In 1645, a pamphlet written by a Cork Jesuit living in Lisbon was circulated in Ireland and was fervently denounced from the pulpits. It argued that the conditions laid down in the famous bull of Adrian IV which had ceded Ireland to Henry II had now been broken, that Ireland was released from its allegiance to the English crown and recommended that the Catholic Irish elect a Catholic king from among their own nobility. The writer drew an explicit parallel with the recent reassertion of Portuguese independence from Spain.[2] Among the Catholic aristocracy of the period, any natural political particularism was likely to develop into outright disaffection as the English revolution progressed and as parliament encroached on what had been regarded as the prerogatives of monarch, nobility or Church. After the final defeat of the Stuart cause in 1690, one Catholic aristocrat of Gaelic origin, Charles O'Kelly, recorded his sentiments. His political perspective was clearly religious and counter-revolutionary, but also had strong proto-nationalist undertones. Because of the completeness of the defeat and the final character of England's estrangement from Rome and the Stuarts, O'Kelly was willing to question the entire legal basis of English rule in Ireland, and even went so far as to claim that the invasion of Henry II had been a usurpation in terms of international law. Rather ingeniously, he put forward an argument which was to be popular among nationalist apologists two centuries later: he argued that the bull, even if it were not an English forgery, which he strongly suspected, could not have granted Ireland to the crown, as Ireland had never been part of the Roman Empire. Therefore, Ireland could not have been transferred legally to the Pope under the provisions of the (supposedly genuine) Donation of Constantine which had supposedly granted the territories of the Western Empire to the Pontiff.[3] O'Kelly's virtually separatist ideas may or may not have been commonplace among Catholic gentry of the period, but they were certainly well elaborated, and he was very willing to seize on historical and legal arguments which undermined the legitimacy of the English link. Another, perhaps more typical, Jacobite writer who wrote around 1711 had a generally royalist but non-separatist outlook and concentrated his attacks on the Cromwellian and 1688 revolutions.[4]

Counter-revolutionary and Jacobite political sentiments of a rather rhetorical kind persisted in Ireland among the Catholic minor gentry, middle classes and peasantry through the eighteenth and early nineteenth centuries. While popular Jacobitism was wildly sentimental and unrelated to the real, mainly agrarian, concerns of the peasantry, the significant fact is that no similar popular rhetoric of loyalty to the Hanoverian dynasty appears to have existed among Catholics. *Aisling* poetry in the Irish language lamented the decline of Gaelic and Catholic power and represented Ireland as a beautiful woman in Saxon captivity, mourning her Jacobite champions and hoping for assistance from the Catholic monarchs of France and Spain.[5] Generations after the shipwreck of the Stuart cause, itinerant poets kept a curiously aristocratic political creed alive and helped to retard the development of any wholehearted acceptance of the new order. Legal discrimination against Catholics, the hostility and contempt of many of the ruling caste for the religion and culture of the defeated Catholics, an intensely exploitative land system, Counter-Reformation Catholicism and residual feudal loyalties all reinforced each other and assisted the growth of a diffuse, anti-Protestant and anti-English popular nationalism. This originally counter-revolutionary and often conservative tradition became the central ingredient in Irish Catholic political culture, underground and in the Irish language in the eighteenth century, and gradually coming into the open in the nineteenth.

Of course, the exact dimensions of this folk mentality or popular ideology are impossible to assess at this late date. It seems that among sections of the peasantry, the belief or vague hope persisted that the seventeenth-century confiscations were illegitimate and would one day be reversed, poetry and prophecy being used to bolster these hopes. These aspirations may not have always been held with great conviction, but they were certainly widespread and quite concrete in quality. Arthur Young, writing in 1780, reported that some of the peasants he had encountered regarded themselves as the descendants and rightful heirs of the old families who had once possessed the land. He also claimed that landless labourers sometimes solemnly bequeathed their masters' estates to their own sons. Young may have been the victim of a leg-pull, but the joke must have been half in earnest; there is abundant evidence for the persistence of a belief that the land settlement of the seventeenth century was somehow illegitimate.[6]

Ideas of a potentially subversive nature, therefore, ran through much of the Gaelic written and oral tradition in the period 1700 to 1850. The tradition was a popular one, and was spread around the island by a class of itinerant bards, teachers and storytellers, most of them literate and acting as entertainers, teachers, political instructors and news-bringers to an illiterate but receptive population. In parts of Munster, the poets' and storytellers' custom of reading aloud from Irish-language manuscripts actually persisted up to the 1860s.[7] Crofton Croker described these 'poor scholars' in the 1820s as wandering around Ireland and setting themselves up as schoolmasters in particular localities. Their political ideas consisted of an historicist nationalism, a hatred of the seventeenth-century settlement and an antagonism to the legal authorities.[8] The members of this ragamuffin intelligentsia were clever enough to dissimulate: if some representative of landed or state authority were present, treasonable sentiments would not be uttered and would be replaced by some appeal to theories of civil rights. At an even humbler level, the popular ballad tradition displayed a similar two-facedness; bilingual ballads existed, in which Irish and English verses alternated, the English verses expressing impeccably loyal sentiments while the Irish verses expressed satirical or subversive political opinions. Sometimes an innocent-sounding title on a broadsheet would preside over a dozen verses of ferocious sectarian or political invective. In the Gaelic tradition, a similar custom existed of addressing Ireland as a young woman in distress so as to conceal the political content of the poem. In the case of the best of these poems, *A Roisin Dubh*, patriotism and sexual love became fused together with great dramatic and emotional effect.

Hedge schoolmasters occasionally acted as scriveners for local secret societies. As learned men, they acted as arbiters in the internal disputes of these groups and were involved in the doings of the Whiteboy, Rockite and Ribbon gangs of the eighteenth and early nineteenth centuries. The 'little tradition' of peasant political sentiment existed in both the languages of Ireland, and made the transition from Gaelic to English quite easily. In one piece of English-language doggerel captured from secret society men in Tipperary in 1816, the influence of Irish-language assonance and metre is quite noticeable. The 'poem', written in a pretentious pidgin English, uses half-understood long words, prophesies the fall of 'Lutheranism' and savagely denounces 'the Gentry of this Place' who were, of course, of 'curst Cromwell's race'. The local magistrate is described as a terrible tyrant who

... surpasses Dioclesian, or Nero's Cruelty;
He is daily meditating to vitiate our Nation,
From every Consolation, so superciliously ...[9]

One schoolmaster whose Irish-language diary has survived has supplied us with a clear statement of his political views. Amhlaoibh Ó Súilleabháin, a Kerryman, was a teacher in Kilkenny in the 1820s and early 1830s. He lamented the replacement of Irish by English, looked in horror at the English-language circulating libraries that were spreading in Leinster and complained about the 'English debt' which King William had imposed to maintain the 'foreign religion'. For O Suilleabhain, Ulster Protestants were foreigners, but farmers, artisans, shopkeepers and merchants were good people who helped the poor. Landlords were evil men who gave little to the poor because they were too busy disporting themselves abroad with their ill-gotten gains. During the tithe campaign, he gave political speeches in Irish in which he rehearsed, in what was even then a time-honoured fashion, the 'Seven Hundred Years of

Slavery' version of Irish history. He advised Irish Catholics to stick together and to defeat the aristocracy by electing O'Connellite MPs.[10]

Another peasant poet, Anthony Raftery, a Mayoman whose poetry, or poetry of his period and area ascribed to him, survived mainly in oral form until it was written down in the later part of the century, was very popular in Connacht in the 1820s. His poems express the usual historicist nationalist sentiments; although the Catholic Gael has been crushed since Tudor times, Pastorini has prophesied the fall of the heretics, informers and Orangemen will be cast down, the Saxons who ignore the laws of God and Patrick shall be defeated and the Ribbonmen shall be repaid for their efforts in rent-free land. Raftery was also traditionally accredited with giving the Ribbonmen rather more moderate political advice than the millenarian tone of his poetry might suggest. He praised O'Connell's constitutionalism and reportedly advised the 'nightwalkers' to give up nocturnal conspiracy and take up legal agitation for civil rights.[11]

Most of this pervasive underground tradition was invisible to the English-speaking social and political commentators of the time and later. Even when it was pointed out, it tended to be dismissed because of its crudity and because it represented the efforts at political thought of poor and badly educated men. The tradition had very practical consequences; it survived the linguistic transition to the English language and was used to legitimise attempts to subvert the Ascendancy and the legal authorities. The memory or pseudo-memory of the seventeenth-century confiscations was perhaps particularly persistent; as late as the 1890s, Diarmuid (Jeremiah) O'Donovan Rossa, the famous Fenian bomber, proudly noted that the 'Rossa' attached to his name was a reminder in his family of lands in Cork which folk memory told them had been taken from their ancestors. Inability to accept defeat, pride in aboriginal descent, contempt for the reformed religion and a perception of the Ascendancy or even Protestants in general as being interlopers were other characteristics of this popular ideology.[12] Until quite late on, religion and nationality were equated: *Sasanach* meant both an Englishman and an Anglican, while *Albanach* meant both a Scot and a Dissenter.

The potentially subversive nature of peasant political ideas has begun, rather belatedly, to be recognised and documented elsewhere. Scott has ascribed their subversive potential to the fact that the peasantry is everywhere an 'old pre-capitalist class' and is not open to outside political ideas. The 'great tradition' of the towns is resisted by the 'little tradition' of the villages and the countryside and an historical hostility to government and to city-based authority is perhaps universal among peasant societies. Scott sees the religious and nationalist myths of the folk culture as being analogous to the class ideologies of urban societies and, because of the localism of peasant society, it is usual to settle disputes internally and to avoid calling in outside authority. Outsiders, unless they make special efforts to win the trust of the countrymen, will be seen as alien. Much of this 'diffuse oppositionism' is not, however, explicitly organised, but is expressed informally through the 'folksongs, proverbs, humor, popular theater and folktales' of country people.[13]

Because of localism, peasant insurrections in Europe before 1800, despite some political content, were usually reactions to outside encroachments such as attempts at clearances or increased exactions by church and state in the form of demands for recruits, taxes or tithes. Peasant political goals were usually restorationist rather than revolutionary, and they were not usually capable of acting out their political ideas on a large scale unless they were helped by non-peasant elements, whether aristocratic or town based.[14] This dependence on outside elements was characteristic of Irish countrymen too, and the political organisation of Irish peasants and farmers was eventually achieved by an alliance of the country people with non-peasant groups such as shopkeepers and tradesmen engaged in commerce with the rural communities, clergy, artisans and urban bourgeoisie.

THE BEGINNINGS OF URBAN RADICAL POLITICAL ORGANISATION, 1750–1800

Because of (or despite) the exclusion of Catholics and Dissenters, the eighteenth-century Irish political system was scarcely an harmonious political organism. Dissenters were excluded from political power to almost the same extent as Catholics and office was monopolised by a small group of Anglican landowners. So total was the hold of this group on parliament and on the apparatus of state that it came to identify itself with the Irish nation and its interests. So complete was the eclipse of Catholicism that the Ascendancy felt self-confident enough to consider loosening the link with Britain and to press for the elimination of London's measures of discrimination against Irish trade. Under the pressure of the American Revolution, Westminster eventually conceded legislative independence to the Dublin parliament and lifted most of the trade restrictions. However, this 'Constitution of 1782' was faulty and unstable. Executive power remained in the hands of the London-appointed viceroy and to achieve the co-operation of parliament, the government used patronage on an enormous scale. This compounded the distortions generated by a rotten borough system, a franchise which—though quite wide in property terms —excluded Catholics up to 1793, and the continued exclusion of Dissenters and Catholics from important political office. This essentially colonial political system underwent a classic decoloni- sation process, rather similar to that which the American colonies had experienced. Groups excluded from the constitution pressed for inclusion, and in particular commercial interests challenged the political monopoly of the landed interest. A voluntary militia, the Irish Volunteers, sprang up and was used by radical groups as a vehicle for articulating reformist and even nationalist demands. Although mainly Protestant, the Volunteers included many Dissenters, and even Catholics were known to have been allowed to join, despite the prohibition on Catholics bearing arms. Later in the 1780s, radical groups armed considerable numbers of Catholics in imitation of the Volunteers.

Under the 'Constitution of 1782', the executive tended to represent the imperial interest as it had done in the American colonies before 1776, and local or 'patriot' interests tended to be represented in parliament on the anti-government benches. However, in the American version of this court versus country polarisation, the colonial assemblies, representing popular, landed and business interests, were able to undermine the executive by bypassing it, encroaching on its legal powers and by the use of bribery. In Ireland, however, the reverse process occurred; the executive corrupted and bypassed the legislature. Because of Ireland's importance to Britain's security, the process of decolonisation was never permitted to reach a logical terminus of separation under Ascendancy or more widely based rule.

The second half of the eighteenth century saw the development of a large number of popular organisations displacing the older guilds, and recognisably the prototypes of the trade unions, friendly societies, conspiracies and political parties of the following century. In the towns, combinations of artisans bent on restricting entry into trade and maintaining existing rates of pay grew up. Those in Dublin dated from the 1750s, and their activities provoked the passing of an act prohibiting trade combinations in 1780.[15] By the 1770s, Dublin journeymen had regularly elected committees, levied fees on members *in terrorem* and prevented the employment of non-Dublin journeymen.[16] Much of the intensity of Dublin combinations and of similar societies in the other towns was due to the increasing pressure of British economic competition under what were effectively free trade conditions, and also to the over-availability of labour. The notion of tariff protection had an obvious appeal to sections of the Dublin bourgeoisie and artisanate. All classes dependent on the cloth and silk-weaving industries were under particular pressure. The weavers of the Dublin Liberties became a conspicuous element in the Dublin mob in the early 1780s and rioted in favour of protection in 1784. Later they were to give noisy support to republican rhetoric and to the United Irishmen.[17]

Similar dislocation due to British economic development occurred in Ulster, and pressure for political participation and for political solutions to economic problems was not confined to the unpropertied population there either. Like the Dublin middle-class groups, a growing Ulster Dissenter bourgeoisie became increasingly attracted to radical political schemes. The outbreak of the French Revolution accelerated the growth of radical political ideas in the towns, much as it did at the same time in England. By 1790, republicanism was making headway among the Dublin proletariat and Drennan was able to describe Napper Tandy, a prosperous woollen merchant and politician, being welcomed by the Dublin mob as he walked through the town 'in all the surliness of republicanism, grinning most ghastly smiles, and as he lifts his hat from his head the many-headed monster raises a shout that reverberates through every corner of the castle [of Dublin]'.[18]

The Society of United Irishmen started as a series of small reformist clubs in Belfast and elsewhere in 1791. The prime movers were groups of Presbyterian merchants, many of them in the clothing business, professional men and journalists. These rapidly linked up with similar groups in Dublin and elsewhere. The original ideology was reformist and anti-sectarian rather than separatist, although some of the early United Men may, like Tone, have harboured secret separatist and republican sentiments.[19] In part, their political enterprise owed much to American, English and French example, but the precedent of the Volunteers was also important. Economic interest and political resentment at the contrast between their considerable economic and professional status and their lack of any political influence also contributed to their politicisation. Another reason for the formation of the Society was a general sense of crisis. Agrarian and sectarian conflict had already begun along the geographical shatterbelt between Protestant and Catholic Ireland. Non-sectarian agrarian unrest was growing in Ulster, and the Dublin mob was becoming more aggressive. As early as June 1790, Tone felt that among both the middle classes and the ordinary people, 'there is a great fund of [political sentiment] ... but stifled and suppressed'.[20] Curiously, despite the traditional dislike and distrust of the Presbyterians and Anglicans for the Catholics, they seem to have overcome fears of any Catholic uprising; presumably the timidity and conservatism of the Catholic lay and clerical leaders alike reassured them. Eventually, the more cautious and fearful left the Society and left it to be taken over by more forward and revolutionary elements.

The founders showed sophistication and energy in their arrangements. Drennan's recommendation for the institution of a Dublin United Irish society included an apt description of the typical semi-conspiratorial Irish political society of that period and of later periods. He wanted a society to be set up in Dublin which would have much of the 'secrecy and somewhat of the ceremonial' of Freemasonry, 'so much secrecy as might communicate curiosity, uncertainty, expectation to the minds of surrounding men, so much impressive and affecting ceremony in its internal economy as without impeding real business might strike the soul through the senses'.[21] Figures on the occupations and religions of the early societies were promptly fed to the authorities by informers. Table 1 presents a reorganised version of R.B. McDowell's collation of one such set of figures.[22] McDowell points out that there was a very heavy representation of people involved in cloth-making and cloth-selling among the business and artisan categories, reflecting the protectionist and radical sentiments of these groups. Cloth merchants and textile manufacturers were prominent among the bourgeois group, and the other noticeable group was that of the professional men, attorneys and barristers being prominent among them. In many ways, the pattern revealed is typical of eighteenth-century radical opinion. Some liberal-minded aristocrats were prominent in the higher councils of the society, and in country areas landed gentry were occasionally supporters, but these were always in a minority and were fringe members of their own class. By religion, the Dublin group divided approximately evenly between Protestants and Catholics.

Table 1. Occupations of Dublin United Irishmen, 1791–94 (N=328)

	%
Landed gentry	0.0
Business, shopkeepers	52.1
Professions	22.9
Artisans	23.2
Labourers	0.0
Soldiers	1.8
	100.0

It became evident in 1794 that the government, because of its fear of France and of internal subversion, was going to permit the

Dublin Castle authorities to continue with mainly conservative and coercionist policies. The Ulster gentry began to show some support for Protestant paramilitary societies, the Volunteers were suppressed and the Dublin United Irishmen were harassed by the authorities. Towards the end of 1796 a new militia force, composed mainly of Protestant and loyal elements, was raised. This new yeomanry did much to provoke the 1798 Rising. The United Irishmen gradually drifted towards more radical and separatist policies. Like many political societies of later times, the organisation shifted from a civil to a military structure. Elements among the Volunteers became radicalised in the early 1790s, and this drift also occurred inside the United Irishmen after the recall of Fitzwilliam and the dissolution of the Volunteers in 1794. In that year the Dublin United Irish Society was suppressed:

> The military organisation of the United Irishmen had no existence till towards the end of 1796; and was, as near as could be, engrafted on the civil. In order to avoid giving alarm, it continued to conceal itself as much as possible under the usual denominations. The Secretary of a Society of twelve was commonly the petty officer; the delegate of five societies to a lower Baronial, when the population required such an intermediate step, was usually the Captain; and the Delegate often lower Baronials to the upper Baronials or District was most commonly Colonel. All officers to Colonels up were indispensably elected by those they were to command; but at that point, the interference of the Societies ceased, and every higher commission was in the power of the executive only. As soon as a sufficient number of Regiments were organised in any county, the Colonels were directed to transmit to the Executive the names of three persons fit in their opinion, to act as Adjutant-General for that county: of those the Executive chose one, and through this organ all military communications were made to the several counties. In consequence of such arrangements not more than one of the Executive need ever be committed with any county, and that only to a person of his own choice amongst them. It so happened that the same member was enabled to hold communication with several Adjutants-General, which still further diminished the work to the Executive.[23]

The development of this important society is discussed later. It became entangled with popular agrarian and sectarian forces and became as much their servant as their master. At this point it is sufficient to note that the Society of United Irishmen was an elaborately organised body in which a serious attempt was made to reconcile the conflicting requirements of internal democracy, centralised command structure and secrecy. It was to be the prototype for several important political organisations of the following century. It was itself heavily influenced by the elective territorial structure of the Volunteers, as were the contemporary Catholic Defenders and the Protestant Orange Order. Like later Irish secret societies and political parties, these late eighteenth-century organisations resembled private armies, and the discipline of later Irish political parties was to owe much to this tradition of quasi-military political organisation. The United Irishmen may also have owed something to the contemporary Jacobin Society, an organisation which was to be the model for many later European party organisations and underground conspiracies.[24]

AGRARIANISM, RELIGION AND REVOLUTION, 1760–1800

In common with other peasant societies, eighteenth-century Ireland had a well-developed tradition of rural combination. The purpose of these local societies was to prevent anyone from acting against what were regarded as being the community's interests. Because of the reinforcing effects of Ireland's religious, ethnic and class divisions, agrarian combination achieved a particular virulence.[25] Violent resistance to English or Dublin law was, of course, nothing new; the early eighteenth century had seen a certain amount of banditry on the part of the last rapparees and tories, the last skirmishers of the guerrilla warfare of the previous century. The spectacular agrarian agitation which broke out in Tipperary in 1760 and which inaugurated a new phase of agrarian conflict had little to do with the Jacobite cause and much to do with attempts by farmers and landowners to clear tenants and convert the land from tillage to pasture. This period witnessed an increase in the demand for Irish cattle because of British population growth and cattle diseases in many continental countries. The agitation was directed at attempts to clear tenantry, at the enforcement of estate rules by landlords, at the attempts by the authorities to extract tithes for the Anglican Church and even at the attempts of Catholic clergy to obtain financial support from the local peasantry. These early agrarian societies of the south of Ireland were referred to generically as Whiteboys or *Buachaillí Bána*, a term which was later applied rather indiscriminately to rather different societies. The name referred to their habit of wearing white shirts or white ribbons during their night-time excursions. Occasionally, women's clothes were used as disguises, faces were blackened and strange passwords were devised to ensure secrecy and anonymity. The first appearances in Tipperary were soon followed by similar outbreaks elsewhere in Munster and, soon after, in south Leinster as well.[26] In Protestant east Ulster, similar agrarian societies emerged in the 1770s, directed against various aspects of the land system.[27] Whiteboyism, while starting as a kind of agrarian trade union, tended to become institutionalised as an illegal local government system and a Mafia-like enforcement agency. There were allegations at the time that the reason the Whiteboys attacked the tithe system was because local farmers and landowners wished to distract their efforts. Others, of course, saw the Pope, the French or the Spanish behind these Mediterranean-style associations. Whiteboy court systems existed, where local people, whether peasants or gentry, might be tried *in absentia* for breaches of the folk law. Arthur Young reported that it was a common practice for the Whiteboys 'to go in parties about the country swearing many to be true to them, and forcing them to join by menaces, which they very often carried into execution'. They were quite capable of imposing levies to pay the law costs of any of their number who had been captured.[28] Whiteboyism was always particularly virulent in Munster and in the south of Ireland generally, but no part of the island was completely free from combination. South Leinster was soon infected and in the late 1770s peasant society in the Midlands was showing open contempt for the legal order.[29] In the mid-1780s, the Rightboy agitation spread over an enormous area in the south of Ireland. Whiteboyism was originally non-sectarian and apolitical, and was a local reaction to alterations in landholding. Enclosures, the shift to pasture and the rise of a rapacious, mainly Catholic, middle tenantry combined with demographic pressures and the absence of a land code to produce continuous agrarian disturbance.[30] Whiteboyism was also sometimes used to promote the private interests of individual leaders.

The Ascendancy often saw political scheming behind the agitation, and at least one judicial murder of a priest was perpetrated by the authorities. It is possible that a vague Jacobitism informed some Whiteboyism, but it is also significant that early Whiteboy notices sometimes appealed to the laws of England as affirming their claims. Ascendancy paranoia, derived from an acute sense of insecurity, automatically translated agrarian grievances into sectarian and political terms. Of course, on the peasant side there were some who were willing to make similar translations. In Ulster in particular, but elsewhere as well, the sectarian perspective took over from the 'class' or economic grievance, even in the popular mind. Agrarian societies in northern areas became better organised and more militant as well as expressing a wider range of grievances. In the Ulster borderlands, it was easy for the balance between the sects to be disturbed by rumour, by any accession of demographic strength to one side or the other, by intensified competition for employment or land or by any perceived change in the other side's willingness to accept the status quo. Because of this religious factor, agrarian organisations in Ulster and contiguous areas of Leinster and Connacht tended to divide along confessional lines and also to link up rather easily over long distances. In the south, by contrast, the societies remained local, non-sectarian and pre-political for rather longer. There were, however, particularly in the north, but even in the south, the beginnings of inter-county organisation and the emergence of common oaths. Furthermore, non-peasant elements attempted to put themselves at the head of peasant societies. Unlike the United Men, who organised themselves from the top down, regional agrarian societies such as the Defenders were organised from the bottom up and, because of this localist and cellular structure, were impermeable; government efforts to break them up were usually unsuccessful. Despite the debacle of 1798, the Defender network was to survive well into the nineteenth century.

Defenderism, a Catholic network of local societies on the Ulster borders, apparently had its origins in non-sectarian local factions or 'fleets' of young men in Armagh in the early 1780s. By 1786, however, there were two networks, one entirely Protestant and the other mainly Catholic, now called Peep-o'-Day Boys and Defenders, respectively. The Peep-o'-Day Boys attempted to enforce the laws prohibiting Catholics from bearing arms, while the Defenders resisted these raids and sought to arm themselves.[31] By 1788, Armagh Defenders were agreeing not to buy from Protestants. The first Peep-o'-Day Boys were mainly based on Protestant weaver communities in Armagh, communities under economic pressure and subject to Catholic competition.[32]

The early United Irishmen, moving out from Belfast and Dublin into the villages and the countryside in their search for popular support, found themselves attempting to combine Catholic and Protestant elements at a time when the sectarian gap was widening. Tone complained that many Ulster United Irish and Irish Volunteer corps were no better than Peep-o'-Day Boys.[33] However, some Protestant United Irish groups in Ulster were, as yet, non-sectarian; in east Ulster, they were sometimes the descendants of local Protestant agrarian societies of the 1770s, the Hearts of Steel.[34] On the Catholic side, non-peasant elements seem to have attempted to organise Defenderism on an ampler scale at quite an early stage and independently of the efforts of the United Men. Travelling agitators used prophecies foretelling imminent pogroms to drum up support for the society. Typically, such prophecies were similar to those of previous generations which had stated that the 'Scotch' were about to rise on a given date and would try to drive all Catholics out of the area.[35] Schoolmasters, shopkeepers and publicans were reportedly involved in early Defenderism.[36] It appears, however, to have been mainly a Catholic agrarian society, spread through north Leinster and the borderlands of Ulster. The substantial truth of this assessment is indicated by the generally spontaneous nature of Defender action and the lack of evidence of much large-scale and effective co-ordination, at least until 1794.[37] Defender action was immediate and often ferocious, particularly when the local land code was broken; in 1789, for example, Defenders were involved in a murderous campaign of resistance to colonisation of a Catholic area by Protestant peasants in Forkhill, south Armagh. Their oath was essentially defensive and included a somewhat ambiguously phrased declaration of loyalty to George III. However, even before 1790, the Defenders had developed an inter-county communications network, a system of secret signs and passwords, a regular lodge system and had appointed county grand masters. The system was spread around the country by journeymen, carriers, itinerant schoolmasters and lower clergy. Some travellers took the Defender oath as a convenient method of getting safe passage, lodgings and employment in a strange area.[38] It fed in particular on hereditary fears of Protestantism and on the not unfounded belief that the government could not, or would not, protect the community from outside attack.

Local factions were often countenanced by the gentry for elec-tioneering and sporting purposes. It was regarded as normal among sections of the gentry to act as patrons of a 'fleet', in a parody of feudal master/man relationships. With the growth of political feeling and sectarian fear in the 1780s, the mainly Protestant gentry were inclined to favour men of their own religion. The aristocratic toleration and encouragement of what was to develop into early Orangeism seems to have been due more to gentry fear of the revolutionary United Irishmen than to any real concern about Defenderism. Early Orangeism had mixed origins. In some areas, it existed among weavers and grew out of Peep-o'-Day gangs, but in other areas it included tenant farmers and its sectarianism had agrarian undercurrents. Originally reflecting a wish to keep Catholics in their traditional subordinate places, it became a major anti-revolutionary force. So effective was its accumulation of social power in the late 1790s that many United Men took the Orange oath as a form of political insurance.[39] Such an option was not open to Catholic members of the United Irish Society. The territorial militia had been thoroughly infiltrated by Defenderism and the United Irishmen, and the new 'yeomanry' was intended as a replacement. This new force was mainly Protestant and dominated by the Orange Order. The state, weak and underdeveloped as it was, was forced to back up a gentry-led religious faction against both the urban radicals and the general Catholic population during the crisis of 1797–8.

The United Irishmen had originally neither sectarian nor nationalist goals; their original aims were reformist rather than separatist or revolutionary. Many of the recruits which the society attracted from the working class and from the villages did, however, have such goals, and the leadership also changed, control falling into the hands of people influenced by the ideas of the French Revolution. As the movement spread, it came under the influence of its own rank and file, who elected leaders who thought like themselves, which often meant like Defenders rather than like the middle-class *philosophes* of Dublin or Belfast who had started the society. Whereas both Defenderism and Orangeism flourished in regions where the two religions confronted each other, the United Irishmen were strongest in the towns and in the more developed areas along the main roads. The society was evidently of a far more developed and co-ordinated type, at least at its inception. In Ulster, it was strongest in the towns and among Protestant areas with strong agrarian traditions in the east. Catholics in Ulster often remained aloof from the society, presumably because of its Dissenter support.[40] Leinster was the only other province in which it was well organised. The Munster organisation never had time to get off the ground, and Connacht appears to have been neglected; Connacht activity in the 1790s appears to have consisted of Defenderism with a veneer of French catch phrases. Generally, the United Irish system was confined to the more modern, commercialised areas, mainly in the east and north of the island, with better roads and more commerce. Where it penetrated beyond these areas, it tended to become indistinguishable from the local agrarian societies and came to act, despite the wishes of its leaders, as a link organisation between dozens of local agrarian factions. The unhappiness of the leaders with the motivation of the Catholic rank and file was considerable, and the organisation was very divided internally. The Catholics, they reported after the collapse of 1798, had been reluctant to join the republican United Irishmen until the development of the Orange system as an armed and licensed agency of the state stampeded them into the radical association. In particular, a series of ferocious Orange pogroms in Armagh in 1796 had an electrifying effect on Catholics in Ulster and even in Leinster and Munster.[41] A fear of Orangeism ran through the entire Catholic community, even in areas where Orangeism had never existed. In Wicklow, on the east coast of Leinster and just south of Dublin, Orange lodges were well organised and had infiltrated the yeomanry quite openly, and many Protestants were also afraid of armed Orangeism. Joseph Holt, a Protestant farmer who became an able United Irish leader during the guerrilla campaign in the Wicklow mountains during the summer of 1798, was forced to join the rebels through fear of being denounced to the yeomanry by an unfriendly neighbour. Holt, like other Wicklow farmers of Protestant stock, was, if anything, ideologically Unionist, although sympathetic to the reformism of the United Men. He considered that the ordinary poor people had no clear political awareness, even when they joined the rebel army; on the other hand, many of the crown's soldiers were, in fact, United Men, 'wearing one face for their country and the other for their king'. Most of the rebel atrocities, he claimed, were spontaneous reactions to yeomanry murders: they were 'wild, uncultivated, ignorant creatures, whom it was difficult to control, and impossible to keep in discipline when excited'.[42] Hay insisted that the rebellion in Wexford was due to similar fears of Orange pogroms which were, in effect, being carried on under the jurisdiction of the authorities.[43] Musgrave reported many instances of such fears in southern areas where Orangeism was weak or non-existent. He claimed that such rumours were sometimes carried by priests.[44]

The local United Irish societies were typically based on the local middle-class groups, whether Catholic or Protestant, rather than on the peasantry proper. Schoolteachers, prosperous farmers and doctors were conspicuous members in parts of Munster.[45] Wealthy farmers and farmers' sons were active United Men in Wicklow in 1797, before yeoman harassment became unendurable.[46] These more prosperous groups were swamped by a mass membership once the Great Fear of Orangeism took hold, and what had been almost a coterie became a mass movement.[47] Irish society was extremely unstable, and the United Men did not help to make it more stable. They were reported to have had emissaries going about the country in 1796, swearing people in and talking about the Orange peril: 'they have songs and prophecies, just written, stating all late events and what is to happen, as if made several years ago . . .'[48] People sometimes joined for mundane reasons, and in some areas it was like a casual fashion. Local officers were elected, and were often popular local figures such as members of the gentry, strong farmers' sons, ballad-singers or free-spending individuals. The cell system, which was supposed to preserve secrecy, was apt to break down as soon as the decision to purchase arms was made, because the blacksmiths knew who the buyers were.[49] In many cases, people were forced to join for fear of being suspected of having secret sympathies with the other side. However, ideological and political awakening also played a part: 'the discussion of political questions . . . and the enacting of several unpopular laws, had advanced the minds of many people, even before they were aware of it, toward republicanism and revolution.'[50] Even people who were forced to join sometimes became quite enthusiastic, perhaps by way of overcompensation. In Co. Derry, there were forcible haircuttings and midnight threats to make people join, but many 'who had resisted originally, after having been sworn, have been tempted to become as active as any of the more violent'.[51] By February 1798, the number of armed members had reached a notional total of 267,296, but much of this membership seems to have been nominal. The best-organised counties were the Ulster ones and, in Leinster, the prosperous agricultural counties around Dublin: Kildare, Wicklow, Carlow and Queen's. Wexford, not reported on this captured return because the Wexford delegate had, very wisely, gone to ground and avoided the raid, was not particularly well organised.[52]

The Rising of 1798 duly occurred and was put down with extreme brutality, with over thirty thousand, and perhaps over fifty thousand, people being killed, many of them non-combatants and most of them by the forces of the state. In Wexford in particular, the Rising took a sectarian turn, and Protestant prisoners were murdered by the rebels.[53] However, the Rising and the state-sanctioned massacres of insurgents and civilians marked the political bankruptcy of the

Ascendancy, although it took more than fifty years for that bankruptcy to be accepted by the British government. London was nevertheless forced to directly intervene to ensure that Ireland did not become an access point to Britain for the French. The appointment of Cornwallis as viceroy and the abolition of the Irish parliament followed shortly on the Rising.

Cornwallis was horrified at the bloodthirstiness of the Irish Ascendancy, remarking in July 1798 that the political elite of the country were 'in general, averse to all acts of clemency and . . . would pursue measures that could only terminate in the extirpation of the greater number of the inhabitants'. He blamed the sectarian turn the Rising had taken, and the more sectarian character of its suppression, on the assumption by the Ascendancy that religion and subversion rather than reformism and insecurity lay behind the unrest. He was sure that to continue with the Ascendancy's mode of government would result in a separation of Ireland from Britain and accepted that something would have to be done to 'soften the hatred of the Catholics for our government'.[54]

Considerable support for the union with Britain came from the Catholic clergy, particularly from the bishops, who were horrified by the appeal which revolution had to their flock and even to some of the lower clergy. London was seen by some bishops as a possible source of reform, Catholic emancipation and protection against the more extravagant excesses of Castle government. Many Orangemen and Protestant landowners opposed the union because they feared that for which the Catholics hoped. The countrymen appear to have cared little for the issue one way or the other, but the union was energetically opposed by many of all religions and all classes in Dublin, who saw it as signifying the decay of their city, the end of any hope of protection and the loss of place. The union was neither opposed nor supported by religious groups, partly because it was not obvious which groups were to lose and to gain by it. It has been argued that the thirty-year delay in granting Catholic emancipation was the main cause of the failure of the union to be accepted by Catholic Ireland. Catholic emancipation had been promised as part of the Union 'package', and the British government did not deliver. It is difficult not to suspect that the breach between Catholic Ireland and the British regime and its Irish allies went far deeper than a few middle-class grievances. Firstly, the land system's pernicious effects grew worse after 1800 and in particular after 1815. Again, 1798 became part of the folklore, '98 veterans were active in later movements, considerable political mobilisation had occurred and the Rising was to be referred to, generations later, as 'the War'. Later wars such as the Napoleonic and Crimean wars were overshadowed by its memory. Cornwallis himself seems to have sensed the depth of the breach and wondered if Irish Catholics could ever be good subjects of a Protestant government: 'What then have we done, if this position be true? We have united ourselves to a people whom we ought in policy to have destroyed.'[55]

The development of agrarian, sectarian and revolutionary societies in the period before 1798 has been described in some detail because this period marked an early phase of the political mobilisation of the population and because these societies served as a series of prototypes or models for later nationalist political associations in the nineteenth century, including societies or parties which had no militaristic intentions. In some cases, these early societies afforded examples to subsequent organisations of how *not* to organise politically. In other cases, a similar uneasy linking together of urban elites and agrarian or sectarian local societies caused a repetition of some patterns evident in 1796–98. The frequent indiscipline of the rank and file once they had been organised, the usually wide gap between the goals of the central leadership and those of the local groups and the contrast that existed between geographically separated local organisations were all themes which were to recur in the nineteenth century. In particular, a new political institution, the disciplined electoral political party, was to evolve during the nineteenth century, in many ways a synthesis of the agrarian and revolutionary paramilitary organisations of the previous century, although a synthesis turned to essentially new purposes. Above all, the 1780s and 1790s saw the first attempts by urban-based political entrepreneurs to mobilise the countryside behind their causes, attempts which were to be repeated in the following century with rather more success than had rewarded the United Men or the shadowy leaders of Defenderism.

03 | THE DEVELOPMENT OF NATIONALIST POPULAR POLITICS, 1800–48

SECRET SOCIETIES BEFORE THE FAMINE: THE RISE OF RIBBONISM

The origins of Irish electoral political parties are inextricably entangled with the maze of agrarian and sectarian local and regional secret societies of the early nineteenth century. As in other developing political systems, the political parties which developed benefited from proto-political local traditions of combination. In the Irish case, the traditions of large-scale conspiratorial and paramilitary organisation had a considerable impact on the parties which emerged later in the century. Regardless of personal preference, nationalist politicians and nationalist revolutionaries alike had to make concessions to the older agrarian, sectarian and nationalist preoccupations which often dominated the popular mind. In the case of some political entrepreneurs, the preferred solution was to embrace some selection of these traditions. As suggested earlier, agrarianism was originally a reaction to threats to local society and local interests. It was often justified, however, in terms that would nowadays be regarded as sectarian or, perhaps, be seen at best as belonging to a tradition of historicist nationalism, referring to the great swordland conquests of the sixteenth century and the Cromwellian conquests of the seventeenth, events which were remembered with extraordinary immediacy by the peasant folk tradition. Rural agitation became chronic after the 1760s, and between that decade and 1890, the island was, with some intervals and with some important regional exceptions, in a state of what might best be described as slow-moving and low-intensity guerrilla warfare.[1] The main causes of pre-Famine agrarian agitation were a lethal combination of unrestricted landlordism, unrestricted subletting and a Malthusian process of population increase pressing on a fixed supply of land.

In the early nineteenth century, as in the eighteenth, the typical secret society was essentially apolitical, and its goals were restricted to preventing certain exactions and land transactions. Its main objectives were still the enforcement of a crude land law on landlord, farmer and peasant alike. Other common objectives were the prevention of evictions and of land-taking by a non-relative of the previous occupier, by an outsider or, sometimes, by a person of different religion. The societies also discouraged rent increases, the tithe system and, in general, any departure from the folk tenant-right code, a code enforced in the absence of any legally recognised official code. These societies were local, and should be distinguished from the roving banditti of the seventeenth century. Furthermore, they seem to have been quite large, often being capable of mustering more than a hundred men, and had a considerable degree of popular acceptance. It seems that this acceptance was partly founded on traditional memories of older, Gaelic assumptions concerning communal land rights, inheritance and gavelkind which cut across the legal property code.[2] Several commentators have suggested, in harmony with present-day Irish popular tradition, that the societies were rather successful in achieving their objectives: one authority has noted that the eighteenth-century societies probably prevented the sort of wholesale clearances which occurred at that time in Scotland.[3] An economic historian has recently suggested that the activities of the late nineteenth-century societies and leagues, together with the pro-tenant legislation that eventually ensued, succeeded not only in preserving the ancestral communities intact but also in drastically slowing down the emergence of full-scale advanced capitalist agriculture in Ireland.[4]

Nationalist-religious rhetoric was usually mixed up with agrarian grievances.[5] Religious feeling could, in particular, be intensified by agrarian bitterness; attempts by landlords to install Protestant tenants could have murder as a consequence. Even before the collapse of food prices which followed the Napoleonic wars, the juncture of agrarian, separatist and sectarian forces which had occurred in the 1790s persisted in an underground form. The period 1798–1815 saw the persistence of Defenderism, or 'Ribbonism', as it came to be known, in the north, and similar networks emerged elsewhere. After 1815, Ribbonism developed a centre in Dublin to rival its traditional centre in Armagh, and in Munster the local factions became more politicised and more accessible to outside agitators. Pro-French sympathy and disaffection from the British cause persisted in Munster and Connacht; in 1807, Cooke saw the authorities in Tipperary as being isolated in a hostile sea of peasantry.[6] Another informant, writing in 1808, was quite definite that the great factions of Munster were developing political prejudices:

> I wanted to know if they would make me a Shaunavest, as that is the strongest party in the country; and they said I could not be admitted one unless I could swear to reside in the country, and that no stranger would be allowed to associate with them at all; that the people got enough from strangers. The Shaunavest party is the lower order of Catholics, who are sworn Republicans; and the Caravats are the Catholic party inclined to royalty; and the Protestants join the Caravats, and the Shaunavests are sworn to destroy the other party if they can; and whenever they meet each other day or night they beat one another most unmerciful, and even kill at times. A man of the name of John Finn, who lives in Tipperary, told me that whenever they go to take arms they generally ride thirty miles ... He is a Shaunavest ... He said when the French come and the people break out the very good friends in some of the militia regiments too ...[7]

In these southern counties, the United Irish tradition was weak, but Whiteboyism was an institution, and after 1815, war veterans contributed their experience and energy.[8] The ruin of many 'middling' tenants who had done well during the wars, together with the lack of any place for the veterans, appears to have contributed to the growing intensity of southern agitation. The growth of O'Connell's movement in the 1820s attracted the factions to non-agrarian political action.[9] Tipperary was again the main southern focus, as it had been since 1760; Foster complained in 1825 that because of its lack of roads or of a responsible gentry class, Tipperary was virtually ungoverned and had been like that since Elizabethan times.[10] John Kiely, parish priest of Mitchelstown in the 1820s, described local magistrates actually adopting local factions and giving them legal protection in return for certain services; the weakness of the authorities led to a certain balance of fear between magistrates and faction leaders. Once stipendiary magistrates were introduced along with a more centralised and impersonal form of justice administration at the petty sessions, this quasi-feudal relationship broke down; the reforms of the 1820s had the ironic effect of breaking the last tenuous links between authority and the factions, thus making them even more available to constitutional and unconstitutional agitators. Kiely described 'Caravatism' spreading from west Limerick into south Tipperary and north Cork, and reported that it was spread along the roads by certain carmen.[11] The moving spirits of Caravatism were 'a peculiar kind of gentry, a kind of middle order between the rich gentry . . . and the peasantry'. These people had prospered during the wartime agricultural price boom and had suffered badly in the post-war collapse of prices. They had received 'the education of persons above their rank; by the fall of the times they were reduced to their original level; without the habit of labour they associated with the lowest description'. In order to hold on to their property they had built up the Caravat network.[12]

In most of the three southern provinces the societies remained local and essentially non-political, never achieving regional levels of organisation similar to those of Ribbonism. Even the variety of names used by the societies attests to this generalisation: Shaunavests, Caravats, Rock Boys, Terry Alts, Threshers, Carders, Whitefeet and Blackfeet. Despite the extreme brutality of their actions, the societies remained accepted by local people, if not exactly popular.[13] Compulsion was sometimes used to get members, and the oaths invariably emphasised loyalty to one's companions, secrecy and preferential dealing with one's brothers. Many were forced to join the Leinster Whitefeet, but others regarded the society as insurance against being put out of their holdings.[14] Popular attitudes to the societies were ambiguous because of the need for protection, and the community was willing to countenance horrific punishments for breaches of the informal land code, partly from fear and partly because it was felt that the community's material basis was at stake. It was reported from Tipperary in the 1830s that a traveller pretended to be 'on his keeping', i.e. on the run from the police, on account of a killing in his own native place, so that people would pity the poor murderer and give him work. It was assumed that no one committed murder without a good reason; foreign travellers were often struck by the fact that they could travel through disturbed areas unmolested because it was known that they were not involved in the local struggle for existence.[15]

However, not all societies remained at these limited levels of organisation. In the north, the Defender network developed into the Ribbon society after 1815. It prospered best in the Ulster borderlands and was most visible in the counties north of a line between Dublin and Galway. Ribbonism also travelled with Irish emigrants to Britain and America, where it evolved into the more open and harmless Hibernian societies. Ribbonism was, of course, a Catholic counterblast to Orangeism and, by the time of its greatest development between 1825 and 1845, it shared Orangeism's addiction to oaths, banners, sashes, emblems and parades. 'Ribbonism' itself was a name given to the society by outsiders, and the term has often been applied to societies unconnected with either of the two great Ribbon societies of the 1830s. The term was derived from the Ulster faction-fighters' habit of wearing a ribbon to distinguish friend from foe; the first reference to the practice occurs in connection with an Orange versus Green affray at a fair at Swatragh, Co. Derry, in 1810.[16] The old Defender net appears to have been reconstructed. In 1816, delegates from the Ulster counties met in Carrickmacross, Co. Monaghan and agreed to set up a revived Defenderism. The delegates were described as 'decent respectable-looking men', 'gentlemanlike-looking men and rode good horses'.[17] From the beginning, lower middle-class elements were involved, typically farmers or shopkeepers. Armagh was a focal point, and representative structures very similar to those of Defenderism and the United Irishmen evolved. A Dublin centre developed and by 1821 'the Ribbon Society in Dublin City was a kind of mixture of trade combinations, old United Irishmen, journeymen from Ulster and wandering schoolteachers' [my translation].[18] Shoemakers, other artisans, carriers, coal porters and publicans were involved in Dublin Ribbonism, which developed Mafia-like characteristics and became involved in petty crime, intimidation and murder.[19] In 1822, a police agent called Coffey infiltrated the Dublin society and caused many of its leaders to be arrested and convicted. This led to a split in the society and the formation of separate Dublin and Ulster societies, which were not reunited until 1838. By the late 1830s, a publican called Andrew Dardis was head of the Dublin society ('The Irish Sons of Freedom'), and his general secretary was one Richard Jones, who was reputed in police circles to have been involved in an attempt to bomb the William III statue in College Green in 1836.[20] The chief of the Ulster organisation ('The Society of Saint Patrick') was one John Rice, a farmer from Carrickmacross. The Dublin society was far weaker and was wrecked by police action in 1839. The Ulster society appears to have dominated the Connacht lodges, and the Dublin society never achieved any penetration of Munster.[21] The weakness of the Dublin or Leinster network appears to have been due to the relative absence of sectarian tension, and may also have been partly due to the success of the constitutional movement in southern areas. The absence of a prior secret net in Munster may be the reason why Fenianism spread so easily in Munster and had more difficulty in Connacht and Ulster where Ribbonism barred the way. There were strong connections with British Hibernianism; Rice's title was 'President of the Board of Erin for the Three Kingdoms'.

Ribbon oaths were similar to Defender oaths, but usually had some overtly nationalistic or confessional sentiments. The usual emphasis on loyalty to one's brothers and willingness to fight by their sides was accompanied by a promise to deal with Catholics or, occasionally, 'liberal' Protestants. Some oaths included declarations of fidelity to the monarch, as Defender oaths had done; informers, however, were adamant that these declarations were 'blinds' and were not actually sworn to at the initiation. The oaths were often only semi-literate, but this does not necessarily indicate lack of middle-class involvement; good spelling is not a necessary qualification for middle-class status, and certainly was not in pre-Famine Ireland. The typical Ribbon addiction to pseudo-Masonic ritual, designed to overawe the neophyte as recommended by Drennan, is well illustrated by this Dublin Ribbon catechism of the 1820s:

Q: Who made you?
A: A tall man with black whiskers and a fair complexion.
Q: How were you made?
A: Neither sitting nor standing, but on my two bare knees, on the banks of the Jordan.
Q: What are your intentions?
A: To regain all lost rights and privileges since the Reformation.[22]

Early Ribbonism spread partly as a fashion and partly through the systematic efforts of organisers, and its spread was assisted by the development of canal and railway systems. The police did not take it too seriously, and felt that it had no real central co-ordinating authority.[23] However, they admitted it was very widespread through the areas of mixed religion and through counties Meath, Louth, Westmeath, King's, Queen's and Sligo by the late 1830s. Elsewhere, they felt, there was less demand for such an organisation, as '. . . in those Counties where they are all Roman Catholics they are all One Way of thinking, and where they are all Protestants . . . they are all of One Way of thinking, and . . . therefore there is no collision.'[24] Others, not all of them Orangemen, were far more impressed by the growth of the society. O'Connell was uneasy about it, and T. W. Ray, his lieutenant, reported to him in 1837 that its leaders were 'decent farmers' and farmers' sons, and that the armed forces had been infiltrated by Ribbonism. Ray wrote:

. . . about five years ago there was a meeting of the Delegates [from the counties] in Dublin—a man named Reilly from Longford—

Fitzsimons from Cavan—Gogarty from Meath—Moore from Leitrim . . . When the system was sufficiently extended in any locality they immediately proceeded to search for arms. The system thus proceeded from the North to Dublin, where it is now at a frightful height . . . The oath administered is of the most solemn to an ignorant mind—the recruit has to go down on his bare knees— to open his clothes and bare his breast—put his left hand on his heart and extend his right hand toward heaven—he is then sworn by the Captain of the Lodge to be true to death to his brethern, not to hear them backbitten, ill-used or maligned, to deal with none but a brother—they also cause him to invoke the Virgin Mary of the Saints —in the Dublin District they swear merely on the Book.[25]

Secret societies were under a general ban of the Catholic Church. Despite this ban, involving excommunication, a very serious penalty indeed in a Catholic country, Ribbonism was very strong, with many thousands of members at its height. In some counties it enjoyed the adherence of a considerable proportion of the male Catholic rural population. Passwords and 'quarrelling words' were valid over long distances and were changed every three months. Each local group or 'body' had a 'body master', and the masters together constituted a parish 'jury', 'council' or 'committee' which was 'a sort of Parochial Tribunal, that adjudicate in all Cases of Complaint and Quarrel amongst the members of the Body, and also issue their Orders to the Ribandmen [sic] in their Parishes which they are bound to obey'. The usual agrarian intimidation, brutal beatings and occasional murder were ordered by these unofficial courts. It took nerve to defy Ribbonism, but some did so. Captain John Armstrong, for example, who had been a notorious informer in 1798, held lands in King's County and ensured his own safety by granting his tenants leases for his own lifetime. 'Thus in the hot-bed of Ribbonism he gloried to the end in a sort of charmed life.'[26] The important role played by publicans in the organisation appears to have been in part an effort on their part to expand custom, but it also helped to expand their social influence and keep contact with the strong-arm men of the parish.[27] Even in Dublin, many publicans were Ribbon masters, as it brought them custom, protection and prestige. Thomas Drummond remarked that the publicans kept up 'a sort of connexion one with another' and used ritual and a certain 'Degree of Mystery' to ensure their influence over their credulous followers. They gave the impression of being in touch with a mysterious but powerful 'Authority' which was working in obscure but efficacious ways for the eventual overturning of the constitution and other eminently popular objectives of that kind.[28]

Rather like an American big-city machine working in reverse, Ribbonism, instead of using patronage to buy activists, succeeded in persuading its activists to contribute sums of money to it. Certainly, many local Ribbon masters found it profitable; one in Meath, on being persuaded to retire in the mid-1830s by the local clergy, asked for an annual pension of £15 by way of compensation for loss of earnings.[29] Thomas Moran, a tobacconist's carman in Dublin, was a lodge master in 1821 and improved his material position noticeably:

> . . . he had been a common fellow driving a car, but in a short time became 'a great swell'—he got a green surtout, blue body coat, canary casimere waistcoat, drab casimere breeches—top boots—a watch, and even a ring—This was the distinguishing dress of the Masters or Captains of the day.[30]

Ribbonism was a protection organisation which very easily turned into a protection racket, and it often amounted to an ingenious and sinister method of pumping a good deal of money out of poor and intimidated men.[31] However, as in all political organisations, different motivations coexisted. Richard Jones, general secretary to the Leinster society, was a hard-working official who attempted to stop feuding between the various Ribbon factions and to build up a united organisation. He was in easy contact with Ribbon societies all over Ireland and the western littoral of Great Britain. Jones was a haymaker's clerk in Dublin's Smithfield Market, and was rated by the police as a clever man who knew shorthand. The police also admitted that Jones, and some of his colleagues, were honest and genuinely political, whatever the motivations of other Ribbonmen. At his trial in 1840, Jones stated that the objectives of the reunited Ribbon Society were to 'free Ireland', 'unite all Catholics' and 'liberate our country'. Jones and Dardis were transported.[32]

Socially, local Ribbon leaders of the 1835–45 period were relatively well-to-do. Furthermore, while the rank and file may well have been composed of the poorest and most marginal, the officers resembled in their backgrounds the kinds of people who were later to be the backbone of the first Irish political party organisations. Trade was the most common denominator of local Ribbon leaders: of twenty-three Ulster leaders named by an informer in 1839, eleven were shopkeepers—mainly publicans— and five were farmers. A further six were artisans or labourers. Of twenty-one leading Ribbonmen in Longford, six were farmers or farmers' sons, one was a publican and seven were artisans or 'dealers'. In Donegal, of twenty-one prominent Ribbonmen, fourteen were farmers, three of these farmers also being 'road contractors'. Another five were artisans or labourers and two were shopkeepers.[33] Ribbonism appears to have been a partially successful attempt by a section of the new Catholic trading class to put itself at the head of what had originally been societies for communal or agrarian defence. It must be emphasised that although not coordinated successfully by any centre, communications between local groups were quite good, and it should also be remembered that they were very large. By the late 1830s, large Ribbon parades were being held openly in many western and northern areas. Five hundred Ribbonmen marched at the funeral of a Ribbon leader in Fermanagh in 1837, wearing 'white bands and green ribands'; in Leitrim in 1838, 'some thousands of the peasantry from the Leitrim mountains' marched in military formation to another funeral through the village of Ballinamore, 'attired in white scarves and hat-bands, preceded by a white garland or ensign decorated with green'.[34] The numbers increased enormously, and the growth appears to have been most pronounced at the western end of the Ulster borderland. By the early 1840s, a Sligo Ribbonman felt able to say that Ribbonism was increasing: 'I never knew it to decrease except here on the first taking of the Temperance Medals—it is impossible to pass the roads at night without being able to account for yourself.'[35]

The announced aims of the Ribbon societies were civil rights for Catholics, disestablishment and land reform. Repeal was borrowed as a slogan from O'Connell. In so far as it had a coherent ideology, that ideology seems to have been confessionalist, anti-Protestant, vaguely monarchist and not different in type from the old-fashioned Catholic nationalism of the seventeenth century. Despite this traditionalism, Ribbonism was quite a modern political society and was also open to proposals involving subversion of the regime.[36]

Ribbonism scarcely appeared in south Leinster or in Munster at all, despite efforts by Jones to spread *his* gospel of Catholic unity, and Munster societies remained at a lower level of articulation until the advent of Fenianism in the 1850s. In parts of Tipperary, old family connections which crossed class lines and linked landless to landed by kinship formed the sinews of combination.[37] Combination of an unusual aggressiveness persisted in Tipperary from 1760 through the nineteenth century and up to the IRA war of 1919–21; it appears to have been due to the survival there of a propertied or securely tenanted Catholic small farmer class of large proportions, linked together by family ties and with the high degree of self-confidence and political awareness one might expect of a nascent 'rural bourgeoisie'. The very strength of local combination may have made the area impermeable to outside organisers such as Jones. Furthermore, the attractions of O'Connellism to the strong farmers of Leinster and Munster appear to have outweighed the attractions of secret societies with vague political programmes. However, the raw material for a society such as Ribbonism existed in the south; it may be that the intensity of labourer/farmer conflict was too great to permit the formation of a cross-class society such as Ribbonism.

POLITICAL MOBILISATION IN PRE-FAMINE NATIONALIST IRELAND

Political scientists have often discussed political mobilisation, or the process by which large numbers of people become involved in collective politics, as part of the more general process of social mobilisation. The central idea of social mobilisation is that economic, social and political modernisation processes such as the intervention of the state in local affairs, the spread of the market and the growth of cities together with the spread of literacy and communications systems uproot people from their local communities and broaden their horizons. In Western Europe, the political mobilisation of general populations coincided with urbanisation and industrialisation.[38] In Ireland, the usual European sequence was reversed; intense political mobilisation occurred long before substantial industrialisation or even commercialisation has occurred. In fact, the Ireland of 1790–1840 was being 'de-urbanised', as the rural population was growing faster than the town population. Ireland also experienced the development of modern, centralised and interventionist state structures long before it had ceased to be a peasant country. This experience of early state-building and 'premature' mobilisation of a rural electorate is a central determinant of the country's subsequent political development. The country shifted directly from subsistence farm to commercial farm economy with no intervening phase of industrialisation, and the resulting political parties and ideologies echoed feudal and peasant loyalties and political perspectives. Public opinion has a marked tendency to crystallise once it is formed, and popular loyalties formed during a period of intense political mobilisation tend to become ingrained.[39] In Ireland, the ideas spread during this crucial period were those of nationalism, civil rights, egalitarianism and a curious blend of conservative Catholicism and political radicalism.

At the beginnings of political mobilisation in the 1800–30 period, what was being transformed into the public opinion of a politicised community was a well-developed, mainly pre-literate peasant political consciousness, shut off from the political establishment by barriers of caste and accessible only to those who could gain the popular trust through service, demagoguery or some strange mixture of the two. Even English-speaking Catholic Ireland was scarcely less cut off from the establishment and, because of its access to the printed word, it was even more easily mobilised by politicians and clergy. The priests were, of course, the only educated group who had the trust of the community before the O'Connellite movement. The power of the priests was not, however, as unlimited as many have imagined. Ribbon and other secret societies regularly ignored the demands or pleadings of the clergy, although, interestingly, Ribbon leaders often put it about that the priests' condemnations of Ribbonism were insincere, and that Ribbonism and the hierarchy were secretly allied. Priests were financially dependent on the local community and their position resembled that of an elected politician. While their authority was considerable, it was also limited, and to maintain it priests were forced to place themselves, whether they liked it or not, at the head of any movement which aroused the deeper political passions of the people. In this emergent public opinion, traditional memories of ancient conquest, the traumatic events of 1798 and the contemporary grievances of tithe-proctors and land agents were mixed together with either too little or too much sense of perspective, depending on one's point of view. Prophecies were popular, and the predictions of the more influential prophecies were relayed to the population by means of storytellers and pamphlets. The prophecies were, in effect, a form of subversive political literature. The prophecies of Charles Pastorini, bishop of Rama, first published in 1771, were reprinted in Ireland several times between 1790 and 1820. Pastorini prophesied that the fall of 'Lutheranism' would occur in 1825. The (forged) prophecies of Colmcille similarly predicted a victorious rising against the Saxon and the restoration of a Gaelic and Catholic political order.[40] Tom Paine's *Rights of Man* was also popular, a lasting legacy of the missionary efforts of the United Men. In the Ulster border-lands, prophecy of a more mundane kind was used, seers in the 1820s asserting that a new Protestant invasion was nigh.[41] Ribbonmen often used prophetic and millenial phrases in their passwords and slogans; a Ribbon notice in Westmeath in the 1820s averred that 'these Orangemen and Peelers had their day and their rule is almost over, and woe be to all who takes their part when the right rule comes'.[42] Raftery's Irish-language poetry in praise of O'Connell and of Ribbonism had strong prophetic and millenial elements in it, old Gaelic political prophecies and material from Pastorini being blended together in an astonishing mishmash.

While the extension of the franchise to the general population occurred mainly after 1867 and was followed by two great waves of electoral mobilisation in the periods 1880–86 and 1918–20, it would be wrong to see the 1880s as marking the beginnings of popular electoral politics in Ireland. Even then, such a tradition had long existed; the archaic forty-shilling freehold franchise of the pre-1832 period had been quite wide, and propertied Catholics had been allowed to vote, if only for Protestants, since 1793. Even before the 1820s, Catholics had been occasionally restive, and in that decade they began to break free of landlord control under O'Connell's tutelage. The extraordinary continuity, strength and archaism of Irish nationalism are due in great part to this very early popular experience of electoral mobilisation; perhaps only in the United States did an even earlier mobilisation occur, and Britain did not follow suit for another generation.

Early British and American political parties grew out of, and into, a fairly well-understood framework of representative institutions. In the Irish case, the already existing popular movement, with a strong and traditional non-constitutional strand in it, was 'steered' into the channel of parliamentary politics. This steering was achieved with substantial rather than complete success. A persistent popular ambiguity towards parliamentary politics, or at least British parliamentary politics, the product of long experience of non-parliamentary government and of old cultural traditions, survived to become a permanent part of Irish political culture. Even under the narrow franchise of the 1832–67 period, very large numbers of people participated in election campaigns: the participating public was far larger than the electorate. The reason for this was, of course, the fact that the ballot was open. The occasionally terrified voters would be escorted to the polls by their non-voting fellow citizens, their choice of candidate would be booed or cheered, factions supporting various candidates would make the election week an occasion for a trial of strength, priests would lead groups of voters to the polls and landlords' agents would let it be understood what would happen to any tenant who voted the wrong way. Bribery and intimidation were, by all accounts, very common and voters were sometimes marshalled

like political sheep. Election day was also a time for carnival; early
nineteenth-century Irish elections were not particularly democratic
events but the point is that they were extremely *popular* events,
and they involved a large proportion of the population in political
life, no matter how marginally.

In the early years of the century, Catholic upper middle-class
groups were politically cautious. The Catholic Committee of the
1790s had stayed aloof from Defenderism and from the United
Irishmen. After the Union, Catholic and Protestant gentry and
bourgeois elements made common cause for repeal of the union
within a few years of the abolition of the Irish parliament. It was,
however, the continued refusal to grant Catholic emancipation
rather than the issue of repeal that brought the higher strata of the
Catholic community into the political arena in reaction to the
studied sectarianism of the English Constitution. Daniel O'Connell,
the first of an extraordinary trio of Irish leaders, O'Connell,
Parnell and de Valera, was also the least separatist, the nearest to
Gaelic Ireland and the one who made the most impact on the folk
imagination. All three were *charismatic* leaders, but O'Connell
approached the nearest to the almost messianic and millenial
status suggested by Weber's use of that word; the adulation given
Parnell or de Valera was secular by comparison, although recognisably of similar quality. All three had exceptional abilities and
insights ascribed to them by the public, but O'Connell was
regarded as a kind of magician. Significantly, he made his first
appeals to popular sympathy by defending poor farmers and
artisans in the courts. His main weapon was rhetoric, which he
used inside the courts and outside. He specialised in demagoguery, ridicule of his opponents and personal vituperation; as
the targets of his abuse were highly unpopular figures, his
popularity increased each time he attacked some establishment
judge or politician. Irish folklore is full of stories in which
O'Connell is portrayed as a *cleasaí* or trickster who, by wit and
cunning, gets the better of the English lords and gentlemen. He
was reported to have so hexed the great gentlemen of the House of
Commons that he was the only man who had ever been permitted
to wear his hat in the House.

The Catholic middle-class leaders, even in the 1820s, still remembered the disaster of 1798 and feared a repetition. The militarised organisation of the United Irishmen was regarded as a model to be avoided, and the shadowy presence of Ribbonism was a forbidding reminder of that tradition. The Catholic Association of 1823 was founded on different lines, had different intentions and was constitutional in its means. According to Sheil, it was intended at the beginning to unite the poor and the better-off. The association was to avoid being a militarised 'conspiracy of the disenfranchised many', as exemplified by the United Irishmen, and it was also intended to avoid being a militarised conspiracy of the enfranchised, as exemplified by the Volunteers of 1782.[43]

Between 1823 and 1847, O'Connell headed a series of organisations aimed at Catholic emancipation, municipal reform, tithes and repeal.[44] The tradition of a militarily disciplined and centralised extra-parliamentary movement persisted and even reached new heights under his leadership, and he was not above using the symbols of old radicalism to help legitimise his own causes; he often made a point of having 1798 veterans on the platform with him and, in the 1840s, used the symbols of the Volunteers in the Repeal Association.[45] For the Catholic emancipation campaign of the 1820s, the organisation of the Catholic Church provided a ready-made political apparatus to mobilise people behind the association. 'Catholic rents' were instituted, large numbers of poor people contributing small amounts per month to the association's treasury. Emancipation, which only affected the upper strata of the Catholic population, was supported by the urban middle class and by the stronger Catholic farmers. It seems to have meant relatively little to the general peasant population.[46] On the other hand, if the Protestants and the English didn't want it, it occurred to many people that it was worth fighting for, and it was represented in quasi-millenial terms as a revolutionary defeat for the Ascendancy.[47] O'Connell was, however, essentially Whig in his political principles and was not really sympathetic to separatism; he appears to have wanted equality within the United Kingdom for Catholics, rather on the lines of the settlement secured by the Scottish Presbyterians. He was not enthusiastic about social as opposed to political reforms, and was hostile to agrarian agitation and to trade unions.[48] Accordingly, his adoption of the repeal issue was belated and cautious. O'Connell was also strengthened by the Catholic Church's fear of Protestant proselytism, which encouraged the bishops to see Irish Catholicism as the religion of an embattled community and to see O'Connell's enterprise as a campaign for religious freedom or even for the preservation of that community.[49]

The first electoral breakthrough took place in Waterford in 1826, the tenantry following their priests rather than their landlords to vote for the O'Connellite candidate. The Marquis of Waterford's huntsman contritely apologised to his lord for having voted against his wishes, explaining that he could not vote against his religion and his country.[50] The new mood of independence spread rapidly. In Munster it ran through Tipperary and into Clare.[51] Witnesses reported that the priests' leadership was usually conditional on their doing what the people wanted them to do and that the voters would, if necessary, ignore the clergy's instructions if it went against their political wishes.[52] By 1829, these electoral demonstrations had broken down Tory resistance to emancipation. More importantly, perhaps, electoral politics in the robust form of massive demonstrations at the polls had proved an effective political weapon and an alternative to physical force. The two traditions, constitutional and non-constitutional, had henceforth to live together, and whenever constitutionalism faltered, the other tradition tended to re-emerge.

The tithe campaign of the early 1830s touched the peasants' interests more directly, and quickly took the form of a vicious land war in many parts of the country. Under the archaic legislation, pasture was exempt from tithing, so that it was the poorer Catholic farmer or cottier who had to maintain the Anglican Church of Ireland. The tithe agitation in Kilkenny started in 1829, touched off by inflammatory speeches made by schoolmasters and 'itinerant demagogues'.[53] With their usual sensitivity, the authorities permitted the police to enforce tithe exactions and several murderous clashes between peasantry and police occurred. Agrarian and Ribbon societies appear to have become better organised and more determined during the years of the tithe war.[54]

O'Connell's later organisations followed the same general lines as the Catholic Association. They used laymen as well as priests as local organisers in a startlingly modern fashion. O'Connell took care, however, to centralise power in his own hands and in the hands of his immediate family and friends: he used his brother and his son as senior organisers. In 1831, for a local campaign of that year, he urged his brother John to get to work: 'You must ransack the country. Speak to the bishop. Engage every voter. Write every priest. Send Maurice [O'Connell] and Charles Brennan in every direction where a voter can be had.' He regarded ten energetic men as sufficient to set up a movement.[55] To counteract the landlord practice of evicting recalcitrant voters, protection funds were set up. Efforts were also made to build up a large card-carrying membership. A ballad of 1840 suggested a way of getting young men to join the Repeal Association which was decidedly gentler than Ribbon recruitment practices:

Come all you pretty fair maids of counterie and town, If any lad should ask your hand your nuptial joys to crown, First put the question to him before you say yes or no, Tell him he's a traitor if he has no card to show.[56]

O'Neill Daunt describes the 'Repeal Missioners' starting off from Dublin in the early 1840s, T. W. Ray bound for Munster and John O'Connell and himself, organisers respectively for Connacht and Leinster, sharing the west-bound canal boat as far as Mullingar.[57] Typically, the organiser met the local Repealers in the priest's house.

The priest tells his guest the effective strength of the district, availing himself, in the detail, of the local information possessed by the parishioners, or the neighbouring clergy, who have assembled at his house. It is then ascertained who will work; who will undertake the duty of Repeal Warden; who will collect the Repeal rent; and who will assume the charge of particular ploughlands, if in the country, or wards, if in a town. The obstacles are also canvassed; the hostility of Lord so-and-so, or of Captain—his agent who swears he will eject every tenant who

gives sixpence to any of O'Connell's devices! . . . The problem is
speedily solved. What need Squire A. or Lord B. know about the
tenants' contributions?[58]

In the towns, O'Connell had rather different problems, however.
In Dublin, the artisans had evolved an ideology which looked back
on the eighteenth-century regime nostalgically as a political
system which had at least possessed the potential for solving their
problems and which saw a Repeal parliament as a means by which
their industries might get support or protection. The artisans
expressed a desire for 'a different society; one in which . . . the
worker's labour was protected, in which worker-employer relations were based on mutual agreement, one where disputes could
be settled by arbitration'.[59] The artisans appear to have been more
interested in repeal than O'Connell was, thus continuing the
tradition of Dublin nationalism based on protectionism and
corporatism.[60] O'Connell applied the same close-knit territorial
organisation of the repeal movement to Dublin, ensuring that
there was a club for every street and a hierarchy of clubs at parish
and ward levels crowned with a general committee at the Corn
Exchange.[61] His relations with the townsmen were, however,
uneasy. In the early 1830s, he tried to capture the Dublin-based
'National Trades Political Union' and got an anti-O'Connell union
leader, Marcus Costello, a job in Gibraltar to get him out of the
way.[62] However, the union lost the confidence of its members and
became increasingly middle class in its leadership. O'Connell's
obdurate opposition to such cherished artisan objectives as the
closed shop and the minimum wage kept his relations with
them uneasy.[63]

O'Connell's parliamentary party was more old-fashioned than
his extra-parliamentary apparatus. Repeal MPs elected between
1832 and 1847 were fairly evenly divided between Catholics and
Protestants. On the Protestant side they were nearly all landowners,
and landed interests were prominent among the Catholic MPs as
well.[64] It was a curious combination: a party of local notables
linked not to local informal caucuses controlled by the MP, but to
a rather advanced mass political machine based on priests and

regularly appointed local officers set up on quasi-military lines, centralised and disciplined by a central caucus controlled by the Liberator. Parliamentary discipline was impressive only by the standards of the period; what was impressive by any standard was the discipline of the extra-parliamentary organisation. As John Whyte has noted, O'Connell relied not so much on his voting strength in parliament as on massive displays of public opinion outside.[65] His 'monster meetings' in support of repeal were spectacular in size, some of them approaching a quarter of a million, well drilled and pledged to temperance for the day after the style of the Father Mathew movement. However, when the British government used the threat of force to back up its ban on the Clontarf monster meeting of 1843, it knocked the props from under O'Connell's entire political position. By threatening force, the government discredited O'Connell's formula of militant constitutionalism and assisted in the re-emergence of unconstitutional politics.

Young Ireland had started off as an intellectuals' faction within the repeal movement, centred around the *Nation* newspaper. Many of the leading lights of Young Ireland were Protestants, graduates of Trinity College and politically far more liberal than the ageing Liberator or the bishops and priests who supported him. Some of them were able journalists, and they organised a network of 'Repeal reading-rooms' around the country, where copies of the *Nation* and other nationalist literature would be available to the newly literate younger generation. The split between O'Connell and Young Ireland actually occurred over education, the bishops being determined to resist non-denominational education, partly out of fear of proselytism. Much of the tension was due to the oligarchic character of the association, power being concentrated in the hands of an O'Connell dynastic cabal. The *Nation* was excluded from the reading-rooms, the radicals were purged and there was an open split. A clear rural-urban division emerged, the rural areas staying with O'Connell and the priests, while the radicals received substantial working-class and other town support.[66] In Dublin, a large proportion of the Repeal Association rebelled openly against O'Connell in 1846. The 'Remonstrance Repealers' first meeting was attended by an audience in which artisans and tradesmen were heavily represented, and seventy-four out of 120 repeal wardens in Dublin signed the Remonstrance protesting against the expulsion of the Young Irelanders.[67] The establishment of a radical nationalist Irish Confederation followed in January 1847. The regular Dublin artisan trade unions actually supported O'Connell, and working-class participation in the Confederation was of individuals and of neighbourhood and kin groups rather than of the unions as a body.[68] The Confederation, which attempted to build a pledge-bound parliamentary party, got support mainly in the towns. The peasantry mourned the Liberator and believed, it was said, that the Young Irelanders had broken their leader's heart: '. . . they would not hear of them as candidates'.[69] Some countrymen were harder headed; the outbreak of the French Revolution in February 1848, combined with the hopelessness of their political situation and the horrifying progress of the Famine, pushed the Young Ireland leaders into a desperate rebellion. The 1848 Rising was an utter fiasco; the leaders were military amateurs and the peasantry distrusted these new leaders or were too demoralised to follow them. Afterwards, however, the example of these young radicals, their ability to publicise themselves and their political views through journalism, their disgust with the machine parliamentarianism of O'Connell and their romantic militancy contributed to the formation of a new and more uncompromising revolutionary nationalism. Significantly, this new nationalism prospered, particularly among the young men who emigrated to the United States after 1848, bringing with them bitter memories of the Famine and the *Nation's* beliefs as to who was to blame.

Not that those who stayed in Ireland were particularly prone to exculpate the government. According to the resident magistrates, the main popular sentiment in Munster after the 1848 Rising was regret that it had failed and irritation at the clergy's opposition to the rebels.[70]

By the time of the Famine, the main institutions of Irish popular politics were virtually complete. The ideas of a drilled electorate, a pledge-bound parliamentary party, a nationwide communications network, a disciplined activist organisation and the possibilities of agrarian or clerical alliances all existed in well-developed form, overlaying but not displacing the older concept of extra-constitutional violent action. Furthermore, popular action independent of clerical leadership was seen as conceivable. What had not arrived was the occasion when all these institutional technologies could be used together.

04 | SECRET SOCIETIES AND PARTY POLITICS AFTER THE FAMINE

THE SOCIAL BACKGROUND

Nineteenth-century Ireland was the scene of enormous social change, and the development of party politics was closely intertwined with that change. Demographic and linguistic changes are perhaps the best documented: the population of the island almost doubled between 1800 and 1847 and shrank again to roughly the 1800 figure by 1900, while the Irish language, possibly the spoken language of the majority of the population in 1800 and spoken by a very large proportion in 1840, was the every-day language of less than one-fifth of the people in 1900 and was retreating very rapidly before English. Other politically important changes occurred. The shift from Irish to English was accompanied by a massive growth in literacy in English and by the growth of a popular press. The development of a better-organised popular Catholicism appears to date from mid-century as well and is con-nected with the extraordinary change in popular religious practice that has come to be termed the 'Devotional Revolution'.

After 1800, the pressure of rural population on the land had increased until it passed subsistence levels in many areas. Subdivision of holdings occurred on an enormous scale, and it has been repeatedly suggested that the process of subdivision was originally tolerated or even encouraged by landlords for electoral purposes.[1] Certainly, the intimidated authorities were later unable to prevent the process which their own policies or non-policies had done so much to encourage; by the 1820s, solutions such as forcible clearances or prohibitions on subdivision had come under the veto of Captain Rock. The willingness of the people to endure privation, the absence of alternative employment and their inability or unwillingness to emigrate in sufficiently large numbers, coupled with the early age of marriage and their propensity to have large families, were also factors that encouraged extreme subdivision and dependence on the potato. Subdivision commonly occurred informally and illegally, by private understandings among the peasants themselves or as part of an uncontrolled and uncontrollable process of subletting by small tenants to even smaller tenants below them again.[2] Pathetic conflicts between tiny 'middlemen' or 'ternybegs' (*tiarnaí beaga* = little landlords) occurred, and conflict between the more and less landed was chronic.[3] The effect of the Famine was to end in a Malthusian way the process which had come to be the central dynamic in Irish rural society. The deaths of perhaps a million people, the immediate emigration of perhaps another million, forcible and voluntary clearances and the advent of a new commercial landholding class, many of whom were Catholics, accompanied a changeover from tillage to a more cash-oriented pastoral economy. Within two decades, Irish rural society had changed completely. To generalise, the enormous classes of small tenants and landless labourers who had dominated the society shrank and the numbers of middle-sized and large landholders grew. This post-Famine configuration had been anticipated in eastern areas before the Famine, and pre-Famine conditions persisted for another generation in parts of the west. Eventually, a new pattern of small to middle-sized farms, varying enormously in commercial viability, emerged, with the exception of certain areas in the east, north Connacht and Munster where huge grazing farms or 'ranches' emerged. The landless labourer survived in the east and south as part of a slowly declining class, and tension grew up, not only between farmers and landlords, but between different types of farmer and between farmer and labourer.

Even family structure was changed to fit in with the new property system. Marriages occurred later and later, until by the early twentieth century the average marriage age of the Irish farming community was one of the highest in the world. Late marriage was geared to farm inheritance and ensured against sub-division. Massive and continuous emigration to the United States was institutionalised for similar reasons.[4] An intensification of certain traditional attitudes towards sex accompanied an increasing tendency towards lifelong celibacy for much of the population.

Another immediate change was the penetration of the country-side by the popular press, a process which had started before the Famine, but which was accelerated in the 1850s by the abolition of a heavy stamp duty on newspapers. The advent of the English-language newspaper raised possibilities of new, standardised forms of popular politics and hastened the spread of political news, ideas and attitudes, making the traditional role of the itinerant school-master redundant.[5]

A change of long-term political importance was the development of a huge and embittered American diaspora of Irish rural origin. Because of literacy, emigrants were no longer 'dead' to people at home, but could stay in contact by letter, send home news and money, offer assistance to relatives who wished to follow them and even offer political advice. An unknown number of these emigrants came back to Ireland and put the experience they had gained in the United States to good use at home. 'Returned Yanks' with their money, self-confidence and new-fangled ideas became stock characters, and the Fenian movement was virtually created by men of this sort. Like other expatriates, Irish-Americans were sometimes more aggressive and determined nationalists than the people at home.

A parallel and profound series of changes in religious culture occurred. The clergy, because of their religious role and because of their status as educated men, were natural social leaders. The relationship of the priest to the community appears to have changed during the middle decades of the century, partly as a result of certain international political developments and because of the papacy of Pius IX, partly because of the social upheaval in Ireland and partly because of a long process of ecclesiastical reorganisation which dated back to the establishment of Maynooth College in

1795.[6] The continued political dominance of Irish society by a non-Catholic caste, combined with the absence of any great social or ideological gap between the common people and the lower clergy, meant that no clear cleavage occurred between popular political radicalism and the Church. Churchmen opposed radicalism and secularism, but Irish popular radicalism was not particularly secularist. In fact, political radicalism affected the Church itself internally and the tension within the Church was at times very great. Many of the bishops, because of their own preferences or because they were responsive to Vatican or government pressure, were more likely to take conservative lines than were some of the lower clergy. The latter were often likely to be influenced by nationalist sentiment.[7] These differences may have been aggravated by social distinctions within the clergy: the bishops often came of older, semi-aristocratic Catholic families, whereas many of the lower clergy were recruited from the families of shopkeepers and tenant-farmers, those key social categories of nineteenth-century Ireland.[8] Furthermore, whereas in the eighteenth century many Irish priests had been trained on the continent, after 1795 an increasing number received their training in Ireland. What the exact effect of this change was is difficult to say precisely, but it may have weakened older attitudes which accepted the political order and distrusted democratic ideas.

The social role of the priests expanded enormously. Education became virtually a clerical monopoly and the Church became the prime mover in the shift towards a more puritanical, socially disciplined, anglicised and thrifty social culture.[9] The clergy recruited on a vast scale. In 1800, there was one priest for every 2,100 Catholics in Ireland. This ratio remained the same until 1850, but by 1870, the ratio was one priest to 1,250 Catholics; by 1900 it was one to an astonishing 900. On the distaff side, the transition, significantly, came earlier; there was only one Catholic nun for every 32,000 Catholics in 1800 and there was one nun for every 3,400 Catholics in 1850. By 1900, the ratio was an incredible 1:400. The religious revivalism of the 1840s was accompanied by a very successful temperance crusade, the Munster-based Father Mathew movement. Temperance had helped the repeal movement by ensuring that the rallies were disciplined and sober; temperance movements weakened Ribbonism because it kept the young men out of the public houses and therefore away from the Ribbon masters. In the 1850s, there was a huge increase in popular participation in Church-organised devotions. Larkin suggests that fear of 'cultural death' led people to seek refuge and a new cultural identity in religion.[10] Interestingly, a parallel religious revivalism occurred in Presbyterian rural Ulster in the late 1850s, apparently fuelled by similar pressures of transition to a property system which made new psychological demands on people.[11] Methodist revivalism occurred in the British urban working class at this time.

David Miller has interpreted the Irish Catholic religious revival in more directly economistic terms as being a form of cultural adjustment to the psychological demands of a new property system: rural modernisation involved a landholding system which set limits to the subdivision process. The prohibition on subdivision in turn affected marriage rates and ages of marriage, and that again involved sexual abstinence, puritanism and social regimentation. The clergy enforced a code of conduct which was, at a deeper level, generated by the land-holding system and by public opinion. Formal religious practice increased as part of this syndrome; Miller points out that mass attendances were noticeably higher in English-speaking eastern areas than in Irish-speaking western ones. His evidence is not completely unambiguous: communications were better in the more anglicised and urban areas, there being more physical obstacles to attendance at mass in sparsely populated rural areas.[12]

Another change was the emergence of a commercially based prosperity among a wide section of the rural Catholic middle class between 1850 and 1877, particularly in the heartland areas of the east and south. During most of this period there was a boom in agricultural prices generated by English urban demand.[13] Parts of the western periphery remained close to pre-Famine subsistence conditions and vulnerable to potato failure, but single-crop agriculture was a thing of the past everywhere else. For the rest of the country, the more intensive monetisation of the economy and the growth of credit meant that a drastic downturn in prices such as occurred after 1877 would have immediate social repercussions and, indirectly, would put pressure on rents whose legitimacy was already traditionally doubtful in the rural political culture.

ELECTORAL POLITICS AFTER THE FAMINE

The first important essay in popular political action after the Famine was both constitutional and agrarian. The Tenant League of the 1850s benefited from franchise reforms of 1850, which widened the electorate in rural areas, and enjoyed the support of the new class of 'solid' tenant farmers. An attempt was made to unite Catholic and Protestant tenants in a movement for the attainment of a tenant right in the southern provinces analogous to that which existed in Ulster. Also, the League asked for impartial valuation and fixing of rents and the legal establishment of the right of the tenant to sell his interest or 'goodwill' in his holding.[14] Despite the good offices of liberal Ulster Protestant leaders, the League did not get substantial electoral support in Ulster. Its main strength lay in the rural and big-farm areas of the south and east, in particular in the eastern counties around Dublin.[15] The Tenant League ran out of steam rather quickly. The absence of patronage, the hostility of the landlords and the rather conditional character of the priests' alliance were among the causes of its failure, but the immediate reason was the bribing of two of its key leaders by the British government. Another reason was the mixture of support bases; much of its clerical support was due to a temporary religious bitterness, the priests being incensed by anti-Catholic demonstrations in England.[16] No new mass movement on the lines of O'Connell's associations emerged.

Electoral politics up to the 1870s were therefore constrained by mechanical factors rather similar to those which had operated in the pre-Famine period. Voting was still open and the electorate was still small. In effect, there were two political parties in Nationalist Ireland: the Liberals, who were essentially the party of the priests, and the Conservatives, who were the party of the landlords. 'Ireland virtually possessed two aristocracies: landlords and clergy wielded their sway over the same people.'[17] Irish elections were still notorious in the United Kingdom for their violence. The voters were often terrified of the political forces that wrestled for their political souls, and the physical effort to vote must have scarcely appeared worth it. In Co. Monaghan, for instance, there were only three polling booths, and the journey to vote was sometimes over twenty miles.[18] One witness of a mid-century Waterford election described soldiers being sent out to escort the unhappy voters, concluding, 'the escort . . . had to go two days' march for the voters, to receive them over from another escort, but the voters had all escaped.'[19] The use of soldiers was widely regarded as adding state to landlord intimidation. The Catholic bishop of Limerick felt in 1869 that the voters had come to regard electoral politics with utter cynicism and were looking to Washington rather than London for redress.[20]

Mobs were often hired for purposes of electoral intimidation.[21] Priests, it was usually admitted, were not averse to a bit of bully-ing, but were usually telling voters to do what they wanted to do anyway.[22] The use of bribery, 'treating', economic threats and similar 'machine' tactics probably permitted pro-landlord and Conservative elements to survive electorally somewhat longer than they would otherwise have done.[23] Threats of violence by both sides were common, as were crude economic threats by landlords.[24]

Landlords often felt that the tenants had a duty to vote for their candidates. Lord Clanrickarde was surprised and deeply hurt by his tenants' refusal to vote for his candidate at the Galway by-election of 1872.[25] Elections were occasions of very great popular excitement, as deep political passions were roused by the cam-paigns and the polling days were treated as a kind of extended holiday. Priests sometimes appear to have been even more suscep-tible than their parishioners to the general mood of excitement and near-hysteria.[26]

Some residual 'feudal' loyalty or regard for individual landlords survived, but it appears to have lingered only among a minority of the Catholic population, most of which looked to the priests or to the nationalist and agrarian agitators for political leadership. However, no lay political leadership of any united kind existed before the introduction of the secret ballot; there had been no real recovery from the collapse of the Repeal Association.

THE RECRUDESCENCE OF REPUBLICANISM: FENIANISM AND THE AGRARIANS

The secret society known variously as the Irish Revolutionary Brotherhood, the Fenians and, most commonly and most officially, as the Irish Republican Brotherhood (IRB) was the creation of people who were, in the main, veterans of 1848. Its links with Young Ireland are clear, and it appears to have inherited some of the various radical urban groups associated with the split in the repeal movement. Young Ireland had, however, been impressed by James Fintan Lalor's argument that the agrarian question was central to the Irish nationalist cause and that political nationalism should be 'hitched' to the motor of agrarianism. The subsequent squalid failure of the Tenant League turned one early Fenian leader, John O'Leary, off agrarian-constitutional politics permanently.[27] The early Fenians were American based and, in Ireland, were clearly a town-based movement which united middle- and working-class men. In the smaller towns and in the countryside, its support was weaker, except in certain areas of the country where local circumstances happened to be hospitable. The rural population outside these areas stayed aloof from early Fenianism: eventually, the Fenians, who had usually insisted on the primacy of the national issue over the agrarian issue, were forced to accommodate themselves to the peasantry and farmers, rather than the reverse. A precursor of the Fenian movement existed in the towns and villages of west Cork and south Kerry in the 1850s, under the title of the Phoenix Society. The members of this series of clubs were young men, typically the sons of shopkeepers, of a less agrarian background and of rather higher status than the rank and file of the old agrarian societies. Schoolteachers were prominent in these clubs and their main activities appear to have been drilling and the study of Irish history, an explosive combination of activities that was to become a traditional preoccupation of Irish patriotic societies.[28]

Irish Fenianism started in Dublin in 1858 and rapidly became a popular movement. In 1859, the *Nation* organised a popular petition for a plebiscite on the union, and parish branches of the National Petition Movement were formed in the city to collect

signatures at church doors after Sunday mass. Several of these
local branches became permanent organisations, some of them
becoming athletic clubs, and were later absorbed into the Fenian
movement.[29] Like earlier associations, the Fenians often used
funerals as occasions for recruitment and political demonstration.
In the United States, the Fenian organisation was the creation of a
group of political exiles who, with elliptical humour, founded the
'Emmet Monument Association' in 1854. The term 'Fenian' was the
invention of John O'Mahony, a Tipperary man of antiquarian
interests and rather aristocratic and romantic political sentiments.
The term is an anglicisation of the Irish word *Fianna* (warriors,
army) and was intended to commemorate the legendary pre-
Christian militia of Fionn Mac Cumhaill. The use of Gaelic
symbolism obscures the fact that the Fenians were a thoroughly
modern movement by the standards of the period, not all that
different in organisation and composition from revolutionary or
radical movements elsewhere. Its ideology, unlike that of Ribbonism,
was liberal, separatist and neither agrarian nor sectarian. Some
early Fenians were liberal Protestants and the American separation
of church and state appears to have influenced their thinking. The
dominant personality of the early Fenian movement was James
Stephens, an 1848 veteran who had spent some time in Paris and
had some contact with Marx. He was, however, no socialist. An
extravagant and self-willed figure, Stephens walked Ireland
incognito in the late 1850s, using the romantic alias of *An Seabhach
Siúbhalach* (The Wandering Hawk), a nickname promptly rendered
into English by the people as 'Mr Shooks'.[30] He was sometimes
taken for a strolling player or a circus proprietor, a not inappro-
priate judgement when the air of make-believe and theatricality
which surrounded so much of the early Fenians is considered.[31]
The organisation of the IRB was intended to be both secret and
military. Stephens reported studying Italian secret societies such
as the Carbonari and claimed to have adapted their cell system to
Irish purposes. There was, however, adequate local precedent.[32]
The cell system, intended to frustrate the police, actually had
disintegrative effects; as no one knew the doings of the IRB
outside his own cell or 'circle', there was a chronic suspicion of

outsiders, even when they were accredited members of the movement.[33] Organisational decay was endemic to Fenianism. In effect, local groups had great independence of the centre and could, like Ribbon lodges, be turned to local purposes; in many cases, local circles became indistinguishable from the Ribbon lodges from which they were so often descended. John Devoy admitted in 1879, '... It is needless to point out that a protracted conspiracy, however good its object, is liable in a thousand ways to be abused for the promotion of personal ends, the gratification of personal malignity, or the advancement of personal ambition.'[34] Before the abortive Rising of 1867, the organisation was artisan and petit bourgeois and had a general appeal to working-class young men. Trade unions, friendly societies, Dublin drapery stores, the building trades, shoemakers' and tailors' premises were good recruiting grounds, medical students ('doctors') also being conspicuous. Many of the young shop assistants in the early organisation were of rural origin.[35] John O'Leary remembered the early Fenians as 'shopmen, small shopkeepers and small farmers'. In the 1860s, successful attempts were made to infiltrate the British army. Of 1,086 Fenians arrested in 1867, only about 10 per cent were farmers, farmers' sons or agricultural labourers.[36] Young artisans were conspicuous among the prisoners brought before the Dublin Special Commission in April 1867.[37] Of 265 Fenian prisoners actually tried, artisans accounted for one-third of the total and labourers for one-quarter. There was also a significant number of small shopkeepers and their employees, together with a group of what would nowadays be described as white-collar workers. Only 4 per cent were farmers or farmers' sons, mainly Tipperary men, and their holdings varied wildly in size from a few acres to well over a hundred.[38]

Another way of assessing the social make-up of the Fenians is to examine county-level membership figures collected by an informer in 1866. The absolute numbers should not be taken too seriously, but the relative sizes of the numbers can be taken as a fair estimate of the relative strength of the IRB in different parts of the country.[39] Standardising the figures by total county population, Dublin scored highest despite its large size and Sligo, a notorious

Ribbon centre fifteen years earlier, was in second place. Cork and Kilkenny were joint third, Antrim and Tipperary joint fourth and Louth was in fifth place. In most of these cases, Fenianism was stated to be stronger in the towns, Clonmel, for example, being a hotbed. All of these counties were urbanised by Irish standards, with the partial exceptions of Tipperary and Sligo. Fenianism was weakest in the counties of Cavan, Clare, Donegal, Kerry, King's, Leitrim, Londonderry, Meath, Queen's, Wexford and Wicklow, in that ascending order of Fenian strength. The four weakest counties and Leitrim were peripheral as defined in Chapter 1, and King's and Queen's were on the western border of Leinster. The weaker counties were generally less urban; the correlation of Fenian membership in 1866 with the urbanisation rate is a very strong .68 (N = 32). Fenianism was mainly a townsman's society, and was initially strongest in Leinster and Munster.[40] An improving landlord in Tipperary described them contemptuously as the 'merest rabble of shopboys, and suchlike' from the towns.[41] Archbishop Croke considered that Fenianism only prospered in rural parishes where the local parish priest was incompetent, eccentric or inactive.[42] The combined effects of remoteness from urban centres, the resistance of local Ribbon groups to new-fangled ideologies and the social control of the clergy together with Fenianism's hostility to agrarianism seem to have been the causes of this pronouncedly urban distribution during the society's first phase. On the other hand, there was little rural hostility to the Fenians, and the would-be guerrillas of 1867 found that country people were willing to shelter them, even if they were unwilling to join them.

The failure of the Rising discredited the physical force option and weakened the leaders' credibility. It also caused the IRB to be less able to resist involvement in conventional politics. The movement tended to disintegrate into local groups, more or less autonomous, loosely in contact with each other and with the central leadership. Individual Fenian circles often became involved in local politics without any sanction from the central leadership. The leaders, badly split themselves and still planning the attainment of a secularist bourgeois republic by rather romantically envisaged open warfare, viewed these local anticipations of the New Departure with some unease. Connacht Fenianism in particular developed into a kind of political party organisation in the late 1860s. Local centres included a Tuam saddler, a Ballinasloe building contractor (Matthew Harris), a journalist, an adventurer/soldier turned journalist (J.J. O'Kelly), a Loughrea 'substantial shopkeeper' (Joseph O'Flaherty), a shoemaker, a clerk, a tailor, a national schoolteacher and an American Civil War veteran.[43] In the Galway by-election which marked the return of aggressive electoral politics in the west, these Fenians became electoral campaigners. The nationalist candidate won and was promptly unseated for alleged electoral intimidation.[44] In Limerick and elsewhere in Munster the IRB was active in elections from the late 1860s onward.[45] In Tipperary in 1869, Rossa was elected on a 'free the prisoners' plank in the face of both clerical and Conservative opposition. At some local contests, the Church's fear of Fenianism had the strange effect of generating local tactical alliances between the IRB and Conservatives against the Liberal candidate favoured by the clergy.[46] In 1879 in Longford, an even more bizarre align-ment occurred, a local aristocratic candidate being backed by the priests against a nationalist who happened to be supported by Fenians and 'outsiders'. Church and property joined together to oppose city-based radicalism encroaching on their local turf. A handbill urged the electors to vote with their priests and not to vote with the 'mongrel Fenian-Orange crew': 'Who are these Dublin spouters? Can any man in your county say he ever saw, or knew, or trusted them or their fathers before them? Can any man say whether ever one of them had an honest father before him? Away with the raiders! It is the battle of religion against Fenianism!'[47] Clerical dismay at the development of a new style of lay 'revolution by election' lasted until the 1880s, and some priests remained unreconciled to the idea of a completely lay nationalist movement unsupervised by the clergy.

The increased rural bias of the IRB which accompanied the mobilisation of a farmer and peasant electorate in the 1870s shows up in the gross figures of Fenian membership by county which have survived. By 1878, the original urban movement had shrunk to a few small groups in the towns, often demoralised and cut off from the main organisation. Almost as though to counterbalance this urban shrinkage, the IRB had grown considerably in western and north-western areas. The five strongest Fenian counties now were, in descending order of strength, Monaghan, Cavan, Sligo, Roscommon and Leitrim, all western borderland counties and all counties with a strong Ribbon history. The correlation of the 1878 figures with the urbanisation rate was –21 (N=31), a correlation certainly weakened by the absence of reliable Dublin figures. There was a correlation of –.01 (N=31) between the 1866 and the 1878 figures, indicating negligible geographical continuity between the two years.[48] This 'Ribbon-Fenian' pattern, which emerged on the eve of the Land War, was to persist for a very long time. These 'Ribbon-Fenian' counties of the west and north-west were to show persistently high rates of participation in agrarian and nationalist organisations over the following century and formed the area of the island where agrarian feeling, sectarian tension, cultural change and peripheral effects overlapped most. John Rutherford, an unreliable writer disliked by the IRB, observed in 1877 that Fenianism, in the ten years after 1867

> . . . made little progress north or west except in a few of the principle towns. The Orangeism of Ulster was a stubborn obstacle in its path; and nearly as stubborn was the Ribbonism of Connaught. The older rebellious association was jealous of the newer . . . Then the views of the newer society were far broader and more liberal. Ribbonism contained much religious fanaticism. On the other hand, the [IRB] . . . deprecated religious strife, spoke slightingly of the priest . . . in short, the liberalism of Fenianism stood much in its way with the men of Connaught; nor was it until a date comparatively recently in its history that it obtained a solid footing in the province *where it is today the strongest.*[49]

What is not mentioned in this and other contemporary accounts is the weakening of urban Fenianism which accompanied the growth of the society's interest in the agrarian question. Many of the original Fenians were quite conventional men, Luby and Grey, for example, disapproving of Stephens' Parisian bohemianism, his vaguely socialistic ideas, his 'self-conceit' and his 'loose attitude to women'.[50] The clergy's fear of their liberalism was due to a confusion of it with continental anti-clerical radicalism. Gradually, they realised that Fenianism was not particularly anti-clerical and equally gradually the IRB discovered the political merits of agrarianism, at a time when town radicals were beginning to discover the attractions of socialism. Gradually, they conquered their unease about electoral politics. Fenians had been allowed to participate in constitutional organisations and could try to get elected to local representative bodies, but getting involved in electoral politics under the tempting terms of the expanded franchise of 1867 and the Ballot Act of 1872 appeared to some leaders to endanger the whole military character of the movement. What was happening, of course, was that an emerging constitutional movement of great power was insensibly swallowing the IRB up, the rebels were being turned into a party organisation of a new and unprecedented type. The old purist Fenians watched the development with unease.[51] John O'Leary in particular looked back on the conversion of the west to Fenianism rather unhappily: '... [Edward] Duffy was the first who made much impression on those intractable and ignorant Ribbonmen, who have, I fear, been much more come-atable for political purposes ever since.'[52] After 1878, the tension between unconstitutional separatism and constitutional agrarianism, paralleling republican versus Home Rule divisions, resulted in a series of splits into 'Old Fenians', 'Ribbon-Fenians' and a fringe of *enragés*, some of whom became dynamitards. The mass of 'Ribbon-Fenians', under Devoy and Davitt, severed their formal connection with the old movement and cast in their lot with Parnell's New Departure.

THE IRB AND IRISH POLITICS AFTER THE LAND WAR
The IRB, however, survived the upheavals of the 1880s and was to have a decisive effect on nationalist politics in the twentieth century. At the risk of breaking the chronological sequence and of anticipating later discussion, this section outlines certain aspects of this extraordinary society's development after 1880. While

becoming involved in the constitutional agrarian movement, the Fenians tried to keep separatist ideas afloat and adopted a policy of getting involved in any organisation which showed separatist potential. With the obvious and all-important exception of the Land League itself, perhaps the most important organisation to be infiltrated by the IRB was the Gaelic Athletic Association (GAA). After 1880, a long-drawn-out rivalry occurred between the IRB and the clergy for control of various local social organisations dedicated to the preservation and revival of the Irish language and tradition. In the case of the Gaelic Athletic Association, founded just after the Land War, the priests were actually defeated by the republicans, and this organisation was to become a central source of recruits to nationalist causes in Ireland in later years. The GAA, by organising young men into football and hurling clubs, acted as a substitute for the old parish factions which had absorbed the energies of the young men in the pre-Famine period. Like the factions, although primarily recreational in purpose, the GAA also acted as a framework within which local social leaders could operate, and had a political undercurrent: the GAA was in many ways the true parent of the IRA of the Anglo-Irish War of 1919–21.

In the years immediately after its founding in 1884, the GAA was confined to the southern half of the island: it was a Munster and south Leinster organisation, absorbing much of the old secret society and factional tradition into itself, and remaining relatively immune to the Ribbonism of the north. Its original strong areas were also those areas of Norman settlement where the ancient game of hurling had survived through feudal and landlord encouragement. Hurling, a game which resembles field hockey, is prehistoric in its origins and is, unlike soccer, difficult to become proficient at unless it is taken up in childhood. For that reason, it was under threat from various forms of football. Football is an English import into Ireland, and in the seventeenth century was confined to an area of medieval English settlement in north Dublin. It tended to displace hurling, however. Michael Cusack, one of the founders of the GAA, solved the problem by inventing a form of football which could, unlike soccer, be played on the same pitch as hurling. This 'Gaelic' football, in which handling the ball is permitted, was organised in parallel to hurling, and had the effect of preventing the spread of English-style soccer into Ireland, with the exception of some of the large towns and the Protestant areas of Ulster. The GAA was nationalist in its politics, but it was originally run by a moderate combination of clergy, Home Rulers and republicans. In 1887, however, it was taken over by IRB elements in a spectacular organisational coup, and for the next few years the GAA was used as a stalking-horse and recruiting ground by the movement.[53] Thus, at a time when Parnell had brought the clergy into the constitutional party to balance the republicans, the republicans were attempting to push the priests out of the GAA, an organisation with enormous long-term potential. At the same convention, the famous 'ban' which prohibited GAA members from playing or watching allegedly 'foreign' games such as soccer, rugby or hockey was imposed.

These measures of segregation helped to perpetuate and aggra-vate traditional hostility to the police and isolated Catholic youth behind the walls of a different football code and the game of hurling. This made them available for nationalist indoctrination and prevented the young men from gaining access to attitudes and ideas which had not been approved of by the nationalist leaders. Eventually, many of the clergy saw the advantages of such a cultural *cordon sanitaire* and came to accept the organisation and to support it; in the beginning, however, relations were somewhat strained. The GAA became thoroughly infiltrated by the Brother-hood at lower levels as well. Even during the 1890–98 period, when Fenianism was generally regarded as being moribund, recruiting continued for the IRB. Although the Fenians saw themselves as innovative and progressive forces in Irish society, the republican society was oddly reminiscent of far older secret societies.[54] For example, a police informer ('Emerald') in Kerry in the early 1890s was offered IRB membership in terms reminiscent of Defenderism: 'When he had been about six months in the GAA he was accosted . . . by Maurice Moynihan, Secretary of Kerry GAA and County Centre of the IRB who asked him if he would wish to become a man. Emerald said that he *was* a man. Moynihan replied that he was only a boy, but that he could make a man of him.'[55]

Local factions based on kin existed within the GAA, and Fenian and Ribbon tendencies coexisted rather than coalesced in parts of the north-west, often in open rivalry with each other. The neo-Ribbon Ancient Order of Hibernians eventually developed into a clericalist counter-organisation to both Orangeism and Fenianism in Ulster.[56] These developments are discussed in more detail in Chapter 6. The penetration of the GAA was impressive, and by 1890 clerical influence within the GAA was weak. Police records indicate that nearly half of the GAA county committee men in 1890 were IRB members, and fragmentary evidence in the RIC files indicates that the IRB men tended to be more energetic and to hold key offices at local level. IRB committee men were rather less likely to be farmers or farmers' sons than non-IRB committee men and were more likely to be publicans or artisans; despite their involvement in rural politics after 1879, the Fenians had held on to something of their non-agrarian character.[57]

The events of 1887 and the grip of the IRB over the organisation led to clerical distrust of the GAA, a distrust which nearly wrecked the athletics association after the Parnell split. Even before the fall of Parnell, however, the police had noticed that the GAA was being weakened even in Munster by clerical displeasure. 'It appears that the priests have been objecting to the people spending their Sundays travelling about to matches and getting drunk instead of attending Chapel etc . . . I think many of the clergy have taken alarm at what was revealed at the Thurles convention, and would be glad to throw cold water on the further progress of the association.'[58]

The Irish Republican Brotherhood, then, became the main 'opposition party' within the nationalist movement, a movement which included every shade of ideological opinion from extreme clerical monarchist to Utopian socialist. Despite the dominant position of the Irish Party and the development of an agrarian 'Ribbon-Fenian' tendency in the 1870s, Fenianism, which saw itself as a secret army but which resembled nothing so much as a conspiratorial political party like the Bolsheviks, persisted as the alternative to constitutional politics because of its influence in sporting and cultural associations. In effect it played Bolshevik to the constitutionalists' Menshevik in nationalist politics after 1890.

05 | AGRARIANISM, NATIONALISM AND PARTY POLITICS, 1874–95

POLITICAL MOBILISATION AND THE AGRARIAN CAMPAIGN

The franchise extension of 1867 had not brought any immediate radical change in party politics. The crucial reform was the introduction of the Secret Ballot Act in 1872, which permitted the expansion of a type of politics which had existed in embryo form previously. A liberal and inter-denominational attempt by gentry, middle-class and ex-Fenian elements to campaign for 'federal' Home Rule was made in 1870 under the aegis of Butt's Home Government Association. This group tried to separate the political demand for Home Rule from issues such as landlord-tenant relationships, amnesty for Fenian prisoners or denominational education. The testing of the political market by these respectable Home Rulers in 1871–2 indicated that although portions of the aristocracy and gentry still preserved their hankering for a Dublin parliament, the popular sympathy for such a proposal and for social and agrarian reform was far more substantial. From the point of view of anyone who wanted to win elections, the popular sympathy was beginning to be more important than any other.[1] Their findings also suggested that what was left of landlord sympathy for Home Rule would be rapidly dissipated by any attempt to link it with the agrarian and educational issues.[2] The general elections of 1874 and 1880 confirmed these expectations. In 1874, a 'Home Rule' label appeared in the Commons for the first time, and the numbers of Home Rulers increased significantly in 1880. At the same time, the social backgrounds of Irish MPs changed drastically: of 105 Irish MPs in 1868, 69 per cent were landlords or landlords' sons, but the proportion in 1874 was only 49 per cent. The number of MPs with professional backgrounds doubled, the proportion of MPs with such backgrounds going from 10 to 23 per cent between 1868 and 1874, foreshadowing the heavy professional representation in the Irish Party of later decades; by the early 1890s, the proportion of professional men in the parliamentary party had exceeded 50 per cent.[3] The democratisation of electoral politics led to the demise of landlord-led politics in nationalist Ireland and also to the end of any real inter-confessional nationalism divorced from social and religious issues.

The pressure of the agrarian issue on parliamentary politics grew as economic conditions changed. Since the Famine, Irish agriculture had enjoyed a boom, but as the population fell, the area devoted to tillage and to subsistence agriculture fell. Grazier ranches and smaller pastoral farms emerged, even in Connacht. Between 1851 and 1873, prices 'moved markedly in favour of animals and against the products of the plough'.[4] This evolution resulted in commercial farmers, whether large graziers or small farmers with an interest in the British cattle trade, emerging as an important and increasingly cohesive social category over most of the country, even quite small farmers in remote areas being tied into the market through the rearing of young stock for sale to larger and less remote farmers. Transportation and retail trade also expanded and there was a good deal of upward social mobility. An increasingly literate and prosperous population, well organised and possessed of a traditional sense of social solidarity, occupied most of rural and small-town Ireland. They were also developing into a public, were increasingly capable of organising themselves for political purposes and of maintaining discipline and solidarity in large numbers for long periods.[5]

This evolution coincided with the secret ballot and with the end of the twenty-year commercial boom. A further circumstance was the return of the potato blight in parts of the west in the late 1870s. In 1877, prices fell and farmers, whose credit had become over-extended during the long boom, looked to their landlords, politically the weakest of their creditors, for relief.[6] The prosperous farmer had no interest in the continuation of landlordism; traditional rancour and material interest coincided. Sudden economic shifts made an anti-rent campaign financially attractive, and cultural changes made a nationwide campaign organisationally feasible. Cultural continuity, on the other hand, supplied the folk memories that questioned the property rights of the landowner, excused agrarian crime and strengthened local solidarity against the outside. The Land War was a classic end result of a 'revolution of rising expectations' and had been prefigured by the galvanising effect of the agricultural crash after the Napoleonic period.[7] A Tipperary farmer, interviewed in the mid-1880s, appears to speak for an entire class: 'My father could pay the rent . . . because he was content to live so that he could pay it. He sat on a boss of straw, and ate out of a bowl. He lived in a way in which I don't intend to live, and so he could pay the rent. Now, I must have, and I mean to have, out of the land, before I pay the rent, the means of living as I wish to live; and if I can't have it, I'll sell out and go away; but I'll be—if I don't fight before I do that same!'[8]

The 'frustrated rising expectations' model predicts that the better-off rather than the more materially deprived will get involved in political action. One would therefore expect that prosperous areas would be more disturbed than poorer areas, where people were presumably too busy keeping body and soul together to get involved in political and agrarian campaigns. To some extent this is true: the really poverty-stricken areas in the west were quiet, but then so were the really prosperous areas around Dublin in east Leinster. In fact, there were several regional patterns of reaction to the general crisis of 1877–79 and there was a complicated interaction among the several classes and regions involved. Both rather poor and rather better-off areas were involved in the campaign, and farmers of many different levels of prosperity were involved in the Land League. Certainly, the upheaval of 1879–82 owed much to social-psychological processes such as the feelings of frustrated material expectations or of relative deprivation which have been mentioned. A sociological factor appears to be important as well; Irish society at the time of the crisis was very close-knit, and the old tradition of militant communal solidarity was still very much alive. A tradition or norm of this kind bound everybody, rich and poor alike, those who hoped to gain materially and even those who felt that the campaign might damage their interests. An internally enforced solidarity bound richer and poorer together against outsiders and at times superseded the interests of those who might be thought of as leaders of the insurrection. Small and large farmers, labourers, artisans and the priests, shopkeepers and teachers who acted as organisers and administrators were bonded together not just by personal material interest, but by group pressure. Outside interference brought this solidarity into action, and it could also be used against an outside agency.

W. Bence Jones had complained bitterly that his tenants looked on a farm 'literally as a possession of an inheritance, not as a business', and felt that, as a well-meaning improving landlord, he was faced with a social culture of tribal and personal loyalties which valued fidelity to one's own clan and encouraged what amounted to treachery toward others.[9] If the landlord attempted to exercise the rights that were theoretically and legally his, local resistance was likely. There is some evidence that landlord intervention became less tolerable during the 1850–77 period. One extreme reaction to unbridled landlordism was assassination, the most dramatic example being the murder of Lord Leitrim, his clerk and his jarvey in Donegal in 1878. The killers were well known locally, but no one turned queen's evidence and the very considerable reward was never paid. After Irish independence, a very pious cross was erected in the area in memory of the assassins who, according to the inscription, 'by their heroism . . . ended the Tyranny of Landlordism in Ireland'.[10] Elsewhere, even well-intentioned attempts by landlords to regulate farming practices generated irritation and an increasing reluctance to tolerate such intervention.[11] The effects of what I have already described as diffuse political alienation should also be considered. The old distrust of government had been noticed by outside observers in every generation since the 1790s, and was not dead in the late

1870s; the British government's legitimacy was still very shaky. In western regions, where near-Famine conditions returned in 1880, local people came to see the government as fulfilling its traditional role of remote and unsympathetic overseer: 'A popular impression ran abroad that the Government . . . were not fully persuaded of the danger, and that their distrust, as well as perhaps the feelings engendered by an intense agrarian agitation in Ireland, had communicated an equal degree of incredulity in England.'[12]

Various indicators suggest that the crisis encouraged high levels of political and agitational activity in very different areas. The first real nationalist successes in representative local government before 1880 were made in the poorer area of Bantry, Co. Cork and in prosperous and traditionally troubled east Limerick. By 1886, however, tenant representatives were entrenched on the Boards of Guardians, or local administrative councils, in a bewildering variety of places: west Mayo, west Donegal and north Kerry, all poor areas, north Leinster, south Kilkenny and Wexford, all prosperous or at least 'snug', and a broad swathe of land in central Munster. Conservative, Liberal or Unionist strength persisted mainly in eastern Ulster and in the areas surrounding Dublin and Cork.[13] Another indicator of popular political mobilisation is provided by the numbers of political clubs, as expressed as a proportion of the population, established under the aegis of nationalist-agrarian movements. The most important of these movements, the Land League, was started by a coalition of Home Rulers, ex-Fenians and agrarians and spread outside Mayo, the county of its birth, with extreme rapidity in 1879. The early Land League was far stronger in Connacht than it was elsewhere, and the more violent campaigns of the Land War were fought in the west. However, it soon became powerful elsewhere, even in prosperous areas of Munster and Leinster as well. The League became, in effect, the first Irish mass political party since O'Connell's time, combining constitutional, non-constitutional and agrarian forces in one movement. Its defenders claimed that it acted as a prophylactic against agrarian violence, and that, where it was strong, secret agrarian societies of the traditional type were weak.[14] This argument could be taken to imply that the League weakened secret societies by doing their job for them or even by absorbing their personnel and, sometimes, their methods. There are many indications that the League did not remain confined for long to the small farmers of the west; the National League, built on the Land League's organisation, was, for example, stronger in terms of branches standardised for population in the midland counties than in the more violent west.

This violence, whether in the form of agrarian outrage or in the form of threats, offers a third measure of political mobilisation. Western and central Munster, together with Galway and Leitrim in Connacht, were the most disturbed areas during the 1879–81 period. A clear west-east gradient is visible, the east being relatively immune from agrarian violence.[15] However, the poverty-stricken province of Connacht, although violent, was outdone by the richer counties of west and central Munster. Nationalist Ireland could be classified into three general regions: the east, where the campaign was weak both in terms of branches and in terms of outrages, the west, where branch-formation was only moderately strong or even weak but where violence was widespread, and lastly an intermediate area where branch-formation was high but levels of violence were usually intermediate. In some parts of this middle zone, notably Tipperary and Leitrim, indicators of violence and of League organisation were both strong, although there is little overall correlation. The relationship between the League and the violent campaign was complex and the ambiguity of the evidence was visible to observers at the time. Nationalists, of course, represented the League as being a substitute for violence, while unionists tended to represent it as the fomentor of the violence, to emphasise the 'outside agitator' theory and also to dwell on the opportunistic and brutal aspects of the campaign. In extreme form, this interpretation represented the agitation as something 'got up' by local malcontents, outside politicians and American-paid agitators and as being a reign of terror imposed by these elements on a basically law-abiding and loyal peasantry.[16] A variation on this argument omitted the flattering characterisation of the peasantry. The nationalists usually emphasised the harsh-ness of the landlords as the basic cause of the agitation, high rents and summary evictions being mentioned most frequently. As

Barbara Solow has pointed out, rents were not all that high in relation to agricultural prices, and the agitation had ensured, perhaps, that they would not keep pace with agricultural prices. Neither side had any real interest in adverting to the non-economic factor of political disaffection; the nationalists were emphasising their own constitutionality, and their opponents often preferred to represent the population as victims or dupes of agitators.

The following tentative analysis of the campaign focuses on agrarian violence, threats and evictions in an attempt to make a preliminary assessment of the relationship between popular violence and landlord eviction policies. It is also suggested that the process by which violence was sublimated led to the formation of abnormally strong political party organisations which were able, for a while, to dominate all local factions and which were not necessarily controlled by coteries of rich farmers. Figure 1 plots the official police figures on evictions and 'agrarian outrages' in Ireland from 1849 to 1913 and furnishes a useful preliminary survey of the dimensions of the agrarian troubles in Ireland over the sixty-five years between the Famine and World War I. It does, of course, mask significant regional variations in the distribution of agrarian troubles at various times, changes which will be considered later. Also, definitions of 'outrage' and 'eviction' varied from time to time and tended to be controversial. For the purposes of this chapter, the pattern of outrages and evictions for the years 1850 to 1890 is the most important.

Evictions had reached enormous proportions by the late 1840s. These Famine and post-Famine evictions constituted a classic attempt at clearance, often at the hands of new owners who were speculating in the estates of bankrupted landlords. These evictions ceased in the early 1850s and eviction rates remained at relatively low levels until the early 1880s. Not all evictions were the barbaric affairs described by nationalist propaganda, but the fact remained that the law permitted barbaric evictions, and that such evictions did sometimes happen. 'Firing outrages' dropped off symmetrically in the 1850s and remained at a low level until 1877, the main exception being the 'little land war' of 1870, when a certain amount of violence occurred, there being no relationship between outrages and eviction rates in that year. The 1877 depression was accompanied by a small rise in the numbers of evictions and a subsequent rise in the numbers of firing outrages in 1878 and 1879. However, in 1881, the numbers of outrages increased out of all proportion to the increase in evictions, and the subsequent rise in the numbers of evictions was a result of the concerted no-rent campaign rather than the cause of that campaign; 1881 proved to be the peak year for shooting, but evictions peaked the following year. Outrages diminished subsequently because of determined police action, because of the efforts of politicians and because of the substantial success of the agitation. The Plan of Campaign of the late 1880s was marked by another peak in firing outrages, and after 1890 'normal' levels were achieved. Figure 1 suggests that the relationship between evictions and violence was far more complex than any simple 'tit-for-tat' model of the process would suggest and also indicates that evictions did not touch off the Land War.

A cross-sectional analysis of the conflict during the years of mobilisation before 1881 was carried out on similar data on evictions and threatening letters available by county. The years chosen for this synchronic exercise were the immediately post-Famine year of 1850, the tranquil year of 1860, the year of 1870, for which Figure 1 suggests no outrages/evictions relationship, the pre-Land War years of 1876–78 and the crisis years of 1879 and 1880. Table 2 gives the correlations between incidence of evictions and of 'Threatening Notices and Letters', the classic indicator of moonlighting.[17]

Table 2. Evictions and threatening messages: zero-order correlations, selected years, 1850–80, thirty-one counties

Year	1850	1860	1870	1876	1877	1878	1879	1880
	0.34	0.42	0.21	0.16	0.44	0.53	0.42	0.66

The correlations in Table 2 merely suggest that a relationship did indeed exist between the two variables and that it became stronger in the late 1870s. However, it gives little help in establishing which variable causes which. Table 3 attempts to establish the causal sequence by presenting the lagged correlations between evictions

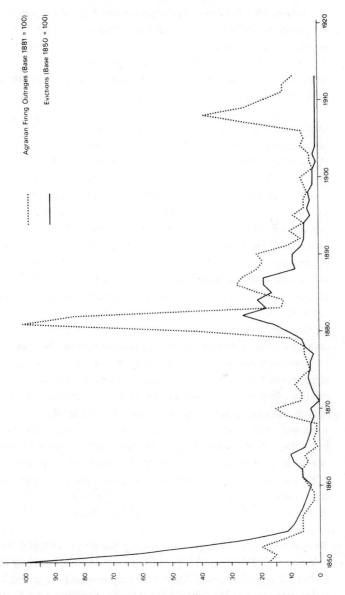

Figure 1. Land Wars: evictions and firing outrages with agrarian motivation, 1850–1913, thirty-one counties

and threats, that is, between eviction rates and the threat rate for the previous year and between threat rates and the eviction rate for the previous year.

Table 3. Evictions and threatening messages: lagged correlations, selected years, late 1870s, thirty-one counties

Year	1877	1878	1879	1880
Previous year's threats: evictions	0.28	0.47	0.56	0.28
Previous year's evictions: threats	0.17	0.49	0.71	0.64

The data presented in Figure 1, Table 2 and Table 3 can, I believe, be given the following interpretation. Prior to the mid-1870s, threats were a response to evictions only in part, and did not focus particularly on this one aspect of a generally unpopular land system. From the year 1877 on, evictions were singled out as an aspect of the system which could be focused on, dramatised and used as a symbol of wider discontent. Table 3 suggests that in the years 1877 to 1880, evictions and threats interacted, but that threats increasingly became a direct and calculated response to any attempt by the landowners to use their ultimate sanction against recalcitrant tenants: for the years 1879 and 1880, the correlations support the hypothesis that threats were a response to previous evictions despite the fact that evictions did not, in practice, increase very much; suddenly, they appear to have become intolerable, and a few well-publicised evictions could touch off a massive increase in local agrarian violence. The correlations between the previous year's evictions and the following year's incidence of threats in Table 3 are quite impressive for 1879 and 1880. Table 3 also suggests that eviction was rarely a punitive reaction to local agitation. Before 1877, then, agitation represented a normal, local and unco-ordinated response to landlord or state incursions or exactions. The adoption of the agrarian issue by the politicians and the organisation of the Land League which preceded the setting up of the Irish Party had the incidental effect of imposing the 'peculiar institution' of 'Whiteboyism', with its preoccupation with local defence and local arbitration, on the grassroots structure of the first modern Irish political party. To anticipate somewhat, arbitration of local disputes, local defence against authority and the enforcement of norms of social and economic behaviour tended to become standard functions of the local political party association, sometimes backed up by traditional sanctions such as moonlighting and the boycott. Subsequent Irish party organisations were to attempt to emulate this model, sometimes with some success.

The 1879–90 campaigns by the Land League and the National League against rents, evictions and the property system itself used traditional techniques of social resistance. These campaigns were, however, larger, more successful and less violent than those of the pre-Famine period. Assassination and assault gave way, with some reluctance, to the boycott, and party leaders appear to have tried to restrain the rank and file. Parnell himself, of course, in a famous speech in Ennis in late 1880, frankly recommended the boycott as a substitute for assassination.[18] This doctrine, in effect a modification of the traditional peasant code, found its way into popular verse, such as T. D. Sullivan's doggerel ballad about a Loughrea land-grabber called Murty Hines:

But when the noble Land League got word of this disgrace,
They sent a man to Murty to reason out the case.
'I own my crime' says Murty, 'but I'll wash out the stain:
I'll keep that farm no longer, I'll give it up again.'[19]

Murty was probably very wise; to be subject to boycott in a west of Ireland community was not a particularly pleasant experience, and in many cases public opinion had the traditional tolerance for harsh forms of boycott. Even the official campaigns were often carried on with great ruthlessness. In some areas the League machine was captured by one local kin-group or faction and used as a weapon in local quarrels. However, discipline was superior to that of previous mass organisations, and the original aims of the organisation were not lost sight of, partly because a leadership with an interest in legality and national cohesion existed and attempted to restrain the movement. The League began to develop into more than a political party and began to look like an unofficial Irish government.[20]

THE DEVELOPMENT OF THE IRISH NATIONAL LEAGUE

The Land League was suppressed by the government in 1882 and was eventually resurrected under a new label as the Irish National League. The revived organisation was, however, firmly under Parnell's control and combined a moderate agrarianism, a Home Rule programme and electoral functions. At the end of 1882 the new organisation already had 232 branches in the RIC area. It was stronger in Leinster and Munster than in Connacht or Ulster and had only one branch in Mayo.[21] Generally, it was stronger in the middle tier of counties and weaker on both the eastern and western littorals.[22] This pattern of highly organised midland counties contrasts with the pattern exhibited by violence; the most violent counties tended to be in the west and west midlands, exhibiting quite a different profile.[23]

Despite the inroads of pasture, western counties tended to be closer to pre-Famine Ireland in social structure, cultural forms and subsistence living; political action tended to be pre-modern, unsustained and sporadic. Capable of sudden surges of energy, the absence of good communications or a large and literate middle stratum ensured that mobilisation would be short lived. Any kind of modern, multi-purpose political organisation beyond the local level would be difficult to sustain and perhaps be beyond the social resources of these communities, even though such an organisation might be welcomed. In the eastern areas, by contrast, the agrarian issue was far less important. The east coast counties had, by and large, escaped much of the rural population build-up during the pre-Famine period, were English speaking and seem to have had traditionally strong ties with the industrial cities of Britain. Farmer/labourer and worker/employer relations were uneasy but could not be politicised very easily, partly because there was no inherited cultural formula that condemned the existing state of things as there was in the midland and western areas, where the Gaelic cultural substratum was so much closer to the surface.

In the midland areas which were intermediately situated on the east-west gradient, however, the potent combination of traditional agrarian cleavages, literacy in English and an active native middle class were more likely to exist in the 'right' proportions to fuel a sustained and aggressive campaign combining constitutional and illegal tactics in the usual fashion. Tipperary and Leitrim were the two counties at the south and north of this central strip of nationalist Ireland, and both had exceptionally high scores on political and violence indices. Both combined agrarianism and the political resources of anglicisation in explosive mixtures. Tipperary was relatively prosperous and Leitrim was on the Ulster sectarian frontier. Neither county was easily accessible from Dublin. In the nineteenth and twentieth centuries, the area around Tipperary in central Munster and around Leitrim and Cavan on the periphery of Ulster formed centres of aggressive political activity, from Whiteboyism through the nineteenth century to the IRA campaign of 1919–21.

Even before the first general election under extended suffrage took place in 1885, the INL had developed well, growing from 242 branches in January 1884 to 592 a year later and, just after the election campaign, 1,262 in January 1886. A few months later it reached its peak of 1,286 branches, or close on one branch for every Catholic parish in Ireland. In the late 1880s, this total tended to be rather lower because the police suppressed many of the rougher, tougher western branches: in 1889–90, they were suppressing all branches in the reorganised and quite violent western counties of Clare and Kerry, many branches in the western counties of Galway, Roscommon and Donegal, and some in the eastern but partly Gaeltacht county of Waterford: the western 'fringe' of nationalist Ireland was more violent and less easily channelled by either the League or the police.[24]

By 1887, despite its expansion, the League still favoured the middle counties, but was now well represented in the west as well. Table 4 correlates the INL branch-formation rate with farm size for 1882 and 1887 in an effort to establish whether the party had any pronounced affinity with any particular class of farmer. The correlations are rather weak, but they do suggest that the INL was indeed based rather more on the 'strong'-farm areas than on the subsistence smallholders of the west. Even for 1887, this generalisation continues to hold true. For neither year, however, is the relationship particularly pronounced; the weakness of the correlations suggests a strong cross-class character. Table 4 also confirms that the small-farm areas were organised for electoral politics rather later than the big-farm areas. David Seth Jones has noted that large farmers and even graziers were present in the Land League in disproportionate numbers.[25] The western subsistence peasantry, despite their vanguard role in 1879–82, were eventually given the role of the subordinate if not always amenable political allies of the medium- and large-size tenant-farmers about to become landowners on a minor scale. However, this alignment was not to be permanent; in particular, over the following generation, small and medium farmers were to gang up repeatedly on the graziers, eventually succeeding in making a substantial dent in the proportion of arable land controlled by large graziers.

Table 4. Irish National League and farm size: correlations between INL branches per 10,000 population and farm acreage, 1882–87, thirty counties

	10–20 acres	20–50 acres	50–200 acres
INL branches, 1882	-.28	0.01	0.24
INL branches, 1887	-.35	-.01	0.26
Increase, 1882–7	0.37	-.22	-.32

Note: Dublin and Antrim counties excluded

Unlike its predecessor the Land League, the INL was under direct parliamentary control from its inception. In 1884, Parnell introduced the local clergy into the county nomination conventions to balance the agrarians and ex-Fenians. The League also accomplished the political subordination of the landless labourers of the south and east.[26]

In the 1885 election, the INL's candidates won eighty-five of the eighty-nine seats contested in Ireland, plus a seat in Liverpool. In effect, the party won the votes of Catholic Ireland and very few of the votes of Protestant Ulster. The INL had an undeniable legitimacy in British constitutional theory; it was centralised on Parnell, it was far more than a mere federation of electoral nomination caucuses and it could claim to contain the vast body of Irish

Catholic public sentiment. Parnell's personal authority in the organisation was enormous, rather like that of O'Connell in the Repeal Association. In particular, he was able to control the nomination of candidates to a considerable extent and, generally speaking, 'the system combined the appearance of local spontaneity with the reality of centralised control.'[27] After 1885, this centralising process intensified. Both the clergy and the local conventions found their political influence further weakened as Parnell managed to gather the reins of power further into his own hands.

However, nominations, although a key matter in the INL as in all political parties and especially in those that effectively enjoy a monopoly of electoral popularity within the voting areas involved, were only one matter with which the League concerned itself. It was still involved in local agrarian matters; although the INL had repudiated the debts of the Land League and denied any legal continuity, there was obviously a continuity of personnel and, to a considerable extent, of political purpose. When non-electoral issues such as local agrarian disputes arose, relationships between local organisations and headquarters were not always so asymmetrical. Headquarters found itself continually being cast in the role of arbiter between local factions and being forced to deliver judgment on the practice of boycotting. Generally, headquarters attempted to moderate the enthusiasm of local 'wild men' and to prevent what it regarded as the misapplication of the boycott weapon, which was sometimes used to prevent people mechanising their farms, employing Protestants or setting up a business which might compete with one already established locally.[28]

In effect, the League found itself acting not merely as an electoral committee, but as local law-giver, unofficial parliament, government, police and supreme court. There was a general willingness, in fact, to appeal to headquarters and, apparently, to abide by headquarters' decision.[29] In 1880, Davitt had triumphantly described the Land League as forming a state within a state, and the National League inherited much of this quasi-governmental character. The mixture of popular assent and intimidation by clique was a potent and only partially controllable one. The younger men who supplied the muscle of the local League often gathered considerable power into their own hands. In a society where age and authority tended to be associated, developments of this kind were regarded as little short of revolutionary. The INL was not the weapon of the more privileged; in Millstreet, Macroom and other areas of north and west Cork in 1887, strong farmers and shopkeepers were targets of the agitation.[30]

The INL was, then, a formidable political machine which owed much of its strength to being built on foundations in the traditional political culture of rural Ireland. Within the nationalist community, no one could, it seemed, stand against it: even the Catholic hierarchy carried on what might best be described as diplomatic relations with its leaders; the local clergy participated in it at grass-roots level but seem to have co-operated with headquarters and ensured that the central office's wishes were respected locally. The bishops rarely tried to tell the leaders what to do: a papal condemnation of the Plan of Campaign in 1888 was openly denounced as an impertinence by the Irish MPs and the clergy themselves were divided on the issue. Labour could not stand against the League either. Urban labour was strongly Parnellite in the tradition of Irish urban nationalism; later, the Irish Democratic Trade and Labour Association was to split on the Parnell issue just as did the Irish Party itself. Labour had no immunity to nationalist politics.[31]

As we have seen, the INL was an alliance of all tenant-farmers in Catholic Ireland and was led by a new breed of professional middle-class politicians. In an important article, Samuel Clarke has pointed out that at local level non-agricultural social groups were important in the cadre of the Land League. Clarke argues that elements of the town bourgeoisie with close trade and credit connections with the farm community were the true leaders of the Land League. Shops and pubs were the natural centres of local social and political life, and their owners had a natural interest in farm prosperity and had a ready-made position in the centre of the local communications net. They were somewhat better educated than the farmers, were usually closely related to farmers and shared their social attitudes. Clarke documented the high proportion of Leaguers arrested in 1881 who came from the 'commercial and industrial' sectors. Most of this over-representation was due to the presence of shopkeepers, publicans and publicans' sons in large numbers. Journalists were similarly over-represented. Clarke concluded that the Land League started off with a discontented section of the town bourgeoisie and was led by them, especially in the western counties.[32] His analysis is convincing, but it could be objected that to explain the prominent part played by publicans and shopkeepers in the Land League by reference to the fact that they shared an interest in the economic welfare of the farming community might be unduly economistic. The leaders of a party do not necessarily reflect the interests of the social category to which they belong, nor do they necessarily reflect the interests of all of their followers; Parnell, a landlord and a Protestant, did not really further the interests of either Protestants or landlords. Some would argue that he did not pursue the economic interests of his electors either.

Shopkeepers and publicans were people who supplied the Leagues with leadership, rather as similar elements had put themselves at the head of Ribbonism fifty years previously, partly to further the interests of the rank and file, partly to further their own interests and partly because they were forced to by circumstance and by the community. In a rural society, people like shopkeepers are powerful, but are also, paradoxically, vulnerable. Their property and persons are, to put it bluntly, easy targets, and they lack the self-sufficiency of the farmers. Rather like the priests, they had little choice but to lead as the followers wished them to lead. Again, although it was in the interests of many who traded with farmers that farmers' purchasing power remain unimpaired, it was of interest to another group of people that farmers and others were available for political agitation; once set in motion, the movement itself became a vested interest. Frank Hugh O'Donnell's disdainful description of the League activists suggests that they were often not so much solid traders worried about their commercial futures as much smaller and more marginal people who saw in the League opportunity of personal advancement; he remembered them as including many poor men, many of them unemployed, with little or no capital: clerks, journalists, law students, teachers, barristers, brewers, travellers, 'small publicans' and spirit grocers.[33] Admittedly, O'Donnell's view of Irish society was rather Olympian.

THE PARNELL SPLIT: THE COLLAPSE OF THE IRISH NATIONAL LEAGUE

The verdict in the O'Shea divorce case, in which Parnell was cited as co-respondent, was handed down in November 1890. Parnell had survived accusations that he had connived at assassination and sympathised with bombers, but he did not survive this case.[34] The Liberals came under immense pressure from nonconformist opinion, and the alliance with the Irish Party's discredited leader was threatened. After a week of agonised debate, the parliamentary party split, the majority opposing Parnell. Soon after, Davitt, the Church and a majority of the rank and file combined against him. The League, however, was already falling to pieces. In three successive by-elections, Parnell appealed to the voters over the heads of Church and Party and was decisively rejected. By then, the split was echoed throughout Irish Catholic society. At elite level, the split involved strong personal loyalties and friendships, and this added to its intractability. The fact that the INL had been so centred on one man, like O'Connell's party, meant that removing him endangered the entire structure. Among the MPs in particular the split generated deep personal bitterness, partly because they were, in a sense, revolutionary politicians; they had come into politics as reformers and campaigners and had had strong ideological convictions: 'amid their varied characters they all possessed something alike in a certain dash of fanaticism.'[35]

There were few noticeable class differences between the Parnellite and anti-Parnellite MPs. It appears that those MPs who remained 'loyal to the Chief tended to be individualists and to be rather on the fringe of the INL machine'.[36] Davitt thought that the Parnellites were those of 'least prestige and experience' in the machine, but also felt that the Parnellites included a majority of the more active local leaders.[37] The League divided into two successor parties that were, even when combined, numerically far weaker than the old INL. An examination of the geographical distribution of branches of these successor parties reveals some interesting differences between the anti-Parnellite Irish National Federation (INF) and the Parnellite Irish National League (INL). The Parnellites were noticeably stronger in the counties around Dublin, plus Roscommon in Connacht, while the INF inherited what was left of the old INL organisation in a belt of counties on the Ulster border (Leitrim, Cavan and Monaghan), plus Queen's and Wexford in Leinster. Table 5 gives correlations between the parties' branch distributions standardised for population and some selected background variables. Dublin data were not available, and Unionist Ulster was omitted. The results are quite suggestive.

Table 5. Parnellites and anti-Parnellites: correlations of INL and INF branches, 1893, with social background variables, twenty-five counties

	INL (Parnellites)	INF (anti-Parnellites)
Irish speakers	−.27	−.58
Employed in agriculture	−.14	0.21
Catholics	0.05	−.51
Low ratable valuation	−.14	0.21

The INF distribution correlates strongly and negatively with Catholicism, indicating its strength in areas where Catholics and Protestants confronted one another. Neither party organisation was particularly western in profile; in this they both resembled their parent party. Where religious communalism was an important factor uniting nationalists, the Federation predominated, and in rural areas generally the clergy could enforce an anti-Parnellite line. In urban areas, where sectarian and clerical pressures were less, the Parnellites could survive. It was almost as though the old opposition between secular and confessionalist forms of Irish popular nationalism was re-emerging.

The by-elections were defeats for Parnell, but the results were not as one-sided as sometimes represented. Furthermore, the coalition which defeated Parnellism was, in the nature of things, a temporary one. To the machine of the old League had been added the organisation of the Catholic Church; clerical influence at the polls in 1891–92 resembled that of the pre-secret ballot days of the 1860s. The canvassing of the priests in favour of the anti-Parnellite candidates was extremely aggressive, reinforcing the *sotto voce* anti-clericalism of advanced nationalist opinion. The folklore of these election campaigns is voluminous, and appears to be based on fact. For example, it was alleged that a priest in Meath had threatened to turn a man into a goat if he voted Parnellite.[38] A priest had to be rescued from a Parnellite mob in Kilkenny in 1892.[39] The Bishop of Ossory admitted to Croke that the people were pro-Parnell and that the priests of Ossory had had to break down that sympathy by the use of 'family, personal and ministerial' influence on the voters.[40] Davitt indirectly admitted the intensity of the pressure the priests were putting on the electorate.[41] A Meath by-election was a particularly spectacular case of clerical intimidation. A Catholic judge subsequently commented

The Church became converted for the time being into a vast political agency, a great moral machine, moving with resistless influence, united action, and single will. Every priest was a canvasser; the canvass was everywhere—on the Altar, in the vestry, on the roads, in the houses. There was no place left for evasion, excuse, affected ignorance, weakness, or treachery. Of the ten polling places, there was but one in which there was not a priest as agent and personation agent, with or without laymen . . . [The Anti-Parnellite candidate] had certainly at least a staff of expert and trained logicians, who were more than a match for his opponent on the many questions that arise over voting-papers and which are of such moment in case of a narrow majority.[42]

One hostile commentator described a priest in Kilkenny standing at the polling-booth door and instructing the voters as they went in, and claimed that illiterate voters, who had to vote openly, were made to vote for the anti-Parnellite candidate.[43] Significantly, this intense clerical activity was not always successful. Despite the pressures, the 1892 general election indicated the existence of a strong minority current of popular support for the Parnellite candidates, and the results appear to reflect an ephemeral Parnellite alliance between disparate sources of radicalism in nationalist Ireland. In the forty non-Ulster constituencies outside the university which were actually contested by both nationalist factions, the Parnellite vote averaged 40 per cent. Parnellites actually won victories in some western agrarian areas, but their most substantial victories or votes were in the towns; the countryside, with the exception of parts of the western periphery, went with the nationalist and clerical establishment. In the cities and towns of nationalist Ireland, i.e. Dublin, Cork, Kilkenny, Limerick, Galway and Waterford, the mean Parnellite vote was 60 per cent of the total nationalist vote, while in the rural contests it was only 34 per cent.

The 1890s was a period of political stagnation. The agrarian question had been substantially settled, and the Church had set its face against political adventure. The great nationalist machines of the 1880s crumbled. The GAA, for example, a particular target of clerical distrust, fell into decay, its number of clubs falling from 777 in 1889 to 339 at the end of 1891.[44] The remaining GAA branches tended to be those more amenable to clerical supervision, and by 1894 the GAA was down to 122 branches.[45] Both the INL and INF had enormous defection rates; by 1894, both parties together could muster only 765 branches, compared with a normal total for any year in the late 1880s of over 1,100 branches.[46] A wholesale political demobilisation occurred. Although the Federation was much bigger than the League, neither successor party showed much vitality. There was a general sense of anti-climax, disillusion and 'paralysis', commonly noted by writers of the period and reminiscent of descriptions of post-revolutionary exhaustion elsewhere.[47] Various attempts were made by both local and Irish-American elements to revitalise nationalist politics, but with little success.[48] American money became scarcer.[49] By the middle of the decade, the nationalist organisations appeared moribund.

There has been a general propensity to view the Parnell split as a decisive event which enabled the Church to fill a political vacuum and which robbed the nationalist movement of its unity and energy. The observation is rarely made that the movement was already in decline before the fall of Parnell. In particular, the constitutional-agrarian politics of the New Departure, which had continued throughout the 1880s in some sense, were certainly in decline by the end of that decade because of political exhaustion, concessions and Parnell's attempts to distance himself from the IRB. The split hastened a decline that was likely to happen anyway. In July 1890, the Mayo RIC reported that the evidence given by Parnellite witnesses, denying IRB involvement, had confused the young men who usually joined secret societies.[50] There was general evidence of growing disunity of purpose in the nationalist ranks, partly because of the defusing of the agrarian issue and partly because of generational tensions resulting from a property inheritance system which discriminated between sons within a farm family. By January 1888, the fusion of the INL, IRB and GAA in Clare had led to the dominance of the young GAA men within the combined movement, much to the annoyance of the veterans.[51] By mid-1889, the notorious agitation around Millstreet, north Cork, had collapsed because so many of the men involved had been given land.[52] There was a general tendency for local IRB circles to degenerate into local Mafias, uncontrolled by the older men or by a central leadership.[53] The agitators were only able to enforce their will where the INL, the clergy and the IRB were in tacit alliance. There was a good deal of evidence that the public were getting rather tired of the agitation and, in particular, those who had benefited from the land reforms had lost enthusiasm. Social pressure kept them in line for the moment, but the vigour had gone out of their support.[54] It is hard to escape the suspicion that the split was actually a relief to some people and that the growth of a propertied farming class was undermining the Parnellite movement long before the divorce case. The split made the decline much more destructive and precipitate than it might otherwise have been, but a decline was apparently inevitable as the land revolution ran out of steam and the winners consolidated their position.[55]

06 | THE RECONSTRUCTION OF NATIONALIST POLITICS, 1891–1910

THE REBUILDING OF THE PARLIAMENTARY PARTY

The period between the fall of Parnell and World War I, often seen as a time when little happened except for endless bickering between the various nationalist factions, was a period in which much political development occurred. The basic political institutions of a post-British Irish state were laid down, local government was democratised and Catholics became involved in the governmental machine in large numbers for the first time. During this period also, the superficially all-powerful Nationalist Party, reunited in 1900, became increasingly involved in imperial politics and increasingly out of touch with people at home. The party never recovered its old vigour and became more and more of a patronage machine, more concerned with council and office politics than with the wooing of the public or of the younger generation. The revolution that eventually destroyed the Nationalist Party was, to a significant extent, generational rather than class in character, and was led by men who had been born around the time of the fall of Parnell. The collapse of Parnellism coincided with the end of agrarianism as a central force in Irish politics. Because of elite bitterness and because the old INL had been so centralised on Parnell, factions became a pronounced feature in the 1890s. Not only were there two successor parties, but the various prominent personalities in the parliamentary group tended to be at odds with each other and to develop their own followings or 'tails'. This internal disintegration was helped by the curious fact that the Irish party system was profoundly non-competitive; in effect, the party system consisted of two single-party systems, one Nationalist and the other Unionist, each with its own bailiwick and therefore, despite much mutual hostility, not in electoral competition with each other. There was little premium on unity in the face of the enemy. T.M. Healy attempted, with some success, to form his own nationalist faction with clerical support, and there was division among the other leaders. The Parnellite group grew weaker, but even Federation organisers found it difficult to raise enough money to pay stipends to those evicted during the Plan of Campaign and forced to exist on party doles.[1]

The slide towards organisational disunity and feebleness was reflected in decentralisation of the party and, in particular, a dramatic loss of control by the leadership over parliamentary nominations. In 1892, the INF created a committee on nominations consisting mainly of the parliamentary leaders. This committee became very vulnerable to local pressures and was forced to accede to local wishes, apparently far more than had been the case in the 1880s. Generally, candidates now had to be self-supporting and be acceptable both to the local clergy and to the more active local nationalists in their constituencies.[2] John Dillon attempted to hold on to the Liberal alliance and the centralised machine, while Healy appealed to the lower clergy and the branches against the parliamentary leadership, urging that the party should not commit itself to either British party.[3] In 1895, Healy openly split with the party and carried some clergy and local organisations with him. There was a further drop in morale, more local restiveness and an even stronger sense of aimlessness. Dillon's attempts to recentralise the party were arrested and local fiefs led by prominent leaders or cliques became consolidated. In 1892, eighty-three of 103 territorial Irish seats had been contested; this figure fell to forty-two in 1895 and reached a nadir of twenty-one in 1906.[4] This reflected an increasing localism and enfeeblement of the party machine rather than any internal unity in the nationalist camp. As Table 6 indicates, by the early 1890s the memberships of nationalist political organisations were far below their 1880s levels and, even when reunification occurred, the successor organisations lacked the unity and power of the Parnell period.

However, the break-up of the INL permitted other organisations to emerge and capture the imagination of the young. Trade unions, cultural-nationalist movements such as the Gaelic League and a revived GAA benefited from the vacuum. Another very significant development was the rise of the neo-Ribbon Ancient Order of Hibernians, first in Ulster and then throughout the country.

Table 6. Nationalist revivals: numbers of (a) clubs and (b) members in good standing, various social and political organisations, 1894–1901, Royal Irish Constabulary area

	IRB		AOH (both factions)		GAA		INL		INF		United Irish League		Gaelic League	
	(a)	(b)	(a)	(b)	(a)	(b)	(a)	(b)	(a)	(b)	(a)	(b)	(a)	(b)
1894	490	6514	118	3794	173	3376	134	6514*	631	47080*	—	—	NA	NA
1895	502	7507	135	4120	244	4050	NA	NA	NA	NA	—	—	NA	NA
1896	509	7215	136	3162	343	7540	NA	NA	NA	NA	—	—	NA	NA
1898	513	8508	158	4864	356	7067	6	160	221	9180	121	1084	NA	NA
1899	491	9108	150	4632	303	8148	—	—	—	—	408	46378	NA	NA
1900	492	8183	159	4875	311	7151	—	—	—	—	892	88293	99	5964
1901	500	8690	171	5723	411	10727	—	—	—	—	1150	84355	258	15086

* Figures for previous year.
Figures refer to all Ireland, exclusive of Dublin Metropolitan Area.

Eventually, a new, more restricted and marginal agrarian campaign developed, organised by the reunited party, relabelled the 'United Irish League', after 1898. Table 6 demonstrates that the loss of vigour in the parliamentary associations was accompanied by a striking growth in non-parliamentary organisations of various kinds, and it also indicates that the IRB survived the period quite successfully. Despite a superficial appearance of passivity, the 1890s was actually a period of quite intensive political organisation, and the years 1890 to 1910 saw the outflanking of the parliamentary forces by societies often unsympathetic to

representative politics. During this period, the Irish Party itself
came to have an unhealthy dependence on one such organisation,
the Ancient Order of Hibernians. The fashionable contempt for
parliamentary politics was, of course, not confined to Ireland, and
romantic political cults flourished everywhere in Europe at this
time. Another event to have a galvanising effect on nationalist
politics was the Boer War, which divided nationalists into pro- and
anti-imperialist camps. Trade unions also grew at this time, but
the most massive increases were in Protestant Ulster, where there
was a noticeable radicalisation of Protestant working-class opinion. However, this did not last very long. Among Catholics, unions
also grew, but the leaders and rank and file were at least as
nationalist as they were socialist.[5]

The United Irish League was explicitly designed to reconcile the
various parliamentary fragments by bringing them together
around a new programme of agrarian agitation, political reform
and Home Rule. William O'Brien was the prime mover, and the
difficulty of the project can be gauged from the fact that the
parliamentary leaders had very different opinions on the land
question. Dillon appears to have regarded the land issue as an
essential motor for the nationalist movement, O'Brien championed the smallholders against the graziers while Davitt, whose
original idea had been state ownership and agrarian socialism, was
not particularly enamoured of peasant proprietorship.[6] O'Brien
attempted to build his UIL on the smallholders of the west,
particularly in areas where land had been consolidated into huge
non-residential grazing 'ranches' producing for the British market.[7]
As the graziers were essentially businessmen and often not
resident on their property, they tended to become targets in land-
hungry areas, particularly once the old anti-landlord campaign
had concluded.[8] Districts where ranch land and smallholdings
marched together existed in north Connacht, north Leinster, parts
of Tipperary and in smaller areas elsewhere.[9] The new agitation
was successful in only a few counties, particularly in Mayo and
parts of Roscommon.[10] The early UIL was almost completely a
western party, with little real vitality outside the smallholder areas;
it was a party of peripheral protest against the relatively satisfied

middle and upper strata of post-Parnell Ireland. The local clergy were usually quick enough to put themselves at the head of the local UIL to ensure no new party dictatorship emerged to challenge them. The UIL resembled the old INL, however, in its organisers; many of them were old INL cadres whom O'Brien had recruited for a repeat performance. In 1900, of twenty-one paid organisers, ten were farmers, farmers' sons or 'evicted tenant farmers' of the old campaign and five more were publicans or publicans' sons, thus repeating the classic mix of Irish populist political movements.[11] There was a good deal of nationalist establishment resistance to O'Brien's movement, but the fact that it relied disproportionately on O'Brien's private means, was rather an artificial movement and concentrated on a very narrow and eminently negotiable issue probably made it inevitable that its organisation would develop into a passive instrument of the parliamentary caucus.[12] The new county councillors who had been elected in 1898 were often pro-grazier, despite the presence among them of many IRB veterans. O'Brien complained bitterly that the Roscommon councillors, some of them old IRB members, resisted his campaign.[13] James Lynam, an experienced veteran of the INL campaigns, reported that the priests were usually hostile to his organising efforts, with the exception of west Clare.[14] In many places, the UIL was merely a revival, twenty years on, of old Land League or INL branches, with many of the same people. The RIC happily noted that the priests were usually able to restrain these ageing firebrands.[15]

A tension, if not a contradiction, existed between the UIL's basic goals; essentially it thrived only in areas where land-hungry men were politically dominant and areas where the older campaigns had left an institutional residue of some kind, but it also aspired to be the means of reuniting the old party. In 1900 the UIL was actually accepted by the parliamentarians as the main support organisation of the parliamentary nationalists, John Redmond, leader of the Parnellite group, becoming leader of the reunited party. However, the Irish Party was now only marginally concerned with smallholders and the UIL tended to be taken over by non-smallholder elements. Sinn Féin and other small radical groups were soon able to outbid the UIL in matters of agrarian radicalism.[16] However, for a few years the UIL did organise traditional agrarian agitations. A few 'grass grabbers' were selected in each area and were made the targets of a boycott. Some of the UIL leaders had kept up their contacts with local secret societies, and these fulfilled their traditional role as enforcers. Interestingly, GAA clubs were reluctant to get involved in the new agitation, a symptom of how marginal the agitation had become.[17] However, in east Galway, meadows were spiked in 1900 and in many western areas the local UIL became a regular local land court, adjudicating on land disputes and issuing decrees which were enforceable in traditional fashion.[18] In a presumably unconscious echo of observers of Irish rural agitation over the previous century and a half, the RIC's inspector-general complained about local attitudes to the rule of these midnight courts. He minuted, 'The injured persons themselves are most reluctant to give the police any assistance or information, and much prefer to submit to this kind of petty outrage rather than do anything to bring themselves in antagonism to the general feeling.'[19]

This agrarian court system became very powerful in some areas, and in 1907 the Nationalist MP for South Leitrim was humiliated by a UIL judgment against him. Outside the west and the borderlands, the UIL developed into a fund-raising caucus for the local MP, was his servant rather than his master and lost much of its agrarian character.[20] One reason why the UIL was tamed so rapidly was, of course, the fact that elected nationalist politicians were now entrenched in the local governmental apparatus and were usually able to use their new governmental and patronage powers to head off any really dangerous agitations; nationalists had won virtually every seat in Connacht and most seats in most councils outside eastern Ulster in the local elections of 1898–99.[21] The rural seats were less likely to be held by IRB or radical nationalists than were the town seats.[22] Unionism received only marginal representation outside eastern Ulster, and the police considered that it received a residual workers' deferential vote for their employers in 1898–99.[23] At subsequent local elections, unionism was virtually eliminated from nationalist Ireland. This new power, a power that even Parnell's party had never had, meant that politicians were less dependent on the electorate or on electoral caucuses than ever before; with majority opinion behind them, they became the natural governors of the nationalist hinterland, lying in siege, so to speak, on the unpopular and unionist Castle administration. The Castle was also weakened by a partial withdrawal of Westminster backing after the Liberals' return in 1906. The nationalist politicians scarcely had to contest elections, and their superficially total grip on local opinion was oddly insecure; local factional groups were able to defy the organisation with impunity. O'Brien was able to take the entire Cork organisation out of the party in 1910.[24] A distaste for what was, in effect, one-party rule at local level appears to have existed in incoherent and underground form throughout the country. However, before 1912 it rarely achieved more than intermittent electoral expression in the form of protest votes for O'Brienite, Labour or Sinn Féin candidates. The Irish Party was in the paradoxical situation of enjoying repeated electoral triumphs and of never holding governmental office, a condition which it usually shared with its unionist opposite number, particularly after 1906. It was reduced to committee politics and rather empty agitation while waiting for the Liberals to deliver on their promise of Home Rule. It was in a false position, a fact that did not become obvious until Irish unionism and its British Conservative allies vetoed Home Rule by threat of force. Even after 1900, the UIL never captured the imagination or interest of the younger generation, who turned either to Labour or to the cultural and militant nationalism of the new organisations.

THE RISE OF THE HIBERNIANS
In one area of Ireland, however, religion-based ethnic identity still could serve as a basis for mobilising popular Catholic opinion on militant lines. This area was, of course, the religiously divided province of Ulster, whose 'peculiar institution' of cross-class religious communalism marked it off in intensity if not in type from the rest of Ireland and Britain. Religious communalism, in its agrarian form, had persisted after the Famine in the borderlands, and the Ribbon societies persisted, although much weakened, in northern areas. In the late 1880s a Ribbon revival of

sorts occurred in Connacht, often the product of English-based organisers ('Nolan of Manchester') operating on the migrant agricultural labourers from Connacht who worked seasonally on English farms. Similar traditional connections existed with Scotland in Ulster, dating back to the 1830s and probably much earlier. In Ulster, Ribbonism appears to have gradually evolved into the more open and respectable Ancient Order of Hibernians in the 1860s and 1870s and was able to resist the encroachments of the IRB.[25] It appears to have been primarily an emigrant or migrant organisation before 1888, but in close contact with areas of origin in Ireland. Its connections were mainly with Britain; there was also an American-based wing of the AOH which had Irish lodges and was pro-Fenian and Parnellite. Its lodges faded away, however, after a few years and it never achieved the vitality of the Board of Erin Hibernians. It did, however, become involved, in a marginal way, with later military adventures by the new nationalists.

The AOH, although the lineal successor to the Ribbon tradition in the north of Ireland, was, in its official *apologia*, careful to deny any connection with the more illegal activities of its predecessors. It was careful to play down its Ribbon ancestors and was fond of claiming an organisational continuity not only with a sanitised version of the Defenders, but also with a sentimentalised version of the old seventeenth-century Jacobite cause.[26] The search for respectability and acceptance by the Church was the keynote of this new Ribbonism of the 1890s. It was strongly opposed to secular ideologies such as those of the IRB or of the new socialist groups, a fact which increased its appeal to certain brands of nationalist politician and to certain sections of the Catholic clergy. The AOH combined its political role with that of a friendly society, and developed a patronage and brokerage machine. It inherited from Ribbonism the usual addiction to fife-and-drum bands, parades, collars, passwords and grand-sounding hierarchical titles. Up to 1904 the AOH came under ecclesiastical ban as an oath-bound society, and the clergy were always divided on its desirability.

The difference in political culture between Catholic Ulster and the rest of nationalist Ireland is well illustrated by the relative success of the AOH and the IRB in penetrating rural areas of the west. By and large, the Hibernians dominated the Ulster areas, while the IRB tended to be more successful elsewhere. The IRB were most unhappy at the re-emergence of this old rival, 'right-wing' nationalist society. In Cavan, in 1890, the AOH challenge was met in characteristic fashion; the local IRB controlled the GAA and staged rows during matches and 'make it so hot for the Ribbon men that they will leave the Club'. After the split, the AOH took an anti-Parnell line, while the IRB were usually Parnellite. However, in more rural areas, local factional rivalries based on kin groups sometimes made nonsense of any ideological alignment. In parts of Leitrim and Cavan, for example, local conversions from IRB to AOH occurred because of a feud between two kin-based factions just before the fall of Parnell. National issues scarcely seem to have penetrated the local opposition. In some of the villages of this part of Ireland, the local IRB and AOH factions appear to have been directly descended from pre-Famine Ribbon or similar local secret societies. Many of the long-distance links to Dublin, Belfast and western Britain appear to have been in existence for similar periods. Also, local secret society leaders appear to have been able to stay in office for very long periods indeed, and even to bequeath their offices to their sons.[27]

Like the Orange Order, the AOH was a right-wing, popular working-class and farmers' organisation for communal defence and welfare. Once the clerical ban was lifted in 1904, the organisation expanded rapidly, although it had shown some dynamism long before the ban was lifted, as Table 6 indicates. The combined Board of Erin and Board of America factions had a total membership of perhaps 5,000 members in 1900, nearly all in Ulster. This figure had climbed to an astonishing 64,000 in 1909. Alone among the parliamentary leaders, Joseph Devlin, the Belfast-based nationalist boss and controller of the AOH after 1905, had a genuine mass organisation to rely on. The AOH provided a militant following which he and the other parliamentary leaders came increasingly to rely on. After 1906, the beginnings of welfarism helped the AOH by increasing the significance of good political contacts and therefore giving it a brokerage role between the public and the civil service. The fact that the Liberals were in office and that nationalists controlled much of local government also gave AOH leaders access to patronage of a petty kind. Under the National Health Insurance Act of 1911, it became a recognised friendly society and became profitably involved in the brokerage of social insurance. Even before the Church and the Liberals accepted it, the AOH had spread quite successfully, overshadowing the UIL in Ulster after 1897 and even rivalling it in southern counties.[28] By 1908, the AOH really was moving south, however; in 1909, it appeared in Roscommon, by 1912 it was active in Mayo and was 'very popular and flourishing' in Louth. It had also made incursions into the Munster counties of Clare, Limerick and Tipperary, and by 1914 it had saturated the entire island, fuelled not so much by sectarianism as by its utility as a patronage, brokerage and recreational association.[29] It appealed to young men of the poorer classes, attracted by the Catholic, nationalist and paramilitary style of the organisation. It also addressed itself to issues such as sectarian Protestant local government in Ulster and elsewhere, rather than to the obsolescent agrarian issues championed by the UIL. The two organisations complemented each other quite well, the Hibernians having a much greater urban working-class appeal.[30] Even in Dublin, the AOH could draw large crowds and stage impressive demonstrations. In 1907, Devlin was able to assure Redmond that a planned meeting of the UIL would be well attended because he would be able to get more than 400 AOH delegates to fill the hall.[31] The AOH also acted as a defence against episcopal attempts to set up a priest-run, or rather bishop-run, Catholic political party in Belfast; in this it had the support of many of the local lower clergy.[32] In Ulster and elsewhere it acted as an unruly but vigorous militant support organisation and was a useful counterbalance for Devlin, Dillon and Redmond against radicals and against O'Brien; O'Brien regarded himself as having been driven from the party by Hibernian hooligans. In 1913, Hibernians were used against Larkin's trade unionism.[33] It had always been a threat to the Gaelic League and to the new Sinn Féin as well, partly because it had a genuinely popular support base. The AOH became particularly disliked by the young revolutionaries of the IRB. The Church was divided on its desirability: on the one hand, it looked like a practical example of Catholic Action; on the other it sometimes was, as Cardinal Logue put it, a vehicle for local thugs, 'a pest, a cruel tyranny, and an organised system of black-guardism!'[34]

The extraordinary growth of the AOH in the first years of the new century also reflected the absence of true competitive politics; it expanded in a political vacuum which other groups, such as Sinn Féin and the socialists, were also trying to fill. Its success encouraged the leaders of the Irish Party to drift out of touch with popular opinion. Preoccupation with elite issues, combined with this comforting sense of having their political rear secured for them by the AOH, increased the tendency of the leaders to take the voters for granted and to think in 'Westminster' terms rather than Irish domes-tic terms. This tendency was also encouraged by the fact that they were mainly ageing men, still thinking in terms of the 1880s. With the wisdom of hindsight, it is easy to see that the AOH's support was unreal. However, it impressed contemporary observers with its apparent grip on popular feeling and its clerical and political con-nections.[35] It also succeeded in socialising many young men to politics of a particular type; up to 1916, it was, after all, probably the dominant popular political organisation even in southern areas of Munster.[36] In the early years of World War I, it was dominant in many southern counties and heavily involved in patronage.[37]

After the 1916 Rising, the AOH melted away outside Ulster, and its members were absorbed into Sinn Féin and the IRA. In many areas, the AOH was the nearest thing to a paramilitary force until the Volunteer movement developed in 1913, and the Volunteers had found it a useful recruiting ground. In Clare in the early years of World War I, the young men were often AOH and pro-War in politics but, after the 1916 Rising, they 'went' anti-War and joined Sinn Féin.[38] In Bantry, west Cork, the entire Volunteer/IRA company was based on a group of young men who had been in the local AOH before 1913.[39] Many prominent leaders of the 1916–23 period, among them Seán MacDermott and Rory O'Connor, had been 'Hibs' before 1913.

Hibernianism was, then, the lineal descendant of Ulster Ribbonism, itself the direct successor of Defenderism. It represented an Ulster, Catholic and 'right-wing' nationalism as against the centrist or left-wing nationalisms of the republican and labour-republican traditions. Essentially an Ulster society, it faded away in the south after partition and lost any residual strength it had had once welfare systems of a more elaborate type developed and made its role as a friendly society superfluous. Another, more immediate, reason for its decline was, of course, its identification with the Irish Party; in 1918, the AOH and the Irish Party shared a common ruin. Not only was the AOH humiliated by the bank-ruptcy of the Party's pro-War policy, it was also systematically harassed by the IRA, who saw it as a rival and as an excrescence of the corrupt machine of the pre-1916 nationalist leadership.[40] The AOH is also significant as a link between the new nationalist organisations and the century-old tradition of popular militant societies. It appears to have had some indirect influence on quasi-military popular movements in nationalist Ireland. More directly, it lingered on as a pro-Treaty support organisation in parts of north Leinster and Ulster after independence. Some Hibernians fought on the Francoist side in the Spanish Civil War.[41] The quasi-fascist Blueshirt movement of the 1930s may, in fact, have owed as much to the Ribbon tradition which it so much resembled as it did to its continental analogues.[42]

Both Hibernianism, the Irish Party and a 'respectable' pro-Empire Irish nationalism were casualties of the British political crisis of 1911–14 and of World War I. The inability of the British government to deliver Home Rule in the face of Ulster and internal British opposition was a symptom of the fact that Ulster's quarrel was also a British quarrel. This inability destroyed the delicate constitutionalism of nationalist Ireland. The British government's political legitimacy in Ireland had always been very fragile, and depended less on a whole-hearted acceptance of the British writ by majority opinion than on an alliance with at least some nationalist opinion. Once that alliance was shown to be untrust-worthy, both the legitimacy of the regime and the acceptability of the leadership of nationalist Ireland were endangered. The Rising of 1916 merely administered a final push to an edifice which was already on the verge of collapse.

07 | THE NEW NATIONALISM AND MILITARY CONSPIRACY, 1900–16

THE DEVELOPMENT OF CULTURAL NATIONALISM AND THE ORIGINS OF SINN FÉIN

The main beneficiary of the weakening of the parliamentary forces was a new cultural nationalism. Various small groups which were to have great influence later on emerged during the political interregnum of the 1890s, particularly in Dublin and the larger towns. New political ideas, or refurbished versions of very old political ideas, emerged from small coteries which often regarded themselves as being non-political or else political only in some new, elevated and uncorrupt sense of the word. In 1893, the Gaelic League was founded in Dublin; James Connolly's tiny Irish Socialist Republican Party appeared in the city in 1896 and Arthur Griffith's little radical nationalist party, Sinn Féin ('Ourselves'), followed in 1905, the result of half a dozen years of journalistic and organisational effort. The Gaelic League was dedicated to the cultivation and revival of the Irish language and tradition. It traced its descent from small groups of antiquarian scholars who from the 1830s on had been studying the Celtic antiquities of Ireland. The work of these antiquaries had immediate political relevance because it suggested that people who had inhabited Ireland before the Anglo-Norman incursion had showed considerable cultural competence. The League never became a political society formally, nor did it ever become a mass organisation like the GAA or the post-1916 Sinn Féin. It was essentially a movement of townspeople, often young and well educated. In some cases, they had had unusual experience in working outside Ireland in business, newspapers, teaching or civil service.

The Gaelic League expanded after the centenary of 1798, like many other patriotic associations, and appears to have enjoyed a real expansion during the years of the Boer War, its membership tripling between 1898 and 1901. Most early Gaelic Leaguers and 'Irish-Irelanders' appear to have had professional or civil service backgrounds. Many had joined the League while living outside Ireland or away from their home place and therefore while relatively free of clerical or establishment nationalist pressures. Such people would also resent impediments to their career prospects caused by entrenched political groups, whether through Protestant discrimination or Catholic old-boy networks. They were, however, relatively free of crude clerical or political threats to their livelihood.

Some early Irish-Irelanders showed their independence of the clergy in strange ways; in 1906, there was a 'Battle of Portarlington', in which the local parish priest was defeated by the local Gaelic League and in which even the bishop was worsted. The issue was the very controversial one of sexual segregation in local Irish-language classes. The League could only finance one set of classes and knew that setting up two series, one for each sex, would bankrupt them. The League's campaign was led by two civil servants who were protected by their status from economic threat; a rebellious shop assistant who was involved in the campaign lost his job because he refused to sign a letter of apology to the parish priest.[1] However, this picture should not be over-generalised; many priests were attracted to the League. Gaelic revivalism seems to have had a particular attraction for middle-class townsmen or returned emigrants. Diarmuid Lynch, for example, a prominent IRB organiser in the years before the Rising, was born in west Cork in 1878 and knew no Irish. He went to London in 1895, became a post office clerk and moved to the United States a year later. In 1898, he discovered an Irish-language class in New York and tried to learn the language, with little success. His regard for the Irish language and for traditional singing and dancing seems to have had as its emotional basis a deep resentment of New York music-hall 'stage-Irishism'. He felt that the Irish at home were not sufficiently worried about the way in which their nationality was mocked abroad. Lynch returned to Ireland in 1908 and was promptly recruited into the IRB by Seán T. O'Kelly. Assertion of self-respect in a foreign community was a powerful stimulus to nationalist feeling. An analogous process affected Ulster Catholics, and even some Ulster Protestants; many of the most active and extreme of the radical nationalist leaders were either of Ulster origin or had important non-Irish connections.[2] The revitalised IRB of the post-1906 period was to a great extent the product of the Dungannon Clubs, an Ulster nationalist organisation whose name referred back to the great convention of the Irish Volunteers in 1782.

The early Gaelic League's mixture of idealistic patriotism, learning and open-air recreation, rather similar to those of youth movements elsewhere in Europe at this period, had a strong appeal to middle-class youth. The League became a forcing school for future nationalist leaders and activists and produced a group of young people who were to be at the centre of every advanced nationalist organisation during the following twenty years. They were to be involved in the Dungannon Clubs, the IRB, the Irish Volunteers of 1913, the Rising, the IRA and the Dáil government of 1919. It has been calculated that about half of those who served as government ministers or as senior civil servants in the first fifty years after independence had been members of the Gaelic League in their youth.[3] In effect, the League educated an entire political class.

Douglas Hyde, first President of the League and a Protestant, had intended it to be non-political and had hoped that it would act as a bridge between Catholics and Protestants. He disliked the League's later association with extremist politics and insisted on separating the goal of reviving Gaelic culture from the goal of political autonomy. He was, however, well aware of the long-term political implications of the movement.[4] The revival of Irish logically entailed the construction of a new national culture with components taken from a dying one. What this new national culture was to look like was not always clear. Certainly, it was to be un-English, which meant, in practice, that English popular culture, English literature and English art, together with the non-

Irish and non-Catholic systems of political and social ideas emanating from London, could easily be represented as being alien and 'un-Irish'. The seeds of cultural apartheid were present even in the early days of the Gaelic League. The ideas of the League appealed to a variety of groups for a variety of reasons; they attracted young men of talent or ambition who felt shut out by Protestant or nationalist establishment forces, old republicans looking for means to keep the old flame alight, social reformers and clergy who regarded English influences as demoralising. Priests appear to have feared that the effect of English popular culture would be to secularise Irish society and threaten the intense culture of popular devotional Catholicism which had grown up since the Famine. The League appealed to two other groups as well, and for opposite reasons; Anglo-Irish intellectuals saw revivalism as an opportunity for them to make a connection with the major Irish community from which class and caste had cut them off, while the new Catholic businessmen saw it as a wholesome antidote to subversive and immoral ideas from outside. Croke had, of course, in a speech which was reproduced in every GAA handbook for two generations, given eloquent expression to this fear of English popular culture. What Ireland faced, Croke had felt, was the prospect of becoming psychologically what it already was politically: West Britain.[5] The snag was, however, that most Irishmen of the 1890s knew nothing about the culture of which they were supposed to be so proud, and those who did know about it were busily divesting themselves of it as fast as they could. Town culture in Ireland was essentially a variant on British provincial culture, the main difference being the religious life and the content of the political culture. The problem was that the Irish really were a little bit British.

Like nationalists elsewhere, the Irish-Irelanders were often clearer about what they disliked than about what they liked. One famous nationalist publicist developed an entire vocabulary of social and political abuse, introducing such terms as '*shoneen*', 'Castle Catholic', 'sourface' and '*bodach*' into everyday language.[6] To be fair, the League was more positive than this, but it should be remembered that social resentments of this kind surrounded the early League. Much cultural work of intrinsic merit was inspired directly or indirectly by the League, and it contained many individuals who were very advanced in their attitudes to education, social status, authority, the role of women and cultural development. It gave self-respect and a sense of purpose to young people who had perhaps not been given sufficient self-respect by the caste- and machine-ridden society in which they lived.

The League's attempt to reconstruct or even invent a national culture was not unique; the use of the historical or even non-historical past to create a new and partly mythical national identity was, and is, an almost universal characteristic of nationalist movements.[7] In the Irish case, the artificiality of the exercise was possibly less obvious than in some others, because the nationalists had the good fortune to have material which was particularly suitable for their purposes. An immediately recognisable Gaelic identity had existed from primordial times and was still present, if only in its peasant form. The revivalists were also fortunate in that this juncture between urban nationalism and an almost medieval peasant culture was witnessed sympathetically by a talented group of mainly Anglo-Irish literary figures. With the collapse of the Ascendancy, many intellectuals of Protestant stock felt impelled to either leave or to attempt to come to terms with the cultural past of the country. Synge and Yeats valued peasant culture because it was non-bourgeois and reflected older and presumably nobler values. Ironically, middle-class Catholics often saw an idealised Catholic piety in the Gaelic tradition, where the Anglo-Irish poets saw pagan heroism. Significantly, the only great Catholic writer of the period, James Joyce, was contemptuous of the new nationalism; his urban Catholic upbringing helped him to see the revival as a new form of cultural imprisonment, and he had no identity problem to solve. Perhaps the greatest irony of all is the circumstance that the best Irish-language novel to emerge from the revival movement was a devastating satire on the encounter between the bemused peasants and the urban Irish-Irelanders, Myles na Gopaleen's *An Béal Bocht*.

The literary movement of the 1890s and 1900s had many non-artistic consequences, not the least of which was to give a fairly typical anti-colonial nationalism an aesthetic and intellectual veneer which it did not really deserve. The romantic vision of a Gaelic resurgence, derived from Gaelic popular tradition, nationalist journalism and Anglo-Irish artistry, had a very powerful hold over the minds of an entire generation of political leaders. The power of the historicist nationalist myth was such that several commentators have been tempted to speculate that it owed that power to the survival of pagan themes such as that of the 'Mother Ireland' figure, the *Sean-bhean Bhocht* of 1798 folksong. A more convincing explanation, perhaps, is that the symbol system of the new nationalism was parallel to that of Irish Catholicism and was a translation of the latter into political terms. Neo-Gaelic nationalism retained the values of self-sacrifice for the group, religious communalism, purity, respect for women, fear of external evils and idealism which were taught by the Irish Catholicism of the period. The use of cultural-linguistic rather than religious terminology obscured in the nationalists' own minds the practical near-identity between their 'Irish' or 'Gaelic' nation-to-be and the mainly English-speaking Catholic community in Ireland.[8]

The cliché version of the nationalist myth was, of course, the Seven Hundred Years of Slavery interpretation of Irish history.[9] This myth was already at least a century old at the time of the 1916 Rising. Successful political myths are usually a strange mixture of truth and falsehood; the Irish nationalist myth had a fair amount of truth in it. However, the truthfulness of a political myth is almost beside the point; a political myth is not a scientific account of events, but is primarily a prescription for political action. It could even be argued that the real antidote for myth is not a scientific account intended to demythologise, but rather another, more appealing myth.[10] In the Irish case, the nationalists found that the past supplied plenty of material and they clothed their cause in potent images derived from earlier nationalist campaigns and from the older and very different lost causes of Stuart and Gaelic Ireland.[11]

The police saw the early League as unimportant and 'made up for the most part of women and children'.[12] Children, however, grow up into men and women, some of whom may be interested in practical undertakings. Certainly, some practical young men took up Irish nationalism. The early Sinn Féiners were by no means a group of visionaries and, despite some crankishness, they did attempt to draft a coherent social and political programme. They also showed a fair amount of practical ability in local politics in Dublin, Cork and elsewhere in the pre-1914 period. Nominally a political party, before 1916 Sinn Féin was actually little more than a coterie of Dublin journalists, minor politicians, politicised students and office workers with some contact with similar groups in provincial centres and with some connections with small agrarian and republican groups who were also at odds with the Irish Party.

Arthur Griffith's programme, which was that of the early Sinn Féin, was political, unlike that of the League. It was also non-republican. Griffith concentrated on James Fintan Lalor's idea of 'moral protest', an idea close to that of present-day ideas of non-violent mass protest. He accepted the sovereignty of the British monarch in Ireland, but insisted that only the King, Lords and Commons *of Ireland* had the right to rule Ireland. It followed that the union of 1801 had been unconstitutional. This doctrine, with its roots in medieval and early modern constitutional theory, was not all that different from the arguments which the American colonists used against Westminster's attempts to legislate for them before 1776. Griffith proposed that the Irish MPs elected for Westminster withdraw from the London parliament, meet in Dublin and constitute themselves as an Irish parliament. They would then proceed to rule the country and the British government in Ireland would, it was hoped, wither away as people gave their allegiance to the new Irish government. His phrase for the resulting system was 'Dual Monarchy', on the analogy of Austria-Hungary. This political proposal was coupled with a classic bourgeois nationalist programme of economic protectionism and industrial development. Although only a small group, Sinn Féin had a considerable impact on nationalist opinion before 1916, and after 1916 it became the basis of a new mass movement. There is, however, only a partial continuity between Griffith's monarchist Sinn Féin and the republican Sinn Féin of 1917.[13] Ironically, Griffith's Sinn Féin was not involved in the Rising which was later named after it; the Rising was the work of the IRB.

FENIANS, VOLUNTEERS AND INSURRECTION

The early 1900s saw a weakening of the Castle's supervision of subversive and nationalist societies. The acceptance of nationalist hegemony at local level and the waning of agrarianism contributed to this relaxation. The police saw the IRB as dying, and insiders also testified to its weakness during the period before World War I. Diarmuid Lynch thought that the IRB was down to about 2,000 'effective' members by 1916.[14] The post-Parnell IRB seems, however, to have had the foresight to keep in contact with the young men and also seems to have selected its members fairly carefully. Its existence was not widely known.[15] The IRB recruited from the GAA, the Gaelic League and other patriotic societies. It was, incidentally, wholly a male organisation; according to Bulmer Hobson, Maud Gonne was the only woman ever sworn into the IRB.[16] The 'firm' had no particular regional profile after 1900, which suggests that it was indeed weaker and was reduced to small cliques scattered around the country and held together by the unusual energy of one or two particularly committed individuals in each locality.[17] Lynch recalled that it persisted in the towns of Munster.[18] It appears that the society had actually foundered in many areas but had recovered something of its older character as a townsman's organisation, outside of a few agrarian 'black spots', where it lingered on in its 'Ribbon-Fenian' form. Membership was often rather passive and nominal before 1912.[19] Richard Mulcahy recalled many years later that the IRB was not really very active and essentially consisted of a roll-call during the 1908–13 years. Under pressure of police surveillance, the 'firm' attempted to protect itself from observation, in part by careful recruitment and in part by a new version of the old cell system.[20] The IRB was under Church ban, and prospective recruits were screened for religious scruples. If they were found to have any, they were immediately dropped.[21]

When Protestant Ulster armed to resist Home Rule in 1912, many of the more military-minded of the nationalists were actually pleased. Churchill regarded the Ulster resistance as treasonable, but many British Conservatives did not agree.[22] The south imitated the north, and the British, having let one side flirt with

treason, watched helplessly while the nationalists armed themselves, getting away with something which, if not quite treason,
could be expected to become treason very quickly if Home Rule
became unstuck. In November 1913, an open Irish Volunteer
organisation was founded, building on the already partly drilled
cadres of the AOH and similar organisations. The provisional
committee of the Irish Volunteers had thirty members and of that
thirty, at least eleven were IRB members and a further four were
Gaelic Leaguers and soon to be sworn into the IRB. Many of the
officers of the Volunteers were IRB and, sensing the danger of the
organisation falling into extremist hands, the Irish Party hurriedly
moved to put itself at the head of the Volunteers, swamping the
original committee with its own nominees. Hobson, however,
recalled that the IRB men held the key positions in the Volunteers
and were the most energetic officers: 'an able and united minority
can run most committees, and the most important work went on
outside the Committee in any case.'[23] The IRB and its fellow
travellers may have been abler than the Redmondites, but they
were not all that united. The IRB was really quite a respectable
organisation and many of the leaders were uneasy about the idea
of starting an insurrection without some kind of electoral
mandate. It was almost as though they could not quite make up
their minds whether they were a military conspiracy or a political
party, not all that unusual a dilemma for an Irish political organisation. Furthermore, not all anti-Redmond nationalists were IRB
men, and they had to be dealt with too. Hobson in the IRB, and
MacNeill outside it, wanted to build up the Volunteers into a mass
organisation which would then be in a position to demand
political concessions without actually having to use force, rather
on the analogy of the Volunteers of 1782. However, there was
another faction in the IRB centred around MacDermott, Clarke
and Pearse, who felt that the World War must not be let go by
without an insurrection: to them, England's difficulty would again
be Ireland's opportunity, and they formed what was, in effect, a
conspiracy inside a conspiracy. James Connolly's little Citizen
Army, the child of the 1913 lockout, was eventually attached to the
insurrectionists' bandwagon.

In 1914, this division between moderates and extremists within the IRB and its allies did not yet exist. Then Redmond, in a speech in September 1914, supported voluntary enlistment in the British army. The Volunteers split, the vast majority following Redmond's lead under the new title of the National Volunteers, and many of them enlisting. An anti-enlistment minority of about 10,000 followed the IRB, retaining the old title of the Irish Volunteers. Table 7 presents an array of correlations between numbers, controlled for population, of Irish Volunteers, National Volunteers and Catholic recruits for the British army at the beginning of the World War, with a standard list of social background variables. To introduce a crude control for 'unionism', the Ulster counties are excluded; Table 7 is intended to assess social influences on political differences among Catholics.

Table 7. Volunteers: military volunteering and social background, 1914–15, twenty-three counties

	Volunteers (MacNeill) 1915	Volunteers (Redmond) 1915	Recruits to British army 1914–15
Agrarian agitation, 1880–82	0.51	−.47	−.48
Agrarian agitation, 1910–12	0.50	−.03	−.08
Distance from Dublin	0.27	−.56	−.44
Irish speakers, 1911	0.24	−.51	−.48
Workers, 1911	0.00	0.35	0.73
Small farms, 1911	−.31	0.07	−.65
Medium farms, 1911	0.00	−.43	−.35
Large farms, 1911	0.29	−.13	0.59

The differences are quite striking in this particular instance. The best discriminator between the two Volunteer organisations was the presence or absence of a Land War tradition in the area, the next best was distance from Dublin, the third best was whether or not the area was Irish speaking and the fourth was the land agitation of the 1910–12 years. Farm size had only a slight effect, as had the proportion of the working-class population. The MacNeill anti-war Volunteers were stronger in areas which had strong agrarian traditions, Irish-speaking areas and areas distant from Dublin. By contrast, the National Volunteers, committed to the War and to moderate Home Rule, had a negative association with Land War traditions, a negative association with Irish speaking and were weaker in areas far from Dublin. The Catholic recruits to the British army echoed the Redmondite pattern of urban and non-agrarian bias, but were far more working class in composition. Militant separatism prospered in rural areas with a long tradition of agrarian unrest and resistance to authority and was weaker in the more anglicised, urban and working-class communities, a classic centre-periphery cleavage within the Catholic nationalist community.

The IRB organisers had long been sensitive to this lingering anti-English and anti-authority streak that persisted in many western areas. Patrick Pearse was particularly sensitive to it, particularly in its Irish-speaking variant. A city man himself, he spent a good deal of his time in the Gaeltacht area of Rosmuc in Co. Galway before the War. He went to great pains to ensure that the neighbourhood in which his thatched weekend cottage was placed was not only Irish speaking but also 'Irish' in political spirit. He inquired about the history of the place and tried to find out what the feeling in the area was about land agitation. People were suspicious of him at first and thought he was an Englishman; he drilled the locals, some of whom had once drilled with the Fenians. He spoke only Irish to them and tolerated no English speaking from them. Pearse was re-enacting in the west of Ireland the encounter between urban political man and his rural following; in a sense, he was a missioner, preaching to the last of the Gael how to be themselves, or at least how *he* thought they should be themselves. The IRB organisers were regarded with what appears to have been a sympathetic bemusement by the locals in western areas. Pearse, Ernest Blythe and other organisers benefited from the old diffuse hostility to the British state that still lingered on and were trusted, despite their odd ideas, because of their fierce nationalism and hostility to the political status quo. As one west Kerry woman put it to Desmond FitzGerald in 1914,

'Yerra, we all know that you and Mr Blight are quite mad, but ye mean well according to yeer lights.'[24]

Long before the horrific battles in Belgium and before the shift in public opinion that took place after the Rising, the authorities had noticed a reluctance of rural youth to volunteer for the army. Catholics volunteered less readily than Protestants, and rural Catholics least readily of all. This rural reluctance, like many other Irish cultural traits, was nothing new.[25] To avoid enlistment was not regarded as being particularly cowardly in rural Ireland, but as evidence of good sense. Among the better-off, the army was regarded as a step down socially, quite apart from any danger it might entail. In the first months of the War, the police reported an abrupt increase in the numbers of young men from the western and north-western counties of Cavan, Galway, Kerry, Leitrim, Longford and Mayo going to America, many of them members of the Irish Volunteers.[26] The police reaction was to introduce new passport regulations and to get the shipping companies to refuse passage out of the British Isles to young men of military age. The effect was to bottle up large numbers of potentially disaffected men in Ireland; most traditional emigration was from poor rural counties and consisted of landless young men, exactly the kind of people who had traditionally been the raw material of secret societies. Emigration had averaged about 30,000 a year between 1907 and 1913; in 1914, it was down to 19,000, the following year to less than 8,000; in 1916, it was under 5,000 and in 1917 and 1918 it was negligible.[27] Many thousands of young men stayed around at home, and the wartime agricultural boom may have helped employment and increased reluctance to volunteer even further. The two classic options open to a politicised young man in rural Ireland, voice, in the form of participation in militant politics, or exit, in the shape of emigration to America, had suddenly been reduced to one: voice.[28]

This analysis is not intended to suggest that the Irish Volunteers were weak in Dublin: on the contrary, Dublin was the centre of the pre-Rising organisation because the city was the centre for any large para-political organisation. The Dublin Irish Volunteers were, in fact, better drilled than their rural comrades and seem to have had more ex-soldiers among them. Outside Dublin, the old Fenian areas of the south-west were the best drilled, followed by the south-east and the midlands; Connacht had numbers, but little military tradition.[29]

Despite the small size of the Irish Volunteers after the split, the units were scattered widely around the country; control was a serious problem both for the Volunteer command and for the IRB. Although political and command hierarchies in the organisation were dominated by the IRB and were given cohesion by the secret society, local factional jealousies were a problem and, of course, the secret organisation itself was divided into conservative and advanced tendencies: some IRB men wanted to build up the organisation so as to force an advanced version of Home Rule out of the British government, while others were planning an insurrection. The insurrectionists took advantage of the secretive ethos of the organisation to keep their own secrets, trusted some local men more than others and attempted to run the Volunteers on military, 'need-to-know' principles so as to ensure that as few people as possible, either inside or outside the movement, got wind of their intentions. Local people, however, sometimes had their own ideas, tended to debate and were not always willing to carry out orders unquestioningly in military fashion. There was a considerable amount of 'civilian' mentality, a problem which the IRA was later to inherit.[30]

The result was that there was the formal command structure of the Volunteers, inside which there was another more or less formal command structure, that of the IRB, and inside the IRB there was a further network of those who were committed to insurrection. The quality of local officers varied enormously because the Irish Volunteers was a territorial force, local prominent people being elected to officer positions.[31] Local direct democracy confronted national-level oligarchical conspiracy, rather as in the old United Irishmen. The principle of election was sacrosanct, and ran against the descending command system which the IRB was trying to operate.[32] Local factional leaders came to dominate companies and to regard them almost as their personal property. In certain rare cases, an even older principle of social leadership operated, and a priest would act as commanding officer.[33] In many cases, the IRB seem to have succeeded in getting their man elected. If the man appointed was not IRB, attempts were sometimes made to co-opt him into the organisation. Denis MacCullough recalled that the pre-existing oligarchical tendencies in the IRB had favoured conspiracies such as that of the insurrectionists. Pearse, a latecomer from the Gaelic League, had not been controllable, 'and of course in the IRB that was the important thing, to control men.'[34] Control or co-operation was usually achieved:

> . . . we controlled the volunteer executive. I was a commandant appointed by the volunteer council. We controlled everything. We operated fellows like you who were obedient . . . The Volunteers were the instrument of the IRB . . . I was elected President, Tom Clarke was elected Treasurer and MacDermott was elected Secretary and we were the three who were supposed to rule the IRB. The IRB controlled . . . practically all the key men down the country . . . all the Commandants down the country that were of importance were controlled by the IRB . . . First they tried to arrange that the men elected would be IRB men and if not that they would come into the IRB . . . I would say that most of the Commandants down the country were IRB in 1915–16.[35]

The IRB attempted to solve, in the classic style of caucus politics, the problem of combining election and oligarchy in the Volunteers. The actual Rising went off at half-cock in 1916, in the time-honoured fashion of Irish risings. This time, however, the confusion was due to deep-seated differences of purpose within the Irish Volunteers and within the IRB itself rather than to unwillingness to obey, bad communications or incompetence, although there was a considerable amount of the latter as well. The insurrectionists imagined a rising rather like those the Fenians had dreamed of, with armies manoeuvering across the countryside.

The Rising was planned secretly by the insurrectionists, and Easter Sunday was picked because the musters could be disguised as normal Church parades; there may have been symbolic reasons for the choice of Easter Sunday as well. The police got wind of the plans and prepared a swoop, and Eoin MacNeill, who was not in the conspiracy, cancelled the Church parades. Dublin, however, went ahead with the Rising, as did other, mainly hard-core IRB areas such as Galway, Wexford, Meath and Tyrone; perhaps one-fifth or about 2,000 of the Irish Volunteers actually participated in the Rising. The fighting was mainly in Dublin, and only a few hundred people were killed. The event had the air of an enactment on stage about it, and of course its real effects were symbolic and psychological rather than military. It was an enactment 'on stage' of Pearse's mythical conflict between Gael and Gall, of a gallant fight against overwhelming odds. The theatrical effect was assisted by the British authorities' decision to court-martial the leaders and execute them. From the British point of view, they were traitors; from the point of view of Pearse and the other nationalist leaders, the executions vindicated their view of the true nature of British rule in Ireland.

No guerrilla war ensued immediately, as the practical men who thought in such terms had been forestalled by the insurrectionists. However, after the Rising the practical men, such as Collins, who wanted a guerrilla war, were to take over the movement, partly by using the British prisoner-of-war camps as recruiting grounds. The British, by executing the leaders, had done as Pearse knew they would do and wanted them to do: by acting as tyrants are supposed to act, they became actors in his play and fit into his mythological framework. By so doing, they ensured the end of their own rule in nationalist Ireland.

08 | ELECTIONS, REVOLUTION AND CIVIL WAR, 1916–23

THE RISE OF SINN FÉIN

A mixture of bewilderment and anger seems to have been the immediate reaction of the general public to the Rising. Irish Party politicians and Church leaders deplored or denounced it, many IRB and Volunteer leaders privately disapproved of it and some, like MacNeill and Hobson within the Volunteer organisation, felt they had been betrayed by the insurrectionists. The Dublin workers' families, many of them with husbands or sons fighting in the trenches, hissed the captured rebels as they were marched through the streets after the Rising. The *Irish Independent*, misconstruing the presence of the occasional socialist among the rebels, called for the execution of more of the leaders. These reactions were, however, short lived, probably confined mainly to the bigger towns and superficial. The executions, the heroic demeanour of the leaders, the fear of conscription and the dislike of 'England's war' made a dangerous mixture, particularly in the context of a rural economy enjoying a wartime boom and an absence of emigration.

The rebel Volunteers, together with some advanced nationalists known to the police, were interned in prison camps in England during 1916–17. They were well treated and used the opportunity to get to know each other, to hold post-mortems on the Rising, to make future plans and, above all, to rebuild their organisation on new and more ample lines. At the same time, a traditional 'free-the-prisoners' campaign was being orchestrated at home, in

Britain and in America. Even before 1916, conspiratorial politics had brought together strange ideological bedfellows: the racialist and pro-capitalist Arthur Griffith apparently got on quite well with the socialist and theoretically internationalist James Connolly, for example. William O'Brien of the labour movement, James Larkin and James Connolly all appear to have been Irish nationalists before they turned to socialism as a political ideology, and in the speeches and writings of all three there is distinct evidence of a strong nationalist undertone; certainly, none of these leaders seems to have really believed that there might be some unbridgeable gap between the socialist revolutionism which they espoused and the revolutionary nationalism with which they had become allied. There is an interesting psychological hypothesis to the effect that beliefs acquired early in life tend to be held more firmly, and tend to be served by beliefs acquired later.[1] It is difficult not to suspect that many Irish socialists came to socialism through nationalism, and that the former ideology was always in danger of being swallowed up by the latter. The mixing together of elites and potential elites that occurred in Frongoch and the other camps during 1916–17 had the effect of minimising the differences between various ideological tendencies and tended to encourage solidarity by emphasising the division between them and their British captors. O'Brien was a good friend of Stephen O'Mara, a nationalist businessman in Limerick; a later tycoon of the Free State, Joseph McGrath, had started his career as a health insurance administrator in the Irish Transport and General Workers' Union (ITGWU).[2] The Transport Union itself had always been nationally minded, had been organised in part by men of IRB affiliation and was to co-operate fairly closely with Sinn Féin later on. Men who were eventually to end up on opposite sides in a civil war were sometimes related to each other, had been in the same class at school, had served in the same Volunteer company or had shared the same hut at Frongoch. As revolutionary elites go, it was a remarkably cohesive group. In general, before 1916, everybody in radical politics knew everyone else, and after 1916, thanks to the camps, they knew each other rather better.

Most of the internees were released before the end of 1916, and found that the mood of the country had changed enormously: at

Easter they had been condemned, at Christmas they were hailed as heroes. Augustine Birrell, the Chief Secretary whose career had been wrecked by the Rising, saw the public mood as nothing really new, but as the contemporary expression of an ancient Irish alienation from British authority.[3] He also thought that this traditional alienation had softened since the 1890s but that the reluctance to grant Home Rule had helped to revive it.[4] Certainly, recruiting of Catholics stopped abruptly after Easter 1916. The police felt that Asquith's acknowledgement that Home Rule must come, together with speeches hostile to the executions from Dillon and from the Bishop of Limerick, had had a galvanising effect on public opinion. Older traditions resurfaced and infected a new generation. Prior to the Rising, there had been the usual veiled hostility to the police in the mainly Irish-speaking areas of west Galway, and a large area actually rose in a badly organised way in sympathy with the Rising. The areas where disaffection was strongest were those 'outside the towns'.[5] Elsewhere in the west and in some other parts of rural Ireland, similar stirrings had taken place.

Throughout 1917 the reconstituted Sinn Féin Party spread through the country, absorbing older groups. The new party had to unite a variety of groups under one banner, some of them not even republican: IRB, old Sinn Féin, Irish Volunteer and ex-Redmondite leaders. Michael Laffan has discerned three phases in the rise of the new pan-nationalist party. During the first phase, from the Rising to December 1916, the organisation was more or less dormant and there was relatively little attempt to respond to or harness the new popular mood. With the return of the Frongoch and Reading internees in December, the party got off the ground, and Laffan sees a second phase starting, one of organisational development and consolidation. The final unification of the various nationalist groups did not occur until the return of the Lewes prisoners in June 1917, among them de Valera. By October, Griffith and Plunkett had stood down in favour of de Valera, and the leaders were recognised 'almost everywhere' as the leaders of 'the great bulk of Irish opinion'.[6] A series of by-elections in 1917 and 1918 demonstrated what acute observers had noticed in late 1916, that public opinion had changed. Sinn Féin won in five constituencies against Irish Party candidates and were returned unopposed in one other. However, the new party's by-election success was not total; a substantial Nationalist Party vote persisted and, in Ulster constituencies in particular, the older party was able to fend off the newer party's electoral challenge. In Waterford, Armagh south and Tyrone east the Sinn Féin candidates were actually beaten, and Sinn Féin only scraped home in south Longford and Cavan east. Only in east Clare and north Roscommon did it have really substantial victories. However, there was an undoubted movement away from the Redmondite Party, and the conscription crisis of 1918 was to act as the accelerator of a process of change in public opinion which was already under way. The old Sinn Féin of Griffith had progressed from twenty-one branches in 1906 to a peak of 128 in 1909, but by the end of 1917 the new Sinn Féin had achieved the old INL saturation point and could boast 1,240 branches.[7] The party maintained this approximate total until mid-1921. Much of the new party was built on the ruins of older mass parties, and it, in turn, was to supply the raw material for successor organisations. The Irish Volunteers were reorganised at the same time, and at the end of 1917 de Valera became President of the Volunteers, uniting the political and military wings of the movement in his own person. De Valera had had only a fringe connection with the IRB and he had never sat in its inner councils. He apparently disliked and distrusted it; the IRB became the instrument of Michael Collins, and this was to affect the form that the final split was to take four years later.[8]

In April 1918, the British government, despite Dillon's warnings, announced its intention to introduce conscription in Ireland. The Irish Party withdrew from Westminster, the Irish trade unions declared against the measure and the Catholic Church not only denounced it but organised a Church-door pledge campaign against it. Intentionally or otherwise, the Church had joined the separatists, the traditional stabilising tension between the moderate bishops and the more radical lower clergy and lay youth was dissolved, the young were released from any restraint and rushed into Sinn Féin. Conscription had intensified the process of remobilisation that the Ulster crisis and the Rising had encouraged. By mid-

1918, the young priests, who had previously kept their nationalist opinions to themselves or expressed them with caution, were making their views noisily known.[9] The threat of conscription faded during the summer, but by then the damage had been done, the priests' restraining influence had been removed and Sinn Féin was unstoppable. The RIC reported that practically 'the entire nationalist youth of both sexes have become obsessed with the idea of an Irish Republic'.[10]

Long before the electoral landslide of December 1918, the Sinn Féiners had evolved an efficient electoral machine. Some major organisational innovations were introduced into Irish nationalist politics at this time. In particular, specific duties such as the organisation of canvass, the management of personation agents, transportation and propaganda were allocated to particular people at local level and also to particular people at regional and national level, a centralised, vertical division of functions which was unprecedented in Irish politics at the time, and certainly had not been approximated by any party organisation since the 1880s.[11] The almost military centralisation of the new party was very noticeable, and contrasted with the localist and decentralised structure of the Irish Party, dominated as it was by territorially based parliamentary 'satraps'. The disciplined, rather impersonal and machine-like style of Sinn Féin became more pronounced after 1918 and was aggravated by the persistent guerrilla campaign which had the effect of militarising the party. Sinn Féin won a devastating victory in 1918, and that fact meant that in 1920 and 1921 it scarcely had to contest seats in areas without a unionist presence: to be nominated was to be elected. Nomination was therefore crucial, and nomination was in the hands of a small caucus centred around Harry Boland, Michael Collins and Diarmuid O'Hegarty.[12]

Boland was de Valera's personal political assistant, trouble shooter and organisational fixer. He had gone to the United States with de Valera in 1919 and within weeks had managed to split and take over the Irish-American nationalist organisation. In 1921, Boland was chairman of the IRB's Supreme Council.[13] In view of the foregoing account of the Dáil nomination procedures, the fact that that Dáil voted against de Valera on the Treaty takes on a certain irony. Boland's loyalty to de Valera was very strong, and he was reported as having voted against the Treaty mainly on the grounds that he felt that he 'couldn't let the long fellow [i.e. de Valera] down'.[14] The extreme centralisation of the movement on a narrow group of key leaders, a development made possible because of the revolutionary events which had produced a popular una-nimity, meant that divisions in the movement would, initially at least, be likely to follow personality differences and clique lines rather than any underlying ideological or social cleavage. The common past experiences of the elites and their common past dilemmas would tend to heighten this effect. Perhaps most importantly of all, the prior existence of a closely knit leadership group was to encourage a sense of personal betrayal when the group finally split in 1921–22.

THE ELECTORAL LANDSLIDE OF DECEMBER 1918

The general election of December 1918 was, in the language of political science, a critical election. Frank Gallagher later remarked that there had never been an election in Ireland like it; he was referring to its plebiscite-like character.[15] Sinn Féin's victory was indeed clear cut, and even Irish Party candidates tended to admit that their defeats had been due less to any kind of intimidation than to a mass conversion to the new party and to its excellent electoral organisation.[16] Admittedly, Sinn Féin did not have it all its own way, and also had some 'unfair' advantages.[17] The party won twenty-five seats unopposed out of 101 seats in 100 territorial constituencies.[18] It actually won just under 48 per cent of the votes cast, and it is possible that the Irish Party held on to much of its traditional support in many areas.[19] However, in the twenty-six counties of nationalist Ireland, Sinn Féin won 65 per cent of the votes cast, and many constituencies were uncontested. Presumably the actual level of support that the party enjoyed in nationalist Ireland was far higher than 65 per cent, and far higher than 50 per cent in all Ireland. Even in the six counties of unionist Ulster, the potential support for the party among Catholics was understated in the results because of an electoral pact between Sinn Féin and the Irish Party.[20] As the electorate had been tripled by granting the vote to the unpropertied and to women over thirty, it could be argued that the Irish Party was defeated by the newly mobilised and enfranchised groups.[21] Dillon felt the party had lost the allegiance of the young.[22]

The geographical pattern of the Sinn Féin vote in 1918 has been mapped by Rumpf.[23] In east and central Ulster, Sinn Féin lost to unionism and also ceded some seats to the Irish Party. It lost a seat to unionism in suburban Dublin and one in Waterford to the Irish Party. The unopposed Sinn Féin seats were mainly in the west, with west and central Munster forming the largest single block of such walk-overs. The new party met with resistance more in the east than in the west, in the towns than in the countryside. The separatists won less than their mean twenty-six county vote of 65 per cent in three out of four Dublin county constituencies, in neighbouring east Wicklow, Waterford City, south Wexford and Louth. In Ulster, Protestant solidarity was total.[24]

The role of the rural and urban working class in this election has been given rather a lot of attention. Labour's decision to stand down in 1918 has been seen as the crucial event which determined its subordinate role in party politics after independence.[25] Labour wished to stand, especially in Dublin, but the local Sinn Féin activists had no intention of entering into an electoral pact with it, and nationalist-minded Labour leaders dissuaded the others from going ahead.[26] The enormous influence of the Transport Union and the acceptance of Sinn Féin propaganda by many of the workers were also factors; after all, Labour, if it had contested the general election, might have been very badly beaten by Sinn Féin and shared the fate of the Irish Party. By staying clear of the nationalist whirl-wind, Labour survived into the era of Irish independence. If Labour had challenged Sinn Féin in 1918, it would have been easy for its opponents to accuse it of secret anti-national sentiments. Another, deeper reason for Labour's defeatism was a structural one: the political organisation of Irish society was far more intense and effective in the countryside than in the towns, and townspeople tended to be less involved in party politics and organisation.[27] After independence, this urban weakness was reflected in the persistently low turnout rates recorded in the larger towns.[28]

Analyses of the election suggest in effect that Sinn Féin won disproportionate support from the newly enfranchised young, the western agrarian counties and, of course, the Catholic as distinct from the Protestant population. Because of the pattern of the non-contests, it appears that the contestants themselves regarded the second generalisation as being valid, and the third is unquestionable. Whether Sinn Féin was a 'youth' party is a moot point. Table 8 presents the correlations between age and religion variables and the voting figures. Because of non-contests and electoral pacts, the calculations were only carried out on the figures for nineteen counties out of thirty-two in all Ireland, the nineteen counties being rather disproportionately non-agrarian but otherwise fairly representative. A particular effort was made to construct an indicator of the presence of young men of military age by abstracting from the 1911 census the proportion of the male population aged fourteen to twenty-four in that year. The other independent variable is the proportion which was Catholic in 1911. For obvious reasons, an agrarianism variable was not used.

Table 8. 1918 Election: youth and religion (N=19)

	Turnout	Sinn Féin	Irish Party
Youth: Males aged 14–24, 1911	−.45	0.33	−.04
Religion: Catholics, 1911	−.33	0.89	0.63

These results are unsurprising, and suggest that Sinn Féin's support was weaker in areas where Protestants were present (presumably because in such areas the Irish Party retained some 'Hibernian' vitality) and that areas with large numbers of young men were indeed somewhat likely to be more in favour of the new party. However, the mild and ambiguous support given to the youth hypothesis is overshadowed by the total dominance of the sectarian pattern: unionism's correlation with religion is a crushing near-unity in the minority of counties that Unionist candidates contested. Sinn Féin correlates almost perfectly with Catholicism. It was surmised that a stronger 'youth effect' was swamped by the presence of the large British garrison in Kildare and by the religion effect. The correlations were therefore recalculated while omitting Kildare, and then calculated again while controlling for religion. Table 9 gives the results.

Table 9. 1918 Election: youth versus religion (N=18)

	Sinn Féin	Irish Party
Youth: Males aged 14–24, 1911	0.17	0.15
Youth, controlling for religion	−.46	−.23

These results suggest that there was no particular relationship between youth and the vote for either party. It should be remembered that the British army was popular with working-class youth, and that Sinn Féin had to propagandise against it. Rural youth was anti-army, but that is a regional, not an age, distinction, for so were rural elders; a Sinn Féin organiser in Louth recalled the gratitude of big farmers whose sons had been saved from the trenches. One is tempted to fall back on the usual political science generalisations about youth and politics, which emphasise the apolitical mentality of most young people, the presence of which is hidden by the activities of a small and noisy minority. In the 1960s in the United States, for example, in similar circumstances of conscription and an unpopular war, young people were divided on the issue, just as were their elders, and opinion polls consistently reflected that fact; the division was not as generational as it looked. In Ireland, the Sinn Féin vote was so huge that it must have included members of all age groups, and the pressure of the huge and efficient Sinn Féin canvassing machine must have been difficult to resist.[29] The analysis suggests that the Sinn Féin vote was based on communities rather than on generations or any distinction between old and new voters; it became more total the more Catholic, the more rural, the more western and the less northern an area was.

These negative findings must be treated very cautiously, but if we assume that young men were less patriotic in the privacy of the polling booth than they were represented as being in nationalist propaganda, the continuity with the pattern of 1914 and the difficulty that the IRA had in recruiting young men during the

Anglo-Irish War fit into place. As the next section demonstrates, the IRA had serious problems of apathy and low morale during the campaign outside their strong areas. Many young men opted to stay out of trouble either by inactivity or by emigration, which started up again in 1920, being particularly heavy in western counties. The IRA during the Anglo-Irish War was a tiny force, its active core being far less than 10,000 even though its nominal membership was over 100,000. After the Truce, IRA veterans bitterly complained of 'Trucileers' and 'Sunshine Soldiers', who emerged to join up when the fighting was over.

THE REPUBLIC OF IRELAND, 1919–23

The Sinn Féin members of parliament elected in December 1918 met in Dublin in January 1919, less those of their number who were in British prisons. No unionist attended. The Sinn Féin MPs constituted themselves as Dáil Éireann (Assembly of Ireland), declared themselves sovereign and also declared a Republic. They also voted a general programme of economic and social reform based on the ideas of Griffith and, to some extent, on social democratic policies. The Dáil government was soon underground and found itself presiding over a guerrilla campaign. Run on a shoestring, it was only partially united in its purposes and only partly in control of events. The guerrilla war, which reached its climax in 1920, was, by international standards, a very small conflict. However, the Anglo-Irish War was occasionally ferocious and was savage enough to brutalise some of its participants.

The first shot was fired in Tipperary, and the central Munster area was the main theatre of the campaign. A smaller theatre existed in the Cavan-Sligo area. Of IRA dead in 1919–21, only one-quarter had addresses in a large town or city, indicating that the force was far more than three-quarters rural, as many of those with town addresses would, presumably, have rural backgrounds.[30] Generally the IRA activity was concentrated at the northern and southern ends of the 'middle west' tier of counties running down the middle of the island from Fermanagh to Cork. Remoteness from administrative centres and from Protestant areas also facilitated IRA action, the correlations between IRA actions and road distance from Belfast and Dublin being .52 and .50, respectively. Possibly because it was nearer Dublin, the central section of the 'middle west' was less active. There were, however, other regional variations. The traditionally agrarian west was not particularly active, nor were the richer eastern counties. Controlling for population, the most active counties were, in descending order, the old Ribbon county of Cavan on the Ulster border, followed by the five contiguous Munster counties of Tipperary, Cork, Clare, Limerick and Waterford. The most inactive was Wicklow, followed by Kilkenny and Kildare in eastern Leinster, followed by the far western counties of Mayo and Donegal. The old two-focus pattern of central Munster and border Ulster had reappeared.

Rumpf has suggested that these were the areas where not only was popular support available, but also local leadership.[31] Such leaders were most likely to appear in 'middle' Ireland, the areas where agrarian memories were strong, but where farms were well above subsistence level, towns were well developed and a stratum of 'strong' farmers existed. He also suggested that the two-focus pattern of IRA activity was connected with the existence in these two areas of well-developed co-operative dairy organisations, both of the areas being centres of these co-operatives.[32] The combination of an agrarian tradition going back to the 1880s and a subsequent tradition of inter-farmer economic co-operation, it was surmised, would be the best predictor of IRA activity. Table 10 gives the results of a test of this hypothesis, and shows that the Land War and co-operatives are both good predictors of IRA activity, but it also suggests that the Land War's ability to predict the IRA variable is unaffected by controlling for co-operatives; the existence of co-operatives may, in fact, be a sign of the existence of structural and cultural factors which are themselves the causes of agrarianism, the IRA activity *and* co-operatives. The pattern which the IRA variable displays repeats a pattern which long antedates the development of dairy co-operatives in the late nineteenth century. However, the British subscribed to the theory that the co-operatives and the IRA were linked: they used to make a point of burning them down.[33]

Table 10. IRA actions, Land War traditions and dairy co-operative organisations, Nationalist Ireland

IRA: Land War, 1880	0.48	(N=23)
IRA: Co-operatives, 1926	0.54	(N=23)
IRA: Land War, 1880, controlling for co-operatives, 1926	0.45	(N=22)

Table 11 summarises the main correlates of the IRA war for nationalist Ireland, demonstrating the general validity of Rump's insight. Table 11 indicates that the presence of middle-sized farmers was indeed important, although it might be suggested that it really indicates that subsistence farming communities generate few guerrillas and many emigrants. The Irish-speaking areas, mainly subsistence areas, were unimportant, as was the GAA variable. Generally, with the exceptions of the distance, co-operatives, Land War and Catholics variables, the correlations with social variables are not strong. This indicates that the IRA was far more than the creation of one rural class, and also that the reasons for the variation in IRA activity seem to have had a lot to do with agrarian traditions plus the physical possibilities of the area. Economic wealth was important only as a 'threshold' factor; below a certain material level no IRA activity could be sustained, just as no party organisations were sustained in the 1880s. It was by no means an agrarian movement, although it had an agrarian aspect, and it was generally hostile to the traditional forms of agrarian activity. Its centre of social gravity seems to have been among the small-town and rural 'lower middle classes' of post-Parnell Ireland, but it also attracted very considerable support from groups both below and above that social level. It benefited from local organisational traditions, some of them of considerable antiquity and dating back, in all probability, to the eighteenth century if not even earlier. Young men, particularly the younger sons of small and medium farmers, who had no alternative to emigration appear to have been particularly active in the movement and, once the conflict was over, many of them emigrated to the United States in time for the boom years of the 1920s.

Table 11. IRA actions and selected social and geographical variables, Nationalist Ireland (N=23)

Distance from Dublin	0.50
Distance from Belfast	0.52
Catholic, 1911	0.48
Irish speakers, 1911	0.20
GAA clubs, 1912	0.32
Small farms, 1911	−0.42
Medium farms, 1911	0.37
Large farms, 1911	0.29

Local factions were, inevitably, the basis of IRA strength in many areas, and non-IRB factions seem to have been less amenable to central control. The east Limerick and Tipperary flying columns were small groups of full-time riflemen living off the land and the community. In east Limerick, there were two family-based IRA factions, one of them IRB and the other not. The two families divided the area between them, and the non-IRB group were initially unwilling to join the 'flying column' which the IRB group had set up. Eventually, the split was healed and the two groups were able to field their maximum force by April 1920: fifty armed men.[34] Similar rivalries existed in Clare, the same territorial and kin tensions existing there too. Collins's centralising and rationalising efforts there encountered stiff opposition.[35] Partly because of this kind of local disunity, areas varied enormously in their effectiveness. East and central Clare, GAA hurling areas, were good, west Clare had no hurling and not much IRA. West Clare and east Galway, despite their reputation as agrarian hotbeds, were poor IRA areas, in the opinion of east Clare IRA, who blamed the incompetence of the local officers.[36]

Physical and geographical factors affected performance; the remote brigades of south and west Mayo, apparently full of fight, could not get their hands on arms.[37] In other areas, not only were officers of poor calibre, locals sometimes consorted with the enemy.[38] Participation was a problem; the south Roscommon IRA commander complained in March 1921 about the draining effect of emigration.[39] However, the real problem appears to have been the shortage of arms and ammunition, and the geographically uneven pattern of the conflict may have been partly due to the fact that the IRA had to rely on captured arms. That, however, also meant that the most eager units would be the best armed and would have accumulated some captured arms in the early months when the authorities were less alert than they later became.[40] Reports to headquarters reflected organisational sophistication and effectiveness, those from Cork and Waterford being the most impressive.[41]

The country rapidly became ungovernable, as was the intention of the IRA leaders. IRA activities contributed to this, but there was also a genuine popular reluctance to co-operate with the RIC and there was a widespread acceptance of the Dáil administration in many areas of the west and south-west, partly for ideological reasons and partly because many people believed that the British were going to leave sooner or later. Even many Protestants and members of the Ascendancy decided to come to terms with the new order. The police became a target of hatred almost immediately. As early as May 1919, the widow of an RIC sergeant killed by local IRA was jeered by the crowd on her way to Mass, and in Munster in general there was a widespread hostility to the police which even the RIC themselves admitted.[42] The old hatred of the 'peelers' was not too difficult to revive, even though the RIC men were generally of Catholic Irish background. The ostracisation of the RIC which was ordered by the Dáil government and enforced by the IRA was defined in April 1919 in terms identical to those of the Land League boycotts.[43]

The Dáil attempted not only to make the British government in Ireland unworkable, but to replace its apparatus. In part this was an attempt to give symbolic and physical expression to its claim to be the legitimate government. Descriptions of the effectiveness of the Dáil underground courts and land tribunals vary wildly, but it is clear that the crown courts were replaced by Dáil equivalents in many areas.[44] The first court was set up in agrarian west Clare in early 1920, and the setting up of such courts in the western counties was motivated by a desire to head off the Connacht agrarian agitation.[45] Even RIC officers sometimes attended Dáil courts; neither RIC nor IRA wanted a new agrarian campaign, the latter because they wished to avoid taking sides in a rural and essentially local class conflict.[46] Sinn Féin expressed sympathy for the smallholder and landless man, but did not recommend a drastic solution and confined itself to an anti-grazier rhetoric similar to that of the early UIL.[47] It is important to note that the Dáil courts, although they recognised British land law, also recognised local 'law'. They put themselves explicitly in a direct line of descent from the arbitration tribunals of the INL and UIL, thus inserting themselves into the folk landholding system. Many large landholders saw the Dáil courts as a means of finally having their holdings confirmed.[48] The Dáil return of counties in which land cases were dealt with by its Department of Agriculture and Land Commission yields a map which is almost identical to that yielded by the RIC return of cases of agrarian agitation during 1920–21: what the west and west midlands lacked in military effectiveness was compensated for in cattle driving.[49]

Neither side could force a military victory. The IRA could make much of the country ungovernable, but the Dáil was only able to replace the British apparatus in a few rather remote, if large, areas in the west and south. The appeal to British and American public opinion, and non-violence at home in the form of the boycott and popular acceptance of republican order, were more important in some ways than the actual campaign of violence itself. Mass solidarity and systematic non-co-operation demoralised the RIC, which suffered many resignations. The IRA, although sometimes merciless to those whom it regarded as collaborators, did not have to use terror, as the vast bulk of the Catholic population accepted it as it had accepted various paramilitary local governments in previous generations. Sinn Féin and IRA leaders such as Collins were able to walk around openly in the towns, be recognised by thousands of people and not be reported to the authorities. The British governmental machine began to disintegrate; the IRA penetrated the RIC and Castle administration, while local government went over bodily to the Dáil in many areas.

The guerrilla campaign profoundly affected the relationships between the various Dáil political institutions. The IRA, nominally subject to the Dáil, came to look upon the civilian side, Sinn Féin, with some distrust and even contempt, and often came to regard Sinn Féin and the Dáil government as organisations which should be subordinate to the army.[50] The civilian movement remained intensely centralised, while the army tended to become decentralised. The militarisation of the entire movement was the reason for this growing monolithism in the Sinn Féin and Dáil structures, as Collins was using Sinn Féin, the IRB and the Dáil as ways of keeping tabs on the IRA, thus cutting across Cathal Brugha, the nominal Minister for Defence. The use of all these parallel structures for the purpose of control by a small central group tended to weaken the structures as institutions and transform them into so many extensions of the central group's network. The IRA, for operational reasons, remained autonomous and decentralised, the local guerrilla chiefs becoming, in effect, the local political chiefs in their areas. They became increasingly inclined to brush aside the Dáil deputies (*Teachtaí Dála*, TDs), Sinn Féin leaders and civilian members of the Dáil government staff. The IRA's sense of superiority was strengthened by the fact that it was an older organisation than either Sinn Féin or the Dáil government, as it was essentially a reorganised version of the Irish Volunteers. As we have seen, the identification of the national interest with the wishes of a military underground was not new. Gradually, IRA officers came to assume that they had the right to control the local Sinn Féin *cumainn* (clubs) and, as the war continued, their ability to do so became greater.

Another ambiguous relationship was that between the IRB and the Dáil. The old Fenian organisation had regarded itself as the government of the Republic. It conceded this authority to the Dáil in 1919, but something of its image as guardian of the flame persisted, and it was regarded with great suspicion by many of the non-IRB activists. This element of paranoia which the secret society's existence generated had an important bearing on the form the Treaty split took. In fact, most of the IRB appears to have melted away into the post-1916 structures. The younger men who were joining the movement joined Sinn Féin or the IRA, not the IRB.[51] As far as the average IRA Volunteer was concerned, the IRB was a remote organisation.[52] The IRA leaders were younger men who represented a generational shift in the movement. Many of them had not had any direct involvement with extreme nationalist politics and many had sympathised with the Irish Party. Many had had experience of active service in the British army in World War I. In some ways they were not unlike other members of their generation who had attempted to remain in army life at the end of the War by joining nationalist paramilitary associations. In a sense, they were not unlike many of the young men in the British forces who had become militarised by the War and who had a contempt for politics, a distrust for civilian leadership and a warrior mystique. The distrust was combined with a rebellion against the older generation as being effete, corrupt, unheroic and, above all, civilian.

The most important relationship was that between the IRA and the Sinn Féin Party. The police assumed that the IRB controlled the IRA and that the IRA controlled Sinn Féin.[53] In fact, the IRA were trying to control the politicians, but the politicians were also trying to control the IRA. Again, many of the participants were unsure as to which role should predominate, Collins's dual role as Minister for Finance and Director of Intelligence being the classic example, particularly when it is considered that he had also usurped the Ministry of Defence, by-passing both the military and civilian hierarchies because of his personal energy and his private network of IRB contacts. Significantly, despite this institutional decay, the formal structures held up fairly well, and the Dáil vote on the Treaty was crucial. The Republic foundered on a constitutional issue, the issue being whether the Dáil or even the electorate had the right to disestablish that Republic. The Republic had no real constitutional machinery or tradition to deal with such a profound issue. Almost every nationalist society and institutional structure split from top to bottom on the Treaty issue, creating a jungle of intra-organisational coups, duplications and secessions. The sinister machinations of the IRB were seen as being responsible for the pro-Treaty vote by many anti-Treatyites.[54] The political institutions of the Republic dissolved under this pressure and the militarisation of the movement which had occurred since

1918 hastened this dissolution. Furthermore, the tradition of secrecy encouraged distrust and paranoia on both sides.

The Truce finally arrived in July 1921 after months of undercover contacts. By this time the Ulster parliament had been opened, presenting the republicans with a *fait accompli* and guaranteeing to the British a permanent entanglement in Ireland. The Treaty of December 1921 accorded dominion status to nationalist Ireland. Certain military concessions were made to the British, and partition was tacitly accepted as a temporary or, perhaps, permanent expedient. Dominion status did not appear to be total independence, although it was later to prove to be. The symbols of the new Irish Free State were an uneasy synthesis of post-British and republican themes, and it could be, and was, easily represented by republican propagandists as a British puppet regime. Most importantly, the Republic was disestablished and an oath of allegiance to the British monarch was included in the proposed constitution of the Free State.

The first rift was between the Dáil government as personified by de Valera and the plenipotentiaries themselves who, having signed the Treaty, felt they had to abide by it. The crucial and unresolved question is why the delegation did not contact de Valera in Dublin by telephone before signing the Treaty. Subsequent argument concentrated on the selection of the delegates, why de Valera himself did not go and why they did not check with him before signing. De Valera explained that he wished to hold himself in reserve so as to be able to rally the radicals in favour of a moderate solution; in effect, he stayed at home to keep the republican radicals in check.[55] Griffith and Collins, as the other two senior figures, had to go, he explained. Both, he felt, would be 'soft' on monarchy, but the two strong republicans in the cabinet, Brugha and Stack, would be impossible for Griffith and Collins to work with. Mary MacSwiney would also be unacceptable, because neither Griffith nor Collins would be able to work with her; 'women in general, I suppose' was de Valera's comment. Barton was intended as a substitute for Brugha and Stack, but 'Duggan and Duffy were mere legal padding'. Childers—an Englishman— was supposed to have a toughening influence as secretary.[56] De

Valera seems to have been admitting that, quite apart from personality conflicts, the republican wing of the movement was rather short on good committee men.

The centralisation of the civilian machine on Collins combined with the localist structure of the IRA was an important conditioning factor affecting the form of the split. Collins's pessimistic assessment of the military situation was crucial in getting acceptance of the Treaty from the IRB.[57] However, although the Supreme Council of the IRB accepted the Treaty, many local IRB centres in Munster refused to accept it.[58] The Dáil vote of January 1922 resulted in a small majority for the Treaty; Mary MacSwiney claimed later that a solid bloc of forty IRB TDs voted for the Treaty.[59] However, the internal unity of the IRB was scarcely total, and anti-Treaty complaints about the Dáil vote appear odd in light of the fact that many of the TDs had been vetted originally at the nomination stage by Harry Boland, himself a senior IRB figure.[60] During the six months after the signing of the Treaty, the entire national front disintegrated in a fashion reminiscent of the collapse after the Parnell split. The general staff of the IRA voted for the Treaty by a majority, but the rank and file voted against it. The civilian organisation went mainly anti-Treaty too, but was a very depleted and militarised organisation at the time. The women's organisation, Cumann na mBan, was stridently anti-Treaty. Dáil, Sinn Féin and IRA all split into two parallel sets of organisations, neither of which could lay unambiguous claim to being the legal successor to the pre-Truce organisations.[61] It appears that those who had been politicised by the military campaign tended to be anti-Treaty, while those whose experience had been in the civilian or bureaucratic side tended to be pro-Treaty or to be at least moderate. IRA leaders in the northern areas tended to be 'Hibernian' and to accept the Treaty on tactical or pragmatic grounds, whereas the southerners tended to take a more fundamentalist line. The women TDs all voted against the Treaty. There was a small, but noticeable, correlation between high social status and pro-Treaty voting among Dáil deputies.[62] The IRA was under-represented in the Dáil, which made the soldier versus politician aspect of the split more pronounced.

The IRA divided slowly and reluctantly. Many individuals and units tried to avoid the dilemma, and the overall effect is as much one of disintegration as of a split into two coherent groups. The lure of America, of the new, paid, Free State army and police and reluctance to fight comrades all combined to erode the pre-Truce IRA. In Munster in particular, local IRA units took control of the local Sinn Féin cumainn to ensure that the party stayed anti-Treaty; a Sinn Féin activist from Clonakilty wrote to Collins in January 1922:

> I can prove that the IRA are using the authority of their officers to compel the members of Sinn Féin to do against their will what they would not otherwise do ... Responsible and highly placed officers of the IRA have informed me that they will not permit their fathers etc. to vote in the coming election ... As a more or less successful attempt has been made to rig all the clubs in South Cork I think that the roll of members etc. should be strictly examined— all the country are still solid for the Treaty but are afraid.[63]

Similar allegations of IRA takeover or interference came from elsewhere in Cork, from Kilkenny and from Sligo. A priest was sometimes chosen as the pro-Treaty delegate, as the only alternative to an IRA delegate; among civilians, only a priest had the ability to resist IRA pressure in safety.[64] The anti-Treaty takeover of Sinn Féin was very effective. By February 1922, only nine constituency organisations in Sinn Féin had advanced the money to pay county organising secretaries to Dublin headquarters. The other twenty-eight had either not collected the money or had kept it. Of the nine, presumably moderate or pro-Collins and pro-Treaty constituency organisations, four were in Dublin and four were Leinster counties near Dublin. In the rest of Ireland, even before the special *ard-fheis* (party convention) of February 1922, the country organisation was cutting contact with Dublin, disintegrating or being taken over by the IRA.[65] Over 1,000 clubs were fully paid up in 1919, but by the end of 1921 only 117 were fully paid up.[66] The RIC saw this development as a generational division, the young and poor intimidating the old and propertied.[67] By early 1922, it was only in the 'home counties' that a coherent civilian Sinn Féin organisation persisted. Elsewhere, the IRA prevented the development of a separate Sinn Féin structure; even as early as October 1921, Sinn Féin's director of organisation reported immense difficulties in setting up a line distinct from that of the IRA communications line; local Volunteers resisted any attempt to set up an independent Sinn Féin line.[68] The *ard-fheis* of February 1922 which accepted the Treaty and the proposed election was that of a rump party. In March, the IRA defied their own general staff and rejected the Treaty at a special army convention. Also in March, de Valera attempted to set up an anti-Treaty *civilian* organisation, a political party called Cumann na Poblachta (Republican Party).[69] This organisation never achieved any real standing, and the IRA remained the only real anti-Treaty organisation. By April Collins was writing to McGarrity complaining that the anti-Treaty IRA were making it impossible for the pro-Treaty people to hold meetings.[70]

At the IRA convention, delegates representing a notional 80,000 volunteers opposed the settlement while delegates representing a notional 30,000 were in favour.[71] The IRA was itself very unevenly distributed, being mainly a Munster force, and one-third of the delegates were from Munster.[72] The southern divisions were most determinedly anti-Treaty. The Connacht IRA was also anti-Treaty, but did not have the manpower or influence of the southern units. In the north-west, Sean Mac Eoin, a famous Longford IRA leader, persuaded many of the local IRA to accept the Treaty.

The Civil War that followed the Free State's attack on the Four Courts at the end of July 1922 was short. By early 1923 the republican cause had been decisively defeated by the forces of the Free State, but the true defeat of the republicans was the acceptance of the Treaty, in both 1922 and 1923, by the electorate. Even the 'Pact' election of 1922 could be seen as decisive, and the subsequent Civil War as an attempt to reverse an electoral verdict by arms. Republicans interpreted the pro-Treaty result of the 1922 election in contradictory ways; on the one hand, as de Valera put it in a phrase that still haunts his political heirs, the majority had no right to do wrong, while on the other the verdict of 1922 had not been a free one because the British had threatened war if the Treaty was not accepted. The new draft constitution was only published on the morning of the poll. Furthermore, Collins had agreed to an electoral pact with the anti-Treatyites and had then broken it in spirit if not in the letter by advising the voters to vote their own choice rather than the package put up by the joint list and recommending that they vote, if they so wished, for candidates belonging to neither faction of the old Sinn Féin. He appears to have agreed to the pact to ensure that the IRA permitted the election to be held at all.

The electorate voted overwhelmingly for the Treaty, and many voted against Sinn Féin. Nearly 40 per cent of the vote went to non-Sinn Féin groups, whether Labour, Farmers' Party or Independent. Admittedly, the verdict was unclear, as the turnout was low, many constituencies were uncontested, there was a lot of intimidation and the franchise was still somewhat restricted.[73] The acceptance by the majority of the population of the Treaty in its essentials is indicated by the election result and also by the brevity of the ensuing Irish Civil War, which always had the air of an army mutiny about it, despite the claim of the republican leadership that they represented the legal government of the Republic. In 1923, after the Civil War, the electorate again voted preponderantly for pro-Treaty parties and the message was unambiguous this time. The entire IRA campaign of 1919–21 had been legitimised in the minds of the Dáil and IRA leaderships as being in accordance with the will of the electorate as expressed in December 1918. It was difficult for most IRA to ignore that electorate when it turned on them; subsequent IRAs have always had trouble with the fact that the voters will not vote for them, and harp unceasingly on 1918, the time the electorate got it right. Eventually the less militarised or more educable of the anti-Treatyites absorbed the bitter lesson of 1922–23; military defeat, electoral unpopularity and four years in the political wilderness were good teachers, and they gradually realised that their Republic really was dead.

09 | THE ORIGINS OF THE PARTY SYSTEM IN INDEPENDENT IRELAND

THE ANCESTRY OF THE IRISH PARTY SYSTEM

The emergence of new political parties in the Irish Free State after independence in 1921 was inextricably linked with the political crisis which accompanied the establishment of the state itself. The split which had divided the nationalist movement into two bitterly opposed sections involved constitutional and symbolic issues rather than the kinds of class or bread-and-butter issues which are assumed to be appropriate in Western party systems. Certainly, despite the intensity of the passions involved in the split, no profound division concerning the correct socio-economic organisation of society underlay the cleavage initially. The concerns of the Sinn Féin political elite were those of the relationship of Ireland to Britain, partition, the quality of the new state's independence and who was to be in control, all issues whose consideration was hampered by the sense of betrayal which both sides had. Why this was so is difficult to explain, but it had much to do with the very oligarchical character of Sinn Féin, which restricted political decisions to a narrow and secret group and, more distantly, with the ingrained and obsessive nature of the drive for independence, which had bent to its service all kinds of political, economic and even aesthetic systems of ideas. It has become common to regard the cleavage between the two major parties in the Republic of Ireland, Fianna Fáil and Fine Gael, as somehow meaningless and superficial. I would argue that the division between these two parties actually reflects a profound distinction in Irish society, a distinction between those who, for class, cultural or other reasons, assume a natural affinity between Ireland and Britain and those who do not, or would rather such an affinity did not exist. This distinction is reflected with fair accuracy in the more Anglophobe Fianna Fáil tradition and the less Anglophobe pro-Treaty, Fine Gael tradition.

The support bases of the parties cannot be clearly distinguished in terms of class, although there was an important class element in the original popular support bases of the two groups. Class is by no means as universal or as natural a basis for polarisation in party systems as is sometimes assumed. In many Western party systems, class differences as a predictor of voting behaviour are often subordinate to those of religion, region, ethnic affiliation or language. Religion in particular is a very important predictor and is a more usual basis for political affiliation than any of the other commonly mentioned factors. Religion may achieve political expression in the behaviour of electorates in the form of a cleavage between those who practice the dominant religion and those who do not, as in Italy or France, or else in the form of an inter-confessional opposition, as in the Netherlands or Northern Ireland. Even countries which are normally regarded as having achieved a state of secularised politics, such as the Scandinavian countries, the United States or the United Kingdom outside Ulster, contain an important religious element in the traditional loyalties of many of their voters.[1] Region, as in the cases of the south versus the non-south in the United States, or centre versus periphery in Norway, is often important, and ethno-linguistic bases for political affiliation are commonplace. Most Western party systems display complex cross-cutting patterns derived from an amalgam of traditional affiliations of this kind. One of the few generalisations that can be made about voter loyalties in liberal democracies is that, once formed, they are surprisingly hard to break; the electoral followings of political parties often show loyalty to their chosen parties over very long periods, and even transmit these loyalties to subsequent generations. Voting preferences and party affiliations are often acquired in childhood rather than in the adult world, and are to an important extent inherited along with much other parental social culture.[2] Even after very violent political and social upheavals, old loyalties have reappeared. Political parties are used by many different people for different purposes in different generations, even though the parties themselves sometimes persist in surprisingly unchanged form. In most Western countries, the political parties are permanent parts of the political landscape and date back to the period in which universal suffrage was granted, typically around the time of World War I.[3] Political parties reflect past crises and can, of course, be transformed, dismembered or replaced in new crises. However, the parties and party systems of the past inform the parties and party systems of the present, even where a massive discontinuity such as those experienced in Germany in 1933–45 or in Ireland between 1916 and 1923 separate the old and the new systems.

In the Irish Free State, the parties which emerged had few obvious direct connections with the organisations of the pre-1916 era and were, of course, operating in a very different political environment. The unionist competitor finally had been removed by partition and the object of political competition had been redefined: the control of an independent state's government rather than the formation of an alliance with a British political party. Single-issue politics gave way very slowly and reluctantly to multi-issue politics. The apparent newness of the post-1922 parties is partly due, however, to an ingrained habit of viewing 1916–23 as a watershed, or a period of massive discontinuity. Affinities and even direct continuities with pre-1916 organisations are stronger than is sometimes assumed, components of older societies were sometimes used to build the new ones, and new parties inherited significant segments of the clientele of older parties. The post-1922 party system is a *second-generation* system, with its own cleavage lines, but those cleavage lines are superimposed on older cleavages, generating a complex pattern. This palimpsest effect, a result of abrupt and violent transition from the politics of protest within a British periphery to the politics of independence, accounts for much of the strange ideological blending that is to be seen in every Irish political party.

The continuities and discontinuities can be conveniently traced at three main levels: the level of political elites, the middle level of activist organisations and the level of the general voting public. At the elite level, it is perhaps easier to see discontinuities than continuities, as none of the old Irish Party's leaders survived the transition and only the Labour Party's elite shows a continuity. The Sinn Féin leaders who became the leaders of the two nationalist parties in the post-1922 state were a generation younger than the leaders of the Irish Party whose political estate they inherited or usurped, and 1918 involved a certain amount of political parricide by election. Some legitimate political heirs also survived: James Dillon, son of John Dillon, was to become a leading figure in, and later leader of, Fine Gael. Dillon joined Fine Gael, the reconstituted version of the pro-Treaty party, in 1933, and had enjoyed the support of the Farmers' Party, the AOH and other Irish Party elements before that juncture. Some Cumann na nGaedheal/Fine Gael leaders besides Dillon had 'Redmondite' backgrounds, most notable being John A. Costello, later to be Prime Minister in Fine Gael-led governments between 1948 and 1957. Even on the pro-Treaty side, however, the continuity with the Irish Party at elite level was rather weak, and the core of the Cumann na nGaedheal/Fine Gael group was solidly Sinn Féin, IRB and IRA in background. Interestingly, however, they tended to attract non-Sinn Féin elements, as will be seen later. On the anti-Treaty side that was to develop into Fianna Fáil under de Valera, there was no continuity with the Irish Party at elite level.

At the level of local activists and branch politics, there is tantalising and incomplete evidence for continuity in structures and even in personnel between the Irish Party and the Sinn Féin of 1917–21. There was evidently a considerable amount of defection from organisations such as the National Volunteers, the AOH and the UIL to Sinn Féin and the Irish Volunteers or IRA; the mass political conversions of 1916–18 must have been accompanied by organisational conversions on a considerable scale. As we have seen, many young IRA men seem to have had formative experiences in the AOH. Another common route, taken by IRA leaders like Emmet Dalton and Tom Barry, was active service in the British army, with or without prior service in the National Volunteers, followed by service in the IRA. David Fitzpatrick reports that 12 per cent of local AOH leaders, 13 per cent of UIL leaders and 23 per cent of National Volunteer leaders reappeared as Sinn Féin leaders in Clare.[4] The RIC reported that younger AOH or UIL activists were more likely to move over to the new formations, and Sinn Féin and the IRA absorbed them in large numbers.[5]

A common characteristic of Irish popular nationalist societies in British times was an immense amount of overlap in membership, particularly, but not exclusively, at elite level. The IRB had tried to weave a net of interlocking elites between the more 'advanced' of these organisations. The organisations complemented, rivalled and supplanted each other at different times. Table 12 maps the affinities between the various nationalist social and political societies of the half-century between the Parnellite election victory of 1885 and the victory of de Valera's Fianna Fáil in 1932, a period which spans the great mobilisations and discontinuities marked by the rise and fall of Parnell, the Rising of 1916, the victory of Sinn Féin in 1918, the Treaty split and the rise of Fianna Fáil in the late 1920s. It also, of course, spans two different regimes, the thirty-two-county united Ireland of British times, and the partitioned twenty-six-county independent state of 1922. The scores used in calculating the correlation coefficients are, in each case, the numbers of clubs in each county, controlled for population.[6] The major omission is figures for the post-1921 Cumann na nGaedheal/Fine Gael pro-Treaty group. To some extent, the early Cumann na nGaedheal appears to have been based less on a branch structure than on a 'local notables' system.[7]

Some caution is necessary in interpreting the correlations in Table 12. For reasons of geographical structure and because underlying rates of political participation for all organisations were higher in some areas, certain counties, particularly those in the north-west, tend to have high scores on all organisational affiliations. The relative rather then the absolute levels of the correlations should be considered. Furthermore, a strong inter-correlation between two organisations can be interpreted as indicating a genealogical affinity between them, a strong rivalry between them or even a similar but unrelated achievement of an organisational saturation point. Despite these caveats, however, Table 12 supplies some intriguing evidence of continuity and discontinuity.

The most striking feature of Table 12 is the strong evidence it offers for the existence of considerable organisational continuity between the Irish National League of the 1880s and the succession of nationalist parties which followed, including the pre-Treaty Sinn Féin and, to some extent, even the post-Treaty party of Fianna Fáil. The Parnellite party as it existed in 1890 at its peak of development is an even better predictor than that of 1886, the INL of 1890 correlating strongly with the Sinn Féin Party in both its pre- and post-1916 forms. Another general feature is the weakness of the AOH's connection with the other nationalist movements because of its Ulster base and lack of an agrarian tradition that could rival that of the Land League. The AOH displays affinities only with the UIL. Another noticeable and unsurprising series of affinities is that between the GAA and various nationalist parties, suggesting that organisation's significant role in the development of nationalist mass movements. The GAA displays a general lack of affinity with the UIL/AOH sets of organisations. The IRB appears to have had an involvement with a variety of nationalist organisations. The correlations between pre-Treaty Sinn Féin and Fianna Fáil are strong, although not quite as robust as might be expected, given Fianna Fáil's claim to be the rightful heir of the old pre-Treaty national front party. The Fianna Fáil pattern is, however, quite striking; not only does the party correlate strongly with the pre-Treaty Sinn Féin in its developed phase, it shows a marked affinity, despite the gap of over forty years and despite partition, with the INL of the 1880s. The Fianna Fáil of the early 1930s, on the threshold of power, had an organisational profile similar to that of the two pre-Treaty umbrella nationalist parties at their highest stages of development. In view of the fact that Fianna Fáil and post-1916 Sinn Féin are usually regarded as new political formations with little or no organisational precedent, this finding deserves a little more detailed analysis.

Table 12. Correlations between selected nationalist social and political organisations, 1886–1931

	INL 1886	INL 1890	IRB 1898	AOH 1898	UIL 1900	GAA 1901	SF 1909	SF 1917	SF 1921	AOH 1920	UIL 1921	FF 1931
INL 1886	1.00											
INL 1890	0.92	1.00										
IRB 1898	0.06	0.36	1.00									
AOH 1898		0.08		1.00								
UIL 1900	0.27	0.59	0.48	−.13	1.00							
GAA 1901	0.15	0.78	0.22		−.29	1.00						
SF 1909	−.07	0.64	0.31		0.38	0.75	1.00					
SF 1917	0.67	0.88	0.41	0.02	0.11	0.62	0.55	1.00				
SF 1921	0.87	0.93	0.44	−.03	0.19	0.69	0.51	0.86	1.00			
AOH 1920	0.16	−.13	−.02		0.40	−.19	0.22	−.05	−.17	1.00		
UIL 1920	0.36	0.31	0.16		−.29	−.29	0.38	0.11	0.19	0.40	1.00	
FF 1931	0.55	0.42	0.33		−.26	−.26	−.03	0.57	0.52	0.26	0.40	1.00

Note: Blank cells indicate N too small for correlation to be useful, and the correlations are based on Ns of between 20 and 32 (generally over 25). Scores are numbers of branches per county controlled for population, normalised where appropriate. AOH 1898 is Board of Erin only.

Figures 2 and 3 present scattergram representations of attempts to fit linear regression equations to the relationships between the INL of 1890 and the Sinn Féin of 1921 and between the latter party and the Fianna Fáil of 1931. For ease of interpretation, the raw scores are plotted, uncontrolled for population; as population changed relatively little, this is not an important source of distortion. The 1889 branch figures for Kerry and Clare are included in the INL figures, for completeness of coverage: the RIC had suppressed the branches in these counties in 1890. These changes have had the effect of altering the correlations slightly from those reported in Table 12, the most important change being caused by the inclusion of Clare and Kerry, both volatile western counties whose organisational scores often varied widely from year to year.

Figure 2 indicates that there was indeed a strong relationship between the INL of 1890 and the Sinn Féin of 1921. Both organisations had analogous problems of their relationships to agrarian forces and to physical force movements. The figure indicates that

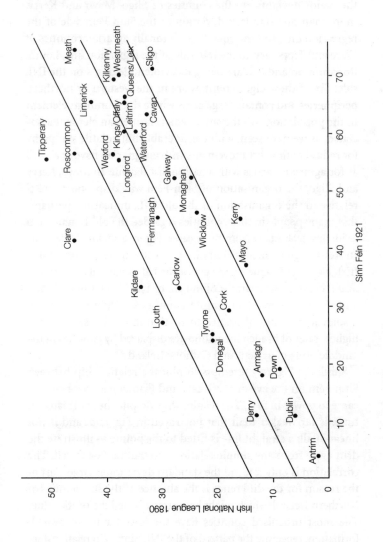

Figure 2. The roots of Sinn Féin: scattergram of Irish National League, 1890 and Sinn Féin, 1921, numbers of branches per county.
r=.81, r²=.65, sd=7.6, y=5.9+.51x, N=32.

the major deviants are the counties of Sligo, Mayo and Kerry, more than one standard deviation to the Sinn Féin side of the regression line, and the equally traditionally agrarian counties of Clare and Tipperary, to the INL side of the regression line, Louth, Roscommon and Kildare being less violent deviants on the INL side. Six of these eight counties are in the western or northern peripheries and contain large areas where the dominant element in the population was the small tenant farmer, an element associated, as we have seen, with considerable but volatile sympathy for radical nationalist movements with an agrarian flavour as well as for agrarian parties with a nationalist flavour. In Mayo, Kerry and Sligo, the organisation of Sinn Féin was 'disproportionate' relative to the organisation of the old INL, indicating, perhaps, that many people in these counties regarded the old League's job as incomplete. Apart from these cases, Figure 2 strikingly demonstrates the general continuity between the agrarian-nationalist Irish National League on the eve of the fall of Parnell and the *soi-disant* cross-class separatist Sinn Féin of 1921 The Ulster counties and the rather more urbanised counties of Dublin and Cork display lower rates of branch formation in both cases, and the highest rates of branch formation are displayed by counties in the 'middle' zone of agricultural Catholic Ireland.

Similarly, Figure 3 attempts to plot the relationship between Sinn Féin on the eve of the Treaty and Fianna Fáil just before it came to power in 1932. The relationship, despite the short lapse of time, is far weaker than that portrayed in Figure 2, and is not linear at all; a straight line is fitted to the points to illustrate the drift away from any simple relationship that had occurred. The correlation is only .43, and the standard deviation is large. Part of the reason for the difference is the absence of the six counties of Northern Ireland, which might have strengthened the relationship. The most urbanised counties have the lowest rates of branch formation, repeating the pattern of the INL/Sinn Féin relationship. The counties of Roscommon, Meath, Monaghan, Kildare and Galway have Fianna Fáil organisations which are too strong, while the counties of Waterford and Kilkenny have organisations that are a little too weak to fit any linear regression model satisfactorily.

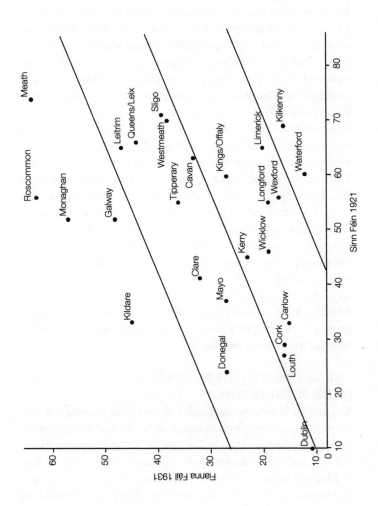

Figure 3. The succession to Sinn Féin: scattergram of Sinn Féin, 1921 and Fianna Fáil, 1931, numbers of branches per county.
r=.43, r²=.19, sd=14.7, y=10.1+.42x, N=26.

The former group of counties includes several which still harboured strong grazier/smallholder tension, most notably Mayo, Meath and Galway, and it seems that Fianna Fáil's espousal in the late 1920s of the anti-grazier cause paid off in the form of strong electoral organisation in some of these areas. Waterford, Kilkenny, Wexford and Limerick, where the new party was relatively weak, were areas where Redmondite or Labour presences persisted. The general pattern suggests a neo-agrarian profile for the early Fianna Fáil, a profile which was more pronounced than that of Sinn Féin in 1917–21 and which combined agrarian traditions of smallholder and labourer land hunger going back to the 1880s. Ecological electoral analyses which are reviewed later come to similar conclusions. The early Fianna Fáil had a strong agrarian smallholder/labourer element although it was, of course, far more than an agrarian party. The pre-Treaty Sinn Féin had held aloof from agrarianism and anti-grazier forces, subordinating the land issue to the political campaign, in part to ensure that the middle and upper classes were not alienated. Fianna Fáil was freed from both of these constraints because, of course, independence was an established fact and the larger farmers and urban middle elements were already committed to the pro-Treaty forces: Fianna Fáil was only the largest party in a multi-party system, rather than being an all-class national front, as the old Sinn Féin had been.

THE LEGITIMATION OF THE STATE AND THE BUILDING OF POLITICAL PARTIES

The new Dublin-based state suffered from serious social and economic problems and from an equally serious weakness of political legitimacy. The Free State was not the all-Ireland Republic which the IRA and previous radicals in the nationalist movement had wanted and dreamed of; it was a partitioned state, controlling only twenty-six counties, and it bore various superficial marks of constitutional subordination. Its economic dependence on Britain was virtually total. The fact that it had its own taxation and tariff powers, effectively total powers over domestic affairs and, as it turned out, full powers over its external relations impressed many less than the shortcomings, real and imagined, of the new state.

More generally, any Irish state that emerged from the Anglo-Irish conflict would have had serious problems of legitimacy and would have been the inheritor of over a century of anti-authority agitation; the political culture was, to put it kindly, slightly less than civic. Even in favourable circumstances, a native government would have been liable to become the target of forces derived from this tradition.

The new state also inherited a tradition of centralised, authoritarian and besieged administration, derived from the colonial character of Ireland's nineteenth-century government. A democratic local government tradition of sorts did exist, but the very fact that the local authorities had been under nationalist control since the turn of the century had encouraged a tradition of hostility between the local councils and the central government, a tradition which the new state inherited. This centre/locality tension had been very important during the independence campaign and had helped, for example, to accelerate the transfer of allegiance of the local councils to the Dáil government.[8] After independence, the new government found the local councils had enjoyed their freedom, and ran into trouble with them; one of the first acts of the Cumann na nGaedheal government was to abolish the corrupt Dublin Corporation and replace it with a triumvirate of bureaucratic commissioners. Other councils suffered similar fates when they resisted government *fiat*. This pattern was repeated many times by both pro-Treaty and Fianna Fáil governments. The fact that many councils in the west were under independent or republican control made matters worse in the 1920s, but Fianna Fáil had similar difficulties and a 'Castle' style of dealing with local resistance was institutionalised. This relationship is dealt with in more detail in a later chapter; at this point, it is enough to note that the state inherited a tradition of alienation from government combined with an equally ingrained tradition of passive dependence on government aid. It could plausibly be argued that the fact that the Free State government actually governed during the first years of independence did much in itself to encourage public acceptance of, if not enthusiastic welcome for, the new regime.

Both the pro-Treaty and anti-Treaty groups set themselves to building new party organisations on the ruins of Sinn Féin and of the Irish Party. The Treatyite group who, in effect, founded the state formed themselves into a new political party in early 1923. This party, Cumann na nGaedheal (Party of the Irish), was later to become the core of Fine Gael. Cumann na nGaedheal governed the state between 1923 and 1932 in alliance with various smaller groups such as the fragments of the old Irish Party, the big-farm group and some unionist fragments. Labour played the role of loyal opposition, while the anti-Treatyites boycotted the Free State Dáil until 1927. Cumann na nGaedheal, the accommodationist wing of the old Sinn Féin, inherited more of the senior people in the old party, most of the central command of the old IRA and IRB and those around the country whose temperament or economic interest impelled them to be tired of revolutionary politics. Equally impressionistic evidence suggests that the younger, poorer and 'true, believer' activists tended to be anti-Treaty. Cumann na nGaedheal suffered from a serious lack of organisational strength at local level, in part because the leadership, which had never witnessed competitive party politics of a normal kind, was insensitive to the need for regular branch organisation and in part because it did not have the enthusiastic unpaid help of the IRA veterans who were to staff Fianna Fáil's organisation in the late 1920s. Cumann na nGaedheal's dominance of the Dáil was somewhat artificial, as it depended on the self-imposed boycott of the Free State Dáil by the republicans and early Fianna Fáil. Outside the Dáil, it tended to become dependent on 'local notable' and clerical support, particularly in rural areas, eventually losing much of its original pro-Treaty Sinn Féiner support and exchanging it for a middle-class and rural large farmer and shopkeeper base. Even by late 1924, the party had appointed only two paid organisers; the old Sinn Féin had had twenty organisers in late 1921. The party also had serious difficulty in persuading its Sinn Féin elements to accept old Irish Party veterans into the ranks of the new party.[9] Mulcahy complained in November 1924 that the attempt to synthesise the Sinn Féin and Irish Party elements in the new Cumann na nGaedheal organisation was suffering from inexperience and 'evil manners' as much as from anything else.[10] However, UIL and AOH elements did not harmonise well with the Sinn Féin veterans.[11]

Several of the early Cumann na nGaedheal leaders, notably Kevin O'Higgins and J.J. Walsh, appear to have had a positive contempt for the whole business of grass-roots organisation.[12] The pro-Treatyites also had the ironic disadvantage of taking over government without having to fight an election of a truly competitive kind. Absorbed in the technical details of fighting a civil war, setting up an administration, negotiating with the British and the unionists, demobilising an enormous military establishment and fending off an army mutiny, the Cumann na nGaedheal leaders subconsciously came to define politics as government and government as administration. The Free State government included many talented figures, and some of them belonged to the Catholic educated middle class that had grown up in the late nineteenth century and who sometimes regarded themselves as the natural inheritors of political power in Ireland. These did not always see eye to eye with those who had come into politics through the IRB or IRA and it took decades before people of Irish Party or Farmers' Party provenance were permitted the same central roles in the party as the old Sinn Féiners. Many people in Cumann na nGaedheal were, however, united at least in their distrust of the IRB, which was believed by some to have penetrated the government; Collins had kept so many strings in his own hands that, when he was killed in late 1922, there was some prospect that the pro-Treaty government would disintegrate. One group within the Free State's army, convinced of an IRB conspiracy, even tried to get in touch with the defeated anti-Treaty IRA, only to be rudely rebuffed.[13] The army mutiny of 1924 occurred partly because of distrust of the government and of the IRB's supposed role within it. In fact, the IRB had virtually ceased to exist by then.

Mulcahy believed that Cosgrave's government lost psychological self-assurance in 1924 because of the mutiny, and that the mutiny was the occasion on which it lost the sympathy of the more energetic and adventurous pro-Treaty elements. Certainly, Cumann na nGaedheal showed less of the 'pro-Treaty republican' character of Collins and several others after 1924 and became the centre of a coalition of not particularly popular sectional groups, many of them with pre-1916 roots and united only in their fear of the 'wild men' of de Valera's party and the reactionary character of their political and social outlook. The innovative abilities of some of the party's leaders were not sufficient to compensate for its increasingly narrow outlook.

The second major group was the Labour Party. Unlike Cumann na nGaedheal, it was not a product of the nationalist revolution, but of the rise of the trade union movement in the years before the War in Ireland and Britain and, more remotely, it could trace its ancestry and its most loyal voter support back to the first organisations of landless labourers in Munster in the 1870s. Generally, the rural labourers, despite their conflict of interest with the farmers, tended to be absorbed into the nationalist forces.[14] Only a negligible proportion of Land League leaders had been labourers, but there were some among the rank and file.[15] The labourers' leaders appear to have adopted an almost mendicant approach to the farmers and had difficulty in coming to an understanding with urban labour.[16] It seems that, as labourers were a declining class with few social allies, even their own leaders were unenthusiastic about their prospects as a political force. Essentially the labourer had three options: he could organise with other labourers for better conditions for labourers as a class; he could try to get land and exit from the labouring class by becoming a farmer; or he could exit from both his class and nation by emigration.[17] The collapse of agricultural prices after World War I, following a boom-and-bust cycle similar to those of the post-Waterloo period and the 1870s, damaged the market power of both labourers and farmers. The labourers' response to their difficulties was as often to leave their class as to organise as a class. Many of them later seem to have come to make common cause with their employers, many others emigrated, while some came to count on Fianna Fáil's promises of land redistribution.

The industrial working class was tiny and concentrated in a few centres. Most workers in the Free State were employed in small concerns, or else in transport, services and agriculture-related activity. Their numbers in 1926 were probably not greater than 13 per cent of the workforce. Many employees were engaged in services such as domestic employment or in the rather small state

sector, and unemployment was endemic. Despite these disadvan-
tages, trade unions had developed fairly well between 1890 and 1920,
but the real growth had been in Ulster. Also, union membership
dropped off sharply after 1920 because of the depression; between
1922 and 1926, the numbers of unionised workers in the Free State
halved, dropping from nearly 140,000 to just over 77,000.[18] The
most significant category was transport and communications,
organised mainly in the ITGWU, Larkin's union, and dominated
by a political outlook that combined socialism with a separatist
nationalist ideology. The 1913 lock-out, the involvement with
Sinn Féin and a split in 1923 between nationalist and socialist
tendencies in the ITGWU weakened the labour movement even
further. Labour as a political movement mirrored the small size,
divisions and ideological subordination of the Irish working class:
in Dublin, much of the working class was republican in outlook
and tended to favour Fianna Fáil in the 1930s. Much of the city's
working class appears to have been depoliticised; the lock-out had
traumatised some, and many had pro-British sympathies due to
social and institutional connections with Britain, British-based
firms or, in many cases, the British army. 'Non-political' brokerage
politics flourished in Dublin, and one famous brokerage TD, 'Alfie'
Byrne, even founded a political dynasty.

Labour had to contend not only with depoliticisation of a
working class which had been bypassed by the nationalists rather
than defeated by them, but also with financial difficulties. Labour
lacked funds partly because of the decline in union membership
and partly because, unlike its nationalist rivals, it could not count
on contributions from business or from the Irish-Americans.[19]
Clerical hostility to 'socialism' and the social stigma attached to
the 'Labour' label were also significant obstacles. Labour became a
rather divided minor party in a system polarised around a blend
of constitutional, cultural, socio-economic and nationalist issues.
The reasons for Labour's weakness have often been debated by
Irish political scientists and historians; it might be more appropriate to inquire into the reasons why it managed to survive at all.

The third and subsequently most successful group was the anti-
Treaty party led by de Valera, reorganised as Sinn Féin in 1923 and

as Fianna Fáil in 1926. The third, or fundamentalist republican, Sinn Féin party was an anti-system party, with a programme of abstention from the Dáil of the Free State, refusal to recognise the political institutions of the Free State and insistence on a line of legitimation from 1916 and 1919 to its own republican 'government' in internal exile. The new Sinn Féin wanted to replace the existing Free State with another political system rather than take it over as a going concern. Sinn Féin consented to contest elections to the Dáil, but refused to sit there on the grounds that it was a usurping legislature imposed by the British. In effect, the Republican Party was attempting to apply to the Free State the kind of boycott tactics that had worked so well in 1918 against Westminster. However, abstentionism had had mass support in 1918; by 1923, there was no unanimous distaste for the new regime. The Church was generally pro-Treaty, emigration had resumed its role as a social safety valve, the Free State had no intention of conscripting anyone, post-revolutionary exhaustion had set in and the boom-and-bust of agricultural prices had occurred. The leaders doggedly held on to their policy of republican fundamentalism until 1926.[20] This purist republicanism contrasted oddly with the outright monarchism of Griffith's Sinn Féin and even with the rather guarded republicanism of the Sinn Féin of 1917–21. The transition from monarchism to republicanism had been popular; the British monarchy was not really popular in Ireland.[21]

Republicanism, however, was not the creed of all citizens of the new state either, and furthermore, it meant different things to different people. To Sinn Féin's left wing, it meant socialism or social democracy, often of a quasi-agrarian, syndicalist and nationalist kind. To others, it simply meant separation from Britain and its empire, together with the possibility of building up an economically independent and culturally distinctive nation-state. To others it meant the ability to build a *cordon sanitaire* around Ireland, preserving it from the evils of secularist and non-Catholic ideas. To many, it meant economic protection against British competition and to some it was the expression of the traditional anti-British political sentiment, occasionally mixed up with romanticism and ideals of self-sacrifice. It was intellectually incoherent.

Seán Ó Faoláin, in a very frank reconstruction of his own mind as a young IRA soldier in 1922–23, described his republicanism as highly emotional and pre-political:

> *We had no concept of the State we wished to found* ... I found myself in the year 1923 acting as Director of Publicity for the Irish Republican Army ... ignorant and inexperienced as I was I had enough gumption to see, within a few weeks, that if what we all knew between us about society and politics, in any intellectual sense, were printed consecutively it would not cover a threepenny bit and that all we ever said, or ever published, with hardly an exceptional article, was ... propaganda without any guiding concept.

The intellectual shapelessness of Irish republicanism enabled it to be expressed politically as a simple and passionate wish to be cut away from Britain. In the case of de Valera himself, this anti-British emotionalism, combined with a sense of personal betrayal by Griffith and Collins, seems to have been a strong component of his anti-Treaty feeling. In a letter to Joseph Connolly in December 1922, he responded to Connolly's tentative proposals for peace:

> When the Articles of Agreement were brought over here, I felt as though the plague were being introduced into the country and every effort I have since made to save the people from its bad effects have been met on the other side by bad faith and the miserable short-sighted tactics of party politics. Frankly I have no hope that our opponents would even now keep any contract they might enter into with us.[22]

The Sinn Féin of 1923–26 was to some extent a genuine revival of the pre-Treaty party, as it itself claimed. Despite its anti-partitionist posture, however, it was a twenty-six-county party, never having more than a dozen branches in Northern Ireland. It was also in very many respects a new party: the old Sinn Féin had had over 1,200 branches in all of Ireland in 1919, and had disintegrated completely by late 1922. By June 1923, the successor party had a mere sixteen branches in all of Ireland. Recovery was rapid, however, and appeared to reflect considerable potential support for some kind of a radical nationalist party; by the end of July, sixty-five branches were affiliated and by October 1923 this total had risen to 729.[23] As Peter Pyne has documented, the new party, despite a promising start, rapidly became demoralised because of its own abstentionist policies and, although these policies appealed to the fundamentalists and the militarists, they found at best only a moderate sympathy among the general population. The Free State had not collapsed, as some republicans had hoped, but on the contrary had showed signs of qualified but definite public acceptance. It passed and enforced laws, it embarked on some imaginative and ambitious development projects, it engaged in foreign relations and generally acted as a government. It was in control of a considerable amount of patronage, was in control of the taxation and grants systems and was, in some sense, clearly not the British puppet which it was represented as being in republican propaganda. In its first months it had relied heavily on coercion to preserve itself, but it rapidly turned to the use of non-violent law enforcement agencies to separate civil from political or criminal law enforcement. This extraordinary achievement in time of civil war was one which had eluded every British administration before 1922 and which has eluded every Northern Ireland government since 1920. By a series of accidents, the new police force was organised as an unarmed force somewhat on the lines of the English 'bobby' system rather than on the lines of the old, paramilitary RIC. Structurally, the new police force, the Gárda Siochána (Civic Guard), inherited the centralised structure of the RIC without its armament or its political segregation from the community. The Gardai were undeniably Irish, contained a considerable number of IRA veterans and were not subjected to the social ostracism which had bedevilled the RIC at times of political tension. The new police participated in the sports events of the GAA, was piously Catholic and also went in for Irish revivalism. As the Garda's historian has commented, the force's use of Irish in the 1920s may not have helped its relations with the English-speaking bulk of the population, but it could be argued that it gave it an important toehold with local political and administrative elites who 'held the

restoration of the Irish language as a sacrosanct aim'.[24] The reality
of the Free State gradually convinced many of the Sinn Féiners that
their revered Republic was really dead.[25] Despite some by-election
successes, the party's supporters were drifting away. The public lost
interest in politicians who had no access to political decision-
makers and who, in fact, seemed to make a virtue of their lack of
such access. Sinn Féin TDs could make little convincing response
to their constituents' material problems in the harsh economic
climate of the times. What was happening was that the electorate's
view of the parliamentary representative as someone who acted as
a go-between from the locality to the remote power-holders of
Dublin was gradually sapping the unworldly outlook of the
fundamentalists.

The activist organisation began to fall apart.[26] In July 1925, the
organisation of Sinn Féin was viewed as being 'not too bad' in
Leinster but as having disintegrated everywhere else because of low
morale. Galway was the only non-Leinster county which showed
any electoral effectiveness.[27] By October, Seán Lemass was blaming
the failure of Sinn Féin, rather unfairly, on the incompetence of its
officials and was urging an extensive overhaul.[28] Further evidence
of collapse was available in the form of the failure of many branch
secretaries to answer headquarters' letters.[29] Under Lemass, Dublin
district was reorganised and the Sandymount cumann proposed at
the 1925 *ard-fheis* in November that Sinn Féin be reorganised to
give Dublin cumainn a pronounced advantage over rural cumainn
in the party's councils, so as to bring the party 'into line with
reality'.[30] Sinn Féin was down to its Dublin leadership and had lost
the country. In November, the IRA withdrew its recognition of the
republican government in internal exile and gave allegiance to its
own army council.[31] In January 1926 de Valera announced his
willingness to sit in the Free State Dáil if the oath of allegiance was
removed.[32]

Sinn Féin finally split in March 1926. The issue, which was
whether or not Sinn Féin would accept seats in the Dáil if the oath
was removed, divided the party almost evenly, the fundamentalists
having a small majority. De Valera and his group had, however,
already decided to set up their own organisation and were

unconcerned about their defeat. Many delegates who had been instructed by their branches to vote for the fundamentalist line came around to de Valera's point of view during the debate, despite the theatricals of Father O'Flanagan, the main spokesman for the fundamentalist viewpoint. With considerable acumen, de Valera's lieutenants advised them to vote according to their branches' wishes and against the de Valera line because it was intended to start a new organisation free of the aura of defeat which clung around Sinn Féin.[33] There was a wish among many of the pragmatists to get away from the histrionics and emotionalism of the group centred around O'Flanagan, Eamon Donnelly, the party's organisational director, and others.[34] O'Flanagan had been a visible symbol of the unity between Irish Catholicism and purist republicanism, and he had been a charismatic demagogue and worker in the 1918 campaign.[35] His quasi-religious political revivalism grated on the nerves of Lemass, who commented years later, 'Father O'Flanagan had been under the impression that he was a kind of spiritual chaplain and political pope to the Sinn Féin Organisation, and that as long as he was alive he was under the impression that the continuity of the Organisation was represented by him.'[36]

What was left of fundamentalist Sinn Féin lingered on, suspended between constitutional politics and the IRA, and has maintained a tenuous continuity up to the present day, its lineal successor being the 'Official' or Marxist Sinn Féin, the Workers' Party. Provisional Sinn Féin is a purist, non-Marxist and therefore more unconstitutional secession from the 'fourth' or post-1926 Sinn Féin. De Valera's new party, Fianna Fáil, was inaugurated in Dublin in April 1926. Its eventual rise to power and to a dominant place in the party system is the decisive event in the development of the new state after the Civil War. It is certain that the new state would have suffered far more than it actually did from flawed legitimacy if Fianna Fáil had not succeeded in detaching most of the republican vote from Sinn Féin, attracted many young men away from the IRA and eventually allied the radical-nationalist vote to a wide centrist support base. De Valera's characteristic fondness for ambiguous political formulae and for the manipulation

of political symbols rather than of political ideas is well epitomised by the name of his new party. The words 'Fianna Fáil'
literally mean 'Warriors of Destiny' or 'Fenians of Destiny' and
form a poetic phrase meaning approximately 'Army of Ireland',
Ireland being the Island of Destiny (*Inis Fáil*, Innisfallen) in the
Gaelic poetic tradition. The name has a variety of symbolic
resonances: the term 'Fianna' combines an echo of the Fenians
with an evo-cation of the pre-Conquest and, indeed, pre-Christian
warrior bands of Fionn Mac Cumhaill. 'Fianna Fáil' was also an
alternative official title of the Irish Volunteers, and every Free State
soldier's cap badge contained the FF symbol which had been
inherited from the Volunteers of 1913. The name asserted the
continuity of de Valera's party with the militant republican tradition of Sinn Féin, the IRA, the Fenians and the United Irishmen.
Whether this assertion was valid or whether such a continuous
tradition existed in quite the form suggested was almost
irrelevant. As a title of the armed forces of the Free State, 'Fianna
Fáil' also suggested an identity between the power of the state and
the new party. A final point in favour of the name was its very
untranslatability, as de Valera remarked later with a smile: 'there
was some virtue in that also.'[37]

Fianna Fáil quickly became the heir to the main body of popular republican sentiment. Among other consequences, this had
the enormously important result that it was not a party organised
or supervised by the clergy at local level. The cleavage between the
hierarchy and the republicans in 1922–23 had been a very serious
one, and had resulted in a separation of popular advanced
nationalism from clerical guidance that was wider than any such
separation since the 1820s, with the possible temporary exceptions
of the early Land League and the pre-conscription Sinn Féin. De
Valera himself was cautiously sympathetic to the political role of
the clergy, and always attempted to work with them rather than
against them. There was a fair amount of muted anti-clericalism
in his party, but it was kept strictly under control, partly by de
Valera and partly by the realisation that an open quarrel with the
Church would be electorally damaging if not actually fatal. The
relationship between de Valera and the Catholic hierarchy was one

of mutual respect and had a curious egalitarian quality, as though the party were a lay church, and de Valera its political pope, to echo Lemass' phrase about O'Flanagan; there even was something priestly about de Valera's public persona. The new party, which relied on veterans of the old IRA to act as party workers, had none of the direct dependence on clerical organisational resources which had characterised the later Parnellite party, the UIL or even important segments of Cumann na nGaedheal. The emergence of Fianna Fáil was a major secularising event in Irish life: despite the party's very extensive concessions to the Church, it resisted, as perhaps no other group could, the virtually theocratic pretensions of the Catholic bishops of this period. Eventually, the existence of competitive party politics discouraged direct clerical participation in electoral politics, as the priest found himself committed to one side or the other, and the hierarchy forbade direct intervention in party politics as being, from their point of view, impolitic. The Church's political influence, though enormous, tended to become passive rather than active, particularly after World War II. Admittedly, the use of the pulpit for political purposes was curbed by the bishops only in 1956, five years after the Church had burned its fingers rather badly in a notorious open intervention in politics. Fianna Fáil's concessions to the Church were due to the pious outlook of its electorate rather than to any particularly clericalist tendencies in its leadership. In part because of the absence of any clerical inhibitions, the party quickly became the main representative of radical nationalism in the system. It was, and is, the only party that still clings to the programme of linguistic revivalism in anything like its entirety. It is the only one of the three major parties in the system whose organisational nomenclature is still in the Irish language. It is also the most persistently anti-partitionist of the three parties.

Fianna Fáil did fairly well at its first election in June 1927, which it contested on a 'moderate abstentionist' platform. The assassination of Kevin O'Higgins, the Free State's Minister for Justice, in August impelled the Cumann na nGaedheal government to rush through a statute which would unseat any prospective TD who refused to take the oath. De Valera was, in effect, pushed into constitutionalism by these events, presumably with partially feigned reluctance on his part. He ceased, in effect, to baulk at the oath and consented to enter the Dáil. A general election ensued in September 1927, and Fianna Fáil's vote jumped an impressive nine percentage points, reflecting the electors' approval of the constitutionalist line. It also indicated the potential popularity of the party which Seán Lemass, in a famous phrase, described as a 'slightly constitutional party'. Even more striking is the fact that the party's vote increased by an average of twelve points in the western periphery which had been so demoralised two years previously, but only by two points in the Dublin area: as the next chapter argues, the new party was recovering the electoral support that Sinn Féin lost, or rather threw away, in the years between 1923 and 1926.

The new party has always been credited with a good and intensive organisation, and the sources of that organisation are of theoretical interest. Fianna Fáil's organisation echoed the branch structures of older pan-nationalist parties dating back to the 1880s, while Sinn Féin in 1924 correlated negligibly with either the pre-1922 organisations or with the Fianna Fáil of the 1930s. This suggests that Fianna Fáil succeeded in evoking the community-wide response that the third Sinn Féin had failed to attract. Fianna Fáil found a ready-made foundation for its organisation, but its leaders had to work to weld it together: 'For more than five years hardly any of us were at home for a single night or any weekend . . . we toured every parish in the country founding Fianna Fáil branches on the solid basis of old IRA and Sinn Féin members. They were all marvellous people.' The party was built up almost directly on old IRA companies, battalions and divisions.[38] A few weeks after the founding of the party, Thomas Mullins, the secretary, accompanied de Valera on a 1,700-mile tour of west Cork in a Baby Austin, Mullins occasionally getting under the old car to do repairs while his Chief waited patiently inside, presumably planning his next campaign speech.[39] There was no link with the ecclesiastical network, and the party encountered some local clerical hostility in its early years.[40]

In formal structure, Fianna Fáil resembled the Sinn Féins and older party organisations. The basic unit was the parish club or cumann, there being theoretically ten members at least for every parish club in the country. In the towns, the organisation was based on the ward. Cumainn were to be registered at headquarters and pay a registration fee of ten shillings. The annual convention (*ard-fheis*) consisted of two delegates from each club, one from each *comhairle ceanntair* (local government constituency council) and one from each *comhairle dáilcheanntair* (Dáil constituency council) together with the party's TDs and the members of the national executive. In practice, the domination of the parliamentary party was not challenged: Fianna Fáil, like many of its predecessor parties, understood itself to be more of a support organisation than a legislative or policy-making assembly.

De Valera's new party actually benefited from the four years in political darkness between 1922 and 1926. The experience of political and military humiliation and the collapse of its political ideas and postures had a hardening, sobering and maturing effect on the Republican Party, taught it the importance of popular organisation and sensitivity to popular opinion and also gave it an internal unity and cohesion which Cumann na nGaedheal lacked. The party also benefited from the IRA and Sinn Féin splits because it was freed from the incorrigible militarists of the IRA and also from the political dreamers of purist Sinn Féin. The new party had had a bitter lesson in the limits of physical force and 'moral force' and in the possibilities of electoral politics. Its initial revulsion against the aridity of abstract political ideas long accompanied it, and it has been noted for an extreme pragmatism. It may be because of these circumstances that the party has, for example, never been unduly worried by the fossilisation of its own original goals. Its original programme was nationalist and populist, anti-urban and neo-Gaelic. Later this programme was supplemented by policies of economic self-sufficiency and development through state aid. The party also developed the welfare system and invested in public housing when in government. The original goals are, however, still proclaimed, in the ironic context of an Ireland still ruled by Fianna Fáil but which is far more industrialised, urbanised, English speaking and probably more partitioned than it was in 1926. The party has long outlived its original ideological purposes.

The two nationalist parties had clear images of each other, in many ways distorted and paranoid. On the pro-Treaty side, de Valera was often seen as the Kerensky of Ireland, as the dupe of gunmen or as a dangerous and incompetent visionary who had precipitated a civil war.[41] Cumann na nGaedheal's leader, William Cosgrave, however, saw de Valera as a captive of forces beyond his control and seems to have thought, as early as 1923, in terms of getting de Valera out of the hands of the militarists and into the constitutional arena.[42]

Fianna Fáil's leaders had a similarly distorted view of Cumann na nGaedheal's leaders. The 'Free Staters' were represented in republican propaganda as puppets of London, and Fianna Fáil leaders appear to have genuinely believed this. Even when governmental power was conceded to de Valera by Cosgrave in 1932, this traitor-in-our-midst mentality persisted in Fianna Fáil. De Valera saw Cumann na nGaedheal/Fine Gael as a British-financed fifth column and represented himself as being surrounded by counter-revolutionary intrigues directed from London: '. . . if we are beaten Ireland for the next fifteen years will be under a dictatorial regime, backed by England . . . You know that the English are in all this; that they are in touch with the opposition leaders . . .'[43]

The original split of 1922 had been on a set of constitutional and foreign policy issues: the desirable and practicable relationships between the new state and the British empire. The intensity of the cleavage at elite level effectively swamped other possible cleavage bases such as left versus right: nationalism absorbed socialism, leaving little trace of the latter. It is sometimes forgotten that it also absorbed liberalism and conservatism as coherent political doctrines. The original dividing point was to become a dead issue, as the constitutional links with Britain were weakened and finally severed in the generation after independence. At the time, however, the constitutional links looked like marks of subordinate status, and the term 'Free Stater' and 'republican' survived to become the popular way of summarising the distinction between those on the Cumann na nGaedheal/Fine Gael side who favoured an accommodationist policy vis-à-vis Britain and those who wished total separation. A left-right cleavage formed part of this division, 'republicans' often being populist, social democrat, socialist or even communist in their social thinking, while 'Free Staters' inclined to liberalism, conservatism or clerical fascism. However, these more cosmopolitan idea-systems tended to be quite subordinate to nationalist-populist sentiment. The term 'republican' has survived to become a general label for a nationalist radical in popular parlance, and even socialists tend to describe their political position as being 'republicanism'.

The mixture of nationalist, populist, class and religious communal sentiment that went to make up the popular political ideology known as 'republicanism' is well epitomised by Fianna Fáil propaganda of the late 1920s and early 1930s. The party's best-known propaganda emphasised industrial and agricultural development, contrasting the woeful conditions under Cosgrave and his British backers with the economic golden age that would follow a Fianna Fáil electoral victory. A Fianna Fáil handbill of 1932 consisted of a series of skilfully drawn cartoons entitled 'The Economic History of the Land of Erin'. It portrayed the evils of free trade in sketches of hungry and miserable Irish workers and farmers emigrating while foreign shipowners grew fat and depicted William Cosgrave, complete with Ascendancy or Castle Catholic top hat, consorting complacently with podgy Freemason bankers.[44] An *Irish Press* cartoon of late 1931 represented despairing Irish workers watching ships unloading imports.[45] An article in Irish included a map demonstrating that the quality of housing in the Free State was far worse in the western and Irish-speaking areas.[46] De Valera, who had always been attracted to the idea of isolationism, condemned the cautious and very partial protectionism of Cumann na nGaedheal and promised a policy of 'all-round protection' in late 1931.[47] De Valera's personal wish for an Ireland shielded from British influence harmonised well with the pressures for protection which had intensified after 1929.

10 | AN ANALYSIS OF ELECTORAL POLITICS, 1923–48

PARTIES AND ELECTIONS IN THE IRISH FREE STATE

The organisations which competed for the votes of the electorate in the new Irish state were the heirs to a tradition of political action which was over a century old at the time of independence. The electorate was, however, in some senses a new one. The electorate of 1918 was three times the size of that of 1910 and was almost certainly composed to a very great extent of first-time voters, none of whom had had the opportunity of forming a voter loyalty to any particular political party, as distinct from a loyalty to the symbols and slogans of the community. Even those who had voted in 1910 had been voting in a system which was essentially non-competitive. In 1923, the franchise was extended to women between the ages of twenty-one and thirty and the transition to full adult suffrage and to one-person-one-vote was completed considerably in advance of the United Kingdom.

The fact that the electorate was a newly enfranchised one, combined with the very basic character of the issues involved in the elections of 1918, 1922 and 1923, indicates that the final phase of political mobilisation, considered by theorists to be a crucial conditioning factor for subsequent voting behaviour, took place at exactly the time when nationalist Ireland ceased being a British periphery engaged in the politics of peripheral resistance and became an independent state. This final phase was, as Sinnott puts it, a 'consensus-generating rather than a cleavage-generating event' in the Irish case. People were mobilised against outsiders (the

British, unionists) rather than against one another, as was the case in many other Western systems. A community that had, within the old United Kingdom, traditionally behaved as a single political party suddenly found itself in an independent political system.

The subsequent split over the Treaty, therefore, divided an elite and electorate which had already been aligned, and the Free State had, instead of a realigning election of the kind documented by V.O. Key, 'an aligning electoral decade, stretching from 1918 to 1927'.[1] I suggest that the original alignment of 1918, itself a re-enactment of previous alignments, so conditioned the form of electoral competition in the Irish Free State that it enabled successor parties to build up cross-class nationalist parties which resembled the cross-class electoral alliance of 1918, such alliances being natural to the political culture, particularly outside the larger towns and in the west. In the medium to long run, Fianna Fáil was to be more successful at rebuilding this party of national solidarity that existed in potential form in the electorate, but even Cumann na nGaedheal bore clear marks of its Sinn Féin descent in the profile of its early electoral support.

If no such pan-nationalist mobilisation, confirming earlier mobilisations, had occurred in 1918, the resulting post-independence party system would have been far more fragmented; even as it was, the locally based Independent TD was an important feature of the early decades of the new political system. One can imagine, in an Ireland which received independence without the experience of groups being welded together by the independence campaign, parties developing around loose regional federations of commercial farmers, western smallholders, agricultural labourers, the urban classes and the Protestant minority. As it was, of course, the tradition of monolithic party organisation, reinforced by 1918, generated political parties which were nationalist, based sometimes on particular classes and sometimes on cross-class alliances, but not indissolubly linked to the interests and political ideas of any particular class. The populist generalities which served Fianna Fáil and Fine Gael as official ideologies reflect this partial autonomy of the political from the social. Irish political parties have shown considerable ability to shift the bases of their political support in the electorate.[2] In a sense, Fianna Fáil and Fine Gael are, structurally and historically, not different political parties, but internal factions of the old pan-nationalist party which still exists in 'ghost' form; the nineteenth-century Irish party system haunts, or underlies, its successor in the independent Irish state in the twenty-first century much as it does its successor party system in Northern Ireland. This nationalist mobilisation, built on pre-industrial allegiances, softened what might have been more 'natural' political reflections of socio-economic divisions, although such divisions did achieve some political expression. Bizarre alliances have characterised Irish electoral politics. The agrarian and localist character of Irish rural society and the proportional representation by means of the single transferable vote (PR-STV) electoral system had the effects of heightening the importance of local notables and, paradoxically, party organisation. The electoral law permitted voters to rank all candidates in order of personal preference and in effect permitted them to express preferences not only for a party label or list but also for individual candidates within a list or even across lists. Irish election results express a strange mixture of party-label voting and personality-voting. Thus a synthesis between party politics and local-notables politics evolved, each of the major parties containing within them a hierarchy of local vote-getters or chieftains, often more in competition with each other than with other parties' candidates.

Despite these disintegrative effects of PR-STV, political party organisations which had developed before and after independence endured. There is, however, some evidence that generational change may be making the organisations weaker as the old bonds between activists weaken. Furthermore, PR-STV tends to convert activist organisations into client groups of individual politicians within parties, thus unravelling old solidarities. This effect was not fully seen until the founding generation began to retire from politics around 1960, and its long-term consequences are not yet clear.

Two features had major conditioning effects on voting behaviour in the first twenty years of the new state. The first was agrarian class, containing within it the distinction between smallholder and commercial farmer as well as that between landholder and landless man. The second was centre-periphery rivalry, the classic dimension in any developing nation-state, reflecting in the Irish case the importance of Dublin as the governmental centre where the dominant English-speaking culture was centred and where colonial authority had been concentrated. In the following analysis, agricultural land valuations are used as an indicator variable for the former dimension and the urbanisation rate for the latter. As a preliminary, Table 13 summarises the regional variations in the votes for the various political groups in the Irish state between 1923 and 1944.[3]

Table 13. Irish Voting Patterns, by region, 1923–44

Election year	Totals %	Centre %	Heartland %	Western periphery %	Northern periphery %
a. Turnout					
1923	59	60	60	55	59
1927(1)	66	65	68	64	65
1927(2)	68	67	69	67	66
1932	75	70	77	75	77
1933	80	76	83	76	81
1937	75	70	78	71	77
1938	76	67	79	74	80
1943	73	68	76	72	75
1944	69	64	71	67	71
b. Sinn Féin III/Fianna Fáil					
1923	28	17	25	39	23
1927(1)	26	24	24	33	27
1927(2)	35	27	33	45	33
1932	45	34	43	55	40
1933	50	43	45	61	50
1937	45	41	42	53	50
1938	52	49	48	61	51
1943	42	45	40	43	43
1944	49	52	46	51	52
c. Cumann na nGaedheal/Fine Gael					
1923	37	50	32	42	41
1927(1)	27	31	22	34	26

1927(2)	39	48	35	41	35
1932	35	39	35	36	29
1933	31	40	29	31	22
1937	35	30	37	35	34
1938	33	34	35	32	29
1943	23	26	26	18	18
1944	21	26	22	17	12
d. Labour and National Labour					
1923	14	5	21	6	7
1927(1)	14	10	21	7	5
1927(2)	10	12	16	4	3
1932	9	8	14	4	3
1933	6	5	11	2	—
1937	11	10	18	4	—
1938	11	9	16	5	5
1943	16	16	22	11	11
1944	12	12	16	6	3
e. Clann na Talmhan (Smallholders' Party)					
1943	9	1	7	17	10
1944	11	—	10	21	9
f. Farmers' Party/Centre Party) (1933)					
1923	14	1	17	9	18
1927(1)	10	—	15	7	11
1927(2)	7	—	10	4	6
1932	3	—	5	2	5
1933	9	1	14	6	8
g. Independents, Independent Farmers, Others					
1923	7	27	6	4	12
1927(1)	22	35	17	20	32
1927(2)	10	14	4	5	23
1932	8	19	3	3	23
1933	4	10	1	—	19
1937	9	18	4	9	16
1938	4	8	1	2	15
1943	10	12	6	10	18
1944	8	9	6	6	25

TURNOUT, 1922–44

The electorate showed clear signs of a learning process. For example, PR-STV caused initial difficulties, but levels of spoilage rapidly declined. The 1920s also saw increasing levels of electoral participation, the major leaps taking place between the elections of 1923 and 1927(1) and between 1927(2) and the election of 1932, in which de Valera's party triumphed. Turnout fell off somewhat after 1933, the year in which de Valera finally got a majority of Dáil seats. Regionally, turnout displayed striking variations. In the first election of 1923, turnout was marginally higher in Dublin and the heartland provinces and marginally lower in the peripheries where the Free State writ did not run quite as successfully. In subsequent elections, however, a striking reversal of this original pattern took place and Dublin came to be overshadowed electorally by the country regions generally and by the heartland region in par-ticular. The frontier region of Ulster also showed high turnout rates, and the highest such rates in the state tended to be in central Munster. Turnout correlated positively and strongly with high land valuations, with the Farmers' Party vote and, despite the periphery's tendency to abstain, with distance from Dublin. It had its own persistent structure; it tended to be high in central Munster and south Ulster throughout the period and, as late as 1948, cor-related positively and strongly with IRA attacks on British forces a generation previously (.40, N=20) and strongly and *negatively* with Land War traditions (–.47, N=20). Turnout, like the IRA war itself, reflected the relatively prosperous 'middle Ireland' of the farming and small-town community rather than either the urban working class or the peripheral communities of the agrarian tradition. Turnout also correlated negatively with emigration and with other indicators of both urban and rural poverty.[4]

SINN FÉIN III/FIANNA FÁIL

It has been demonstrated that strong statistical links existed between support for Sinn Féin in 1923 and traditions of agrarian and militant activity. Sinn Féin benefited from the electoral support of the poorer and more western areas, which had a history of rural poverty and agrarianism. 'It was not supported strongly by the industrial proletariat, who were largely confined to the cities, nor by non-agricultural workers throughout the country'; it was essentially a party of the 'rural lower-middle class', of smaller farmers, shopkeepers and 'traders' vulnerable to economic depression.[5] While this description of the Sinn Féin of 1923 focuses nicely on the petit-bourgeois character of much Irish republicanism and although the party of de Valera has continued to gain disproportionate support from these groups, it soon broadened its base of support. Tables 13 and 14 make it evident that Fianna Fáil did indeed inherit the general support base of Sinn Féin, but soon broadened its base of support considerably. In 1923, Sinn Féin won only 17 per cent of the Dublin vote, whereas it won 39 per cent of the vote in the western periphery. Apparently because of its continued, if ambiguous, abstentionism, the party lost much of its periphery support at the first 1927 election. The second 1927 election saw much of this support return to it. From then until World War II, Fianna Fáil retained this very noticeable western bias, very like that of Sinn Féin in both 1918 and 1923. After 1938, the party's western support sagged, even relative to its national support, and its vote in the Dublin area exceeded its national average for the first time in 1943. The disappearance of Fianna Fáil's western base coincided with the rise of a new western-based party, Clann na Talmhan (People of the Land), a western small-holders' party which combined peripheral protest with the usual agrarian grievances.

This partial loss of its western base was probably an advantage for Fianna Fáil, as it was able to dissociate itself from the rather sterile small-farm protest politics of the 1930s and move into a central position in Irish society, benefiting from the mood of national solidarity that World War II encouraged and accommodating itself to more clearly modern political interests such as those of the business and working classes of the towns, the new and growing public sector and the protected industries set up under the new tariff regime in the 1930s. By 1945, Fianna Fáil's position in the party system appeared unassailable and it was faced by a Fine Gael which appeared to be disintegrating, a badly split Labour Party and Clann na Talmhan, an almost anti-political party. By 1945, Fianna Fáil's vote was correlating only with large family size, Irish speaking and low levels of rural emigration, indicators of the kind of stabilised rural society in which 1930s nationalist ideologues felt Irish people should live. On St Patrick's Day, 1943, de Valera praised this small-farm society in glowing terms; Ireland would be 'the home of a people who valued material wealth as the basis for right living, of a people who were satisfied with frugal comfort and devoted their leisure to the things of the spirit.' He had dreamed of a land whose countryside 'would be bright with cosy homesteads, whose fields and villages would be joyous with the sounds of industry, with the romping of sturdy children, the contests of athletic youths and the laughter of comely maidens, whose firesides would be forums for the wisdom of serene old age.'

Table 14. Sinn Féin/Fianna Fáil: agrarian class and centre-periphery correlates, 1923–44, general elections (N=22)

Election year	1923	1927 (1)	1927 (2)	1932	1933	1937	1938	1943	1944
High land valuation	−.56	−.51	−.57	−.42	−.65	−.39	−.63	−.03	−.06
Urbanisation	−.41	−.41	−.49	−.60	−.48	−.31	−.42	−.08	−.04

Tables 13 and 14 indicate that exactly at this time Fianna Fáil was becoming far more than the party of the stabilised middle and small-farm sector and was evolving into a national party, albeit one with a pronounced rural ethos. The national-populist rhetoric of the 1932–48 period, throughout which Fianna Fáil monopolised governmental power under de Valera, appealed to many non-rural elements as well, and appeared to many as a defence against the secularist and urban ideas of the outside world.[6] The result was the creation of an extraordinary electoral empire; it is as though de Valera had succeeded in reconstructing the national fronts of 1886 and 1918 on newer and more enduring foundations. By means of traditional habits of social solidarity and a mutual-benefit alliance with the Church, de Valera momentarily appeared to have converted nationalist Ireland into a Fianna Fáil country, with a Fianna Fáil constitution and cultural ethos to match; the educational system was harnessed to inculcate national-populist ideals and neo-Gaelic culture, and the political purposes behind much of the history and Irish-language teaching are obvious. By 1948, when the first generation of post-independence voters was reaching maturity, Fianna Fáil's vote defied class distinctions and no longer bore any noticeable Land League or IRA war imprint. As Table 19 indicates, the party was still faintly traditionalist and rural in its electoral profile, but it straddled the wide lower middle and skilled working classes. This empire was built in part at the expense of other groups; in particular, Fianna Fáil absorbed much of Labour's support. It appears that Labour's rural vote actually split, some of it going to Cumann na nGaedheal/Fine Gael, some staying with Labour, while Fianna Fáil took the rest; those labourers who hoped for land joined, or voted for, Fianna Fáil, while those who perceived the destructive effects of de Valera's policies on the cattle trade and their equally destructive effects on labourer employment turned to Fine Gael.[7]

Once in government, Fianna Fáil was able to broaden its appeal by adding the material benefits of government in the form of grants, employment and protection to its non-material attractions, such as its chauvinist rhetoric, and thereby attract a general following. The small farmers tolerated the Economic War because they stood to benefit from protection, and the new industrialists and their workers welcomed the tariff barriers, the housing schemes and the welfare system. In the late 1930s, the party drifted free of its earlier land-hungry, small-farm base.[8]

CUMANN NA NGAEDHEAL/FINE GAEL

Unlike Fianna Fáil or Labour, the early Cumann na nGaedheal's electoral support showed no clear geographical pattern; it was stronger in Dublin and Cork, but was quite strong in parts of the west in its early years and was weak in many big-farm areas. This was due, of course, to its de facto electoral alliance with the Farmers' Party and other conservative groups.[9] Its support shifted greatly in the early years and its transformation into Fine Gael in 1933 coincided with its absorption of the Centre Party and its alliance with the AOH rump. It also allied itself with the Blueshirts, a quasi-fascist agrarian movement led by army veterans. Because of these events, there was little continuity between Cumann na nGaedheal's vote in 1923 and Fine Gael's in 1937.[10] The original Cumann na nGaedheal vote had resembled Fianna Fáil's in possessing a pronounced western 'tilt', reflecting its share in the old Sinn Féin mobilisation which had been pronouncedly western biased as well. It appears to have combined a pro-Treaty Sinn Féiner vote with an urban middle-class vote. It was only later that it became heavily large-farm in support. The party's most persistent support has been in middle-class Dublin, and its leadership has always been heavily Dublin, in contrast to Fianna Fáil's tendency to evolve a nationwide leadership. Table 15 shows the party's lack of clear relationship to either class structure or to urbanisation.

Table 15. Cumann na nGaedheal/Fine Gael: agrarian class and centre-periphery correlates, 1923–44, general elections (N=22)

Election year	1923	1927 (1)	1927 (2)	1932	1933	1937	1938	1943	1944
High land valuation	−.19	−.41	−.13	0.17	0.16	−.14	0.11	0.24	0.01
Urbanisation	0.01	−.17	0.07	0.28	0.43	0.00	0.17	0.37	0.09

Cumann na nGaedheal appears to have lost much of its original Sinn Féin support to Fianna Fáil once de Valera came, in effect, to accept the Treaty settlement, and it, in turn, encroached on the electoral bases of its own allies, thus evolving into a conservative party with a non-Sinn Féin base led by ex-Sinn Féin elites.[11] Fianna Fáil propagandists remarked unkindly of the party's ability to swallow up its allies.[12] Fine Gael built far less on the Sinn Féin mobilisation, and far more on older mobilisations, than did Fianna Fáil. It was not until the 1960s that a 'Tory Radical' group in the party tried to shift the party to the centre or even to the left of Fianna Fáil, which had drifted steadily right in the intervening years. Fine Gael developed a semi-permanent marriage of convenience with the Labour Party in the late 1940s, and the 'Dev versus the rest' pattern of Irish politics dates from that period.

Labour, though nominally to the left of Fianna Fáil, resembled Fine Gael in that its leadership was strongly urban. During the first generation after the national revolution, the leaderships of both nationalist parties were very urban, reflecting the urban character of the old revolutionary movement's leaders. The contrast between Fianna Fáil's leadership and those of the other parties has become increasingly marked since the first generation of politicians retired in the 1950s and 1960s. Fine Gael's front-bench, and to some extent Labour's as well, has become clearly Dublin centred whereas Fianna Fáil's has displayed the opposite tendency and has come to favour the countryside and, in partic-ular, the west and north-western counties which have traditionally been the poorest, most politicised and most 'Ribbon-Fenian' in the country.

This simple statistical contrast between Fianna Fáil and 'the rest' reflects a profound and important difference between the largest party and the other two: Fianna Fáil has a tradition of spreading its ministerial posts around the country so as to cover the country electorally, to favour certain local factions as against others and to ensure that the party retains its status as a general 'country' party. Its ministers sometimes appear to be more concerned with looking after a region and acting as its spokesman in Cabinet than with actually governing the country. This feature of Fianna Fáil speaks for the strength of its local organisation and, perhaps, for its leadership's unwillingness or inability to impose its preferences on local activists or on any bloc of voters. By way of contrast, Fine Gael remained very much a 'centre' party at elite level, as did Labour. The party seriously declined during the 1930s and 1940s, its vote going from 40 per cent in 1923 to a mere 20 per cent in 1944. By that time, it was becoming a Dublin and Cork middle-class minor party with a few rural allies. Its experience in gov-ernment between 1948 and 1951 rejuvenated it electorally. It appears to have regained much of the vote which it had lost to Independents and minor parties and it also built up what appears to be a new liberal wing. Unlike Fianna Fáil, Fine Gael never quite developed the militarised, voter-directed and monolithic unity characteristic of the classic Irish nationalist party.

Table 16. Centre-periphery contrasts, Irish Cabinets, 1923–73

Proportion of Cabinet sitting for:	(a) Constituencies in heartland for centre	(b) Constituencies in western or northern peripheries	
	%	%	N
Cumann na nGaedheal Cabinet, 1923	54.5	45.5	11
Fianna Fáil Cabinet, 1932	62.5	37.5	8
Inter-Party Cabinet, 1948	84.6	15.4	13
Inter-Party Cabinet, 1954	76.9	23.1	13
Fianna Fáil Cabinet, 1968	40.0	60.0	15
Fianna Fáil Cabinet, 1971	50.0	50.0	14
National Coalition Cabinet, 1973	93.3	6.7	15

THE LABOUR PARTY

Labour's support was predominantly rural until the 1960s, being concentrated in the heartland region and in central Munster, areas with large numbers of rural labourers. Table 17 indicates its affinity with large-farm areas and its relative lack of urban support. In the 1920s, its vote correlated strongly with the Farmers' Party vote, reflecting its dependence on the same agrarian class conflict. Labour declined catastrophically during the 1930s, and thereafter began to attract some town support. However, it was not until the 1960s that the towns turned to Labour to any great extent, and internal disunity within the party prevented it from capitalising on urban discontent with Fianna Fáil. The reasons for Labour's

Table 17. Labour Party*: agrarian class and centre-periphery correlates, 1923–44, general elections

Election year	1923	1927 (1)	1927 (2)	1932	1933	1937	1938	1943	1944
High land valuation	0.61	0.60	0.68	0.60	0.24	0.46	0.57	0.66	0.24
Urbanisation	0.09	0.11	0.31	0.10	−.02	0.04	0.11	0.35	−.22
N	21	20	16	17	15	14	19	22	14

*Includes Independent and National Labour

electoral weakness have already been rehearsed.[13] The party is, electorally, a survivor of a pre-1918 mobilisation which survived partly because of 'leaks' in the Sinn Féin coverage of the country in 1918; in the 1920s, the party did somewhat better in areas which had been non-contests in 1918.[14]

Because of the tiny Irish working class, the conservative Catholic ethos of the culture, the party's lack of a strong nationalist tradition and because of chronic disunity in the party due to 'nationalist' and 'socialist' tendencies, Labour did well to survive as a minor party; as late as 1943–44, it was vulnerable to 'red smear' tactics by Fianna Fáil and split disastrously. In 1948, this split very nearly became a permanent division between 'national' and 'official' Labour.[15] As suggested earlier, the real puzzle is the party's extraordinary ability to survive, despite its inability to please any part of its small clientele completely.

THE FARMERS' PARTIES

Farming was the occupation of over half of the population of the Free State in 1926. The farming vote supplies particularly good insights into the concerns of the electorate during this period. The agricultural community did not behave as a political unit, as it might have done in a more highly urbanised political system, and most of its members voted for one or other of the two nationalist blocs. The two farmers' parties, that of the 1920s and the Clann na Talmhan of the 1940s, had different leaderships, ideologies and social bases, as Table 18 indicates. As the market for agricultural produce declined and as Fianna Fáil hostility toward cattle farming became government policy in the 1930s, so did the political reaction of the farmers.[16] Cumann na nGaedheal's pro-commercial agriculture policies were replaced under de Valera by policies favouring the small- to middle-sized farm and 'mixed' agriculture and by an 'Economic War' with Britain that nearly wrecked the cattle trade. The first, 'big' farmers' party was eventually absorbed into Fine Gael, but Independent farmers' TDs were an important part of Irish politics until the 1960s.

Clann na Talmhan was a very different organisation. During the years of World War II, economic pressures on the small-farm communities of the west grew, partly due to wartime conditions, but partly due to the decreasing viability of the farm with less than thirty acres; during the 1880s, the standard of living which such a farm offered had appeared attractive, but by the 1940s it appeared less so. Emigration from the west to the British war industries was very large, the average age of western farmers increased and the entire egalitarian small-farm community set up by the Land Acts in the west seemed decreasingly viable. The west's problems also looked insoluble to the political authorities: Connacht was a barren and overpopulated region, and there was little that could be done about it. The growing concern of government with the towns, Fianna Fáil's close connections with the new business class and the growing importance of rational-bureaucratic considerations in the making of policy combined with Fine Gael's association with large-farm and town interests to make both parties appear decreasingly attractive to westerners. If the rest of Ireland was insensitive to the needs of the Connacht farmer, then the Connacht farmer would have to organise. Formed in 1938, it became a significant minor party in the Dáil in 1943. It benefited from the same wave of agrarian discontent that put Oliver Flanagan into the Dáil from the midlands in the same year on a 'monetary reform' ticket. Both the Clann and Flanagan were later absorbed into Fine Gael. Clann na Talmhan strongly favoured the periphery, resembling the old UIL of William O'Brien to some extent in this at least. Its policies included fixity of tenure for tenant farmers, tillage subsidies (tillage was compulsory during the war), derating of small farms, old age pensions at sixty-five instead of at seventy and, interestingly, the abolition of pensions for government ministers.[17] The party was based on a declining and ageing community whose standard of living, while perhaps regarded as sufficient during the years of the land reforms, had become relatively insufficient with the development of industrial employment in Britain and even in parts of Ireland. Its programme was anti-political and anti-urban, its leaders' speeches being peppered with condemnations of politicians, civil servants, Jews, Freemasons and 'money grabbers'.[18] The party was almost completely confined to the old land-reform areas of the country.

Table 18. Farmers' and Smallholders' Parties: agrarian class and centre-periphery correlates, Farmers' Party, 1922–32, Centre Party, 1933 and Clann na Talmhan, 1943–44, general elections

Election year	1923	1927 (1)	1927 (2)	1933	1943	1944
High land valuation	0.23	0.50	0.35	−.03	−.44	−.65
Urbanisation	−.23	0.18	0.11	−.43	−.55	−.49
N	22	19	14	18	16	15

Table 18 shows not only the different electoral bases of the Farmers' Party and of Clann na Talmhan, but also that the Centre Party of 1932–33, usually regarded as a continuation of the large farmers' party, was actually a link between that party and the Clann; the Centre Party vote correlates with the farm vote of 1932, but not with the farm vote of the 1920s. Furthermore, Clann na Talmhan appears to have been very much a smallholders' party and not, as has been sometimes suggested, a cross-class party of peripheral protest. The party's vote in 1943 correlates with the Fine Gael and Fianna Fáil votes of 1938 at respectively −.02 and .29, suggesting that the party's vote was not closely related to either, that it took somewhat more from Fianna Fáil and that the western electorate was quite volatile. The Fine Gael vote in the west collapsed, but Fianna Fáil's was damaged too, and there appears to have been a complex realignment in the west, with Fianna Fáil losing some votes to the new party and recouping its losses at Fine Gael's expense. Between 1938 and 1943, Fianna Fáil lost farming votes everywhere, but particularly in the west, losing most percentage points in four western counties, Leitrim, Kerry, Galway and Mayo, while gaining points most successfully in the urban counties of Dublin, Wicklow and Cork; the party was trading its rural populist base for a 'national' base.

THE BREAK-UP OF THE TREATY PARTY SYSTEM

World War II profoundly affected Ireland's internal politics, despite the country's isolation and neutrality. The fact that Northern Ireland participated in the War widened the mental gap between the two parts of Ireland. The fear of invasion and the sense of being a rather friendless and weak nation-state in a world at war increased the traditional sense of communal solidarity and also helped to heal divisions of the previous generation. Pro-Treaty and anti-Treaty politicians who had not spoken to each other for twenty years found themselves on the same wartime committees or even serving in the same army; the wartime army was the place where many Civil War antagonisms were reconciled. The actual fact that the state succeeded in achieving a precarious neutrality increased its legitimacy by demonstrating that it was, indeed, sovereign, thus rendering the Treaty controversy obsolete. The new Constitution of 1937 had refrained from declaring a republic and the state was not declared openly to be a republic until 1949, and then by a government led by the old pro-Treaty party. The state had, of course, been as independent as was feasible for a long time by then. The old parties did not fade away, however; what faded away was the original social class component in the old cleavage between Free Staters and republicans.

The 1943–48 period marks the final disintegration of the 'Treaty system' and, as had happened previously in Irish history, the parties long outlived their original reasons for existence. What John Whyte has described as 'politics without social bases' dates from this period. In 1945, a presidential election campaign had indicated a considerable potential vote for a third-party candidate. The third-party vote of 1945 appears to have been an incongruous mixture of disgruntled western republicans and small farmers, urban liberals, Labour supporters and urban radicals. A final strange realignment occurred, and a new republican party, Clann na Poblachta (People of the Republic), was formed in 1946. The radical wing of Fianna Fáil, IRA veterans of the 1930s, urban liberals and reformers and anti-clericals made common cause. The party was strongly welfarist and anti-partitionist; de Valera saw it as a serious threat. The final irony was that the party's main contribution to Irish life was the revival of Fine Gael, the old Free State party, and its re-erection as a major opposition party. Clann na Poblachta was led by Seán MacBride, who had been chief-of-staff of the IRA for a time and who accepted constitutional politics only when the 1937 Constitution came into force.[19] The party's leadership was as variegated as its vote. A bitter teachers' strike in 1946 made it attractive to radical and nationalist elements in the teaching profession. It attracted other professionals who found that neither Fianna Fáil nor Fine Gael were particularly receptive to new blood or ideas. Fianna Fáil's leadership was ageing and was determined to prevent younger men replacing them. In the usual fashion of old revolutionaries, they distrusted the younger generation because that generation could never go through the purifying experiences of revolution; Clann na Poblachta represented, in part, a generational conflict of a kind common in Irish politics. Unlike Clann na Talmhan, the new party had some intelligent and innovative political ideas. The social background of its candidates resembled neither the farmer-dominated list of Clann na Talmhan nor the trade union-dominated Labour parties, but resembled those of the two nationalist parties.[20] Its candidates' backgrounds resembled a citified version of Fianna Fáil's, with fewer farmers and more urban professionals; it lacked the broad country base of de Valera's party.[21] In the 1948 election, Clann na Poblachta won 13 per cent of the vote, its support being geographically 'twin-peaked'; it won votes from traditional anti-partitionist republicans in rural areas and from urban radicals.[22] Republican and liberal wings of 'Clann' did not get on well, and the party soon started to disintegrate. It entered office in 1948 as part of a strange anti-Fianna Fáil coalition government comprising Fine Gael, the two Clanns and the two Labour parties, thus breaking Fianna Fáil's grip on power and also demonstrating that de Valera was not electorally invulnerable. Labour had split into National and mainline Labour, and Fianna Fáil worked hard behind the scenes to detach National Labour's few TDs from the new alliance; there is some evidence that these efforts very nearly bore fruit. The consequences of such an outcome are, of course, incalculable, but it is interesting to speculate on the possible development of a party system in which Labour was permanently divided between nationalist and socialist wings and in which Fine Gael, the Clann and the main part of Labour remained in opposition. The leader of the National Labour Party, James Everett, is said to have subsequently admitted that he was under great pressure from

Fianna Fáil. If Everett had joined forces with Fianna Fáil, both the republican and the labour traditions would have found themselves divided between government and opposition. The fact that it actually happened to republicanism and nearly happened to labour is itself an indicator of the extent to which the politics of government had replaced the politics of abstentionism and protest twenty-five years after the Treaty. Table 19 indicates, by the weakness of the correlations, how the traditional predictors of political loyalties had become ineffective after one generation of party competition. Fianna Fáil, the biggest and most catch-all of the parties, had the weakest correlations. Clann na Poblachta and Fine Gael, allies in the new Inter-Party government, had affinities with opposite ends of the social and political spectrum, indicating that that spectrum was no longer regarded as particularly divisive in Irish political culture. Another contrast was that between the two Clanns; Clann na Talmhan had no noticeable Land War affinity, but Clann na Poblachta had, and the agrarians had no IRA affiliations. Clann na Poblachta echoed the traditional set of affinities of Fianna Fáil, whereas Clann na Talmhan was clearly a non-republican, agrarian 'sectional' party with no specifically political tradition behind it. None of the correlations in Table 19 are pronounced, and if considered in terms of the 'Dev versus the rest' criterion, the relevant correlations—those for Fianna Fáil—are negligible. The alliance system of 1948 cut through the republican tradition and nearly cut through the labour tradition as well. Each side was a cross-class, cross-region and cross-tradition coalition, the main difference being, of course, the monolithism of the Fianna Fáil side. There were some differences in traditional affinities, and the two sides developed distinct political sub-cultures in the years after 1948, sub-cultures which are difficult to map or sum up, but which are easily recognisable. The most persistently successful variable in distinguishing Fianna Fáil from most of the others and, in particular, from Fine Gael has been a cultural one; it has always been supported disproportionately by Irish speakers.[23]

Fianna Fáil has always expressed a more missionary attitude toward the goal of restoring Irish as the national language, despite

Table 19. General Election, 1948: correlations between party votes and selected social background variables

	Turnout	Fianna Fáil	Fine Gael	Clann na Poblachta	Clann na Talmhan	Labour Party	Labour and Nat. Lab.
Workforce in agriculture	0.27	0.30	–.46	0.03	0.35	–.40	.40
Farm equality score	0.13	0.26	–.38	0.20	0.36	–.61	–.69
High land valuation	0.40	–.01	0.58	–.50	–.41	0.26	0.16
Land War, 1880	–.35	0.27	–.38	0.31	0.09	–.25	–.23
IRA, 1919–1921	0.40	0.18	–.02	0.16	–.45	0.11	–.15
Irish speakers, 1901	–.35	0.35	–.26	0.30	0.21	–.03	–.14
Persons per room, 1936	–.59	0.22	–.14	0.57	0.34	–.17	–.42
Radio sets, 1946	–.03	–.22	0.58	–.18	–.28	0.25	0.21

Note: Ns vary from 18 to 22, but are 12 or 13 in the case of Clann na Talmhan.

the fact that the language is clearly dying and has lost an immense amount of ground since 1900. In 1961, Fine Gael withdrew its support for compulsory Irish in schools, but Fianna Fáil has clung to the policy of linguistic revival through the school system. Linguistic revivalism has always been a curiously impractical feature of Fianna Fáil, a party not renowned for its attachment to broad political ideas or to non-pragmatic ideological stances. The determination of this proverbially voter-directed party to cling to the policy of linguistic revival is rendered still more curious by the fact that the idea of reviving Irish is not very popular, and this has enforced a reluctant moderation on government policy.[24] The explanation appears to be that the population at large declare their approval for linguistic revival but do not intend to do anything about it themselves. In effect, the language has become a symbol of the nation, rather like the British royal family, and it is not possible to oppose it without looking faintly unpatriotic. Fianna Fáil's success in holding on to voters who entertain vague sentiments of national piety and of support for symbols of national identity appears to be a long-standing, if not readily quantifiable, ingredient in the party's secret of political success.

11 | THE ROOTS OF PARTY AND GOVERNMENT IN INDEPENDENT IRELAND

THE CENTRAL PLACE OF PARTY IN IRISH POLITICS

In the nineteenth century, Irish nationalist politics revolved around the assertion of communal rather than individual rights. 'Freedom' came to mean the freedom of the group to exist and to assert itself; religious freedom referred, in effect, to corporate privileges for a church and its flock, national freedom to the independence of a national state. Even in the previous century, agrarian groups such as the Whiteboys expressed the will of the group as against that of the individual, their efforts often being directed against wayward members of their own group rather than against outsiders. Inter-communal violence and tension had existed prior to the nineteenth century, but the most continuous and characteristic activity of Irish political societies was the attempt to achieve and, if possible, maintain and enforce internal solidarity and a united front in the face of outsiders.

In one sense, the churches were the first Irish political parties, and it is natural to expect Irish political parties to resemble churches. Certainly, the Catholic Church supplied much of the organisational sinew for the O'Connell movement and its priests were to be directly involved in local-level party politics up to at least the 1930s in the area that was to become the Republic of Ireland and up to the 1970s in Northern Ireland.[1] The same general observations could be made of the Protestant churches. In the nationalist community, the Church could wield massive direct political power not only through its participation in party politics but also through its role in shaping and organising public opinion through the educational system, the pulpit and the popular press. Because of its suzerainty over the educational system, the Church was able to determine much, if not all, of the political socialisation of the Catholic population. An interesting and unresolved question is whether the Catholic Church's influence in education has discouraged or encouraged the growth of an assertive Irish nationalism through its part in the formation of public opinion. It could be argued that an educational system run mainly by laymen would have been far more extreme in its nationalism than were schools under direct or indirect clerical management. Certainly the Church defended the identity of the ethnic-religious group for essentially religious reasons and, at times, for nationalist reasons as well. The two sets of motivations sometimes became indistinguishable in practice, but at other times there was a definite tension between the two. The Church also preached submission to the civil power and usually condemned violence. After the Famine, the Church's increasing control over education was accompanied by a decreasing capacity to control nationalist politics. Significantly, it recovered much of its direct political power only when the lay leadership was split and demoralised after Parnell's fall. Even during the following two decades, there was resistance to the concept of a purely clerical or episcopal political leadership, not least from elements of the clergy, and there was a steady, if reluctant, ceding of the area of conventional politics to the politicians, the Church holding onto its bailiwick in education.[2] Lay leadership was never challenged again in the overwhelming way it had been in the 1890s; the Church retained enormous political power, the Church-state relationships after 1922 were those of approximate equals rather than those of a secularised political system, but outright theocracy was avoided and the new state was ruled by laymen.

The lay political leadership derived its support from the electorate, as drilled and organised by party organisation, something which was true both before and after independence. The fundamental Irish political institution was therefore the mass, militant and cross-class political party, which has been central to Irish politics since the emergence of a mobilised popular public opinion in the early nineteenth century.[3] The party was, and to an important extent still is, the institution by which violent, constitutional and semi-constitutional forces were united and, at least for a time, reconciled. There are two main conventional interpretations of the Irish nationalist political tradition.[4] The first is the romantic view of it as one of 'protest, resistance and violence' against foreign oppression; the second sees it as subordinated to a more important tradition 'built around the development in Ireland of representative institutions of government.'[5] The second view, which interprets Irish political development as being essentially legalistic and constitutional, is plausible, particularly in view of the fact that Irish nationalist leaders generally used constitutional means to agitate for the restoration of parliamentary institutions in the nineteenth century. Parliamentary government under 'devolved' or sovereign constitutional arrangements was the goal of Irish political leaders, and even the physical-force men tended to think in constitutional terms to a great extent.

This 'parliamentary' interpretation of Irish political development, while a welcome advance on the romantic view, has certain difficulties. Firstly, violence has played an enormously important role in Irish politics, both in a symbolic way and as part and parcel of mass movements, even those mass movements customarily regarded as being eminently constitutional. Also, this interpretation sets up what is very nearly a false opposition between physical force and constitutional agitation, as though one were always a substitute for the other: in fact, the two modes of action were often used simultaneously and were sometimes mutually sustaining.[6] It could even be argued that one could not have existed without the other.

Another difficulty with the 'parliamentary tradition' interpretation is that it tends to over-emphasise the adhesion of the Irish leaders to the forms and spirit of parliamentarianism. Irish nationalist leaders, whether constitutional, revolutionary or some murky blend of the two, often, and perhaps typically, had an exploitative and opportunistic attitude towards English political institutions and towards parliament in particular. During the nineteenth century, parliament, in the Burkean sense of a deliberative assembly considering and devising laws for the community as a whole, was outside the experience of the entire Catholic community, and of most of the Protestant community as well. Majorities in the British parliament were determined by British political forces, and only very marginally by their Irish equivalents. Ireland, with its idiosyncratic problems so remote from those of Britain, was often discussed, but always by power-holders who were essentially outsiders and not really dependent on Irish public opinion. The island's government was, in fact, not really parliamentary at all, but executive centred. The Irish parliamentary experience in the nineteenth century consisted to a considerable extent of the opportunistic use of the House of Commons as a *point d'appui* to wheedle or force concessions from British administrations. O'Connell's party in parliament, the prototype for later Irish parties, was small, and the emancipation and repeal campaigns were based less on votes, resolutions and debates in the House than on the weight of an organised and violence-inclined public support, channelled into political associations and backed up by the unspoken, but well-understood, threat of mass violence. Significantly, O'Connell's 'parliamentary' campaign was broken by the threat of state violence against the mass demonstrations of the Repeal Year. Parnell's great innovation, one which horrified contemporary parliamentarians, was the determined and ungentlemanly exploitation of loopholes in parliamentary procedures to prevent parliament from functioning normally. This unparliamentary parliamentarianism was reinforced by a mass political agitation outside parliament, which could scarcely be described as non-violent, although it did use some non-violent techniques. Parnell's chief instrument in this war against parliament was, of course, the pledge-bound and disciplined parliamentary party, acting and voting as a bloc under his direction and linked to an increasingly adventurous and militant mass support organisation at home. This disciplined political party, which contained within itself parliamentary, extra-parliamentary, agrarian and frankly unconstitutional components, owed its monolithic and militarised character as much to Irish traditions of militant solidarity for purposes of communal defence as it did to the parliamentary traditions of either Ireland or Britain. It was, far more than parliament, the characteristic Irish political institution and was, almost literally, an *anti-parliamentary* party.

This focus on the mass political party which organises popular sentiment along disciplined lines, emphasises internal unanimity and which combines in one organisation popularity, aggressiveness and oligarchic tendencies enables us to escape from the usual dichotomy between violent and non-violent political action. From 1879 on, the pan-nationalist political party, in its most successful phases, united all agitational tendencies under one roof in the most pragmatic of ways and blended militarist and non-violent modes of political action. A consequent traditional ambiguity towards political violence has haunted political leaderships. Parnell's relationship with the 'Ribbon-Fenians' was the archetype of this uneasy and powerful combination of the two modes. The former 'men of violence', whether Fenian or 'Ribbon' in background, supplied much of the manpower for the Land League and its successor organisation. The ex-revolutionaries, while not usually allowed to contest parliamentary elections, were enjoined by the 'Ribbon-Fenian' IRB leadership to 'gain control of all local bodies such as municipal corporations.'[7] The use of non-violent and violent methods of political action to *force* others to concede or to co-operate was particularly evident during the land wars of the 1880s, and it epitomised the characteristic Irish blend of legality and violence, of majority consent and coercion of deviants. A similar development occurred in Protestant Ulster.

The enormous importance of the political party and the consequent relative disregard for the autonomy of parliamentary institutions were products of the divorce between the mainly nationalist popular political leadership and the mainly unionist holders of executive power in the government of Ireland that was characteristic of the Irish political constitution in the nineteenth century. Under the union, the Irish constitution consisted of a separation of powers between a non-popular executive and a popular, non-governing party of elected politicians, perpetually shut out of the government of the country. This constitutional experience conditioned the forms that the political institutions of independent Ireland were to take. When Dáil Éireann was founded in 1919, it did not immediately achieve anything like the same 'above-party' corporate identity that its Westminster counterpart enjoyed, let alone the institutional autonomy of the Congress of the United States. From the beginning, Dáil Éireann was a partisan assembly, set up by the MPs of one Irish political party and boycotted by the members of the other major party: it was the creation of Sinn Féin and was effectively monopolised by Sinn Féin until the Treaty. The IRA began their campaign in 1919 with scant regard for the Dáil, and the Dáil government had some difficulty in keeping army, party, parliamentary and bureaucratic roles separate from each other within the underground government, a fact which added to the legal and institutional confusion of the Treaty split. When the Dáil voted on the Treaty, the result was not so much a majority for the Treaty as *two* bodies claiming to be Dáil Éireann, one for each wing of the Sinn Féin party. The Dáil was reflecting its character as the supreme body of a pan nationalist political party rather than as a true inter-party parliamentary assembly in the Anglo-American tradition. After 1922, parliamentarism did succeed in establishing itself, but again by means of force as well as non-violence and in its crystallised form the parliamentary system in Ireland is not as developed as the received Anglo-American models would have prescribed.

Between 1922 and 1927, the Dáil was dominated by the pro-Treaty party, and British colonial traditions of executive dominance tended to reassert themselves through the dominance of the executive over the legislature. These traditions were reinforced by the circumstances of civil war and continual civil emergency. Since then, however, this relative dominance of the executive over the legislature has become entrenched and permanent. One symptom of this is the relative vulnerability of the *Ceann Comhairle* (Speaker) to party, and another is the chronic underdevelopment of parliamentary committee systems in both the Dáil and Senate. Again, the redrawing of constituencies required to keep representation consonant with demographic changes was, until 1980, an executive monopoly rather than the responsibility of a nonpartisan or bipartisan parliamentary or judicial committee. The limitation on this monopoly of the executive was constitutional rather than parliamentary.

In actual practice, the main activities and arguably the true purposes of the Dáil have been to act as a register of party strength, a sounding board for public opinion and as a not always very effective court of final appeal for legislation devised privately by the governing party and the civil service. Early attempts to make certain 'extern' ministers directly responsible to the Dáil rather than to Cabinet failed because of the brute fact of the Cabinet's central place in the system. Similar attempts to entrench a parliamentarianism independent of the Cabinet in the form of a strong, deliberative second chamber quickly came to nothing. The weakening of the Senate and the creation of a weak presidency under Fianna Fáil in the 1930s completed this rapid assertion in independent Ireland of a party-based executive ascendancy.[8] In recent years, this tradition of executive dominance has come under a challenge from the courts, which have been experimenting with processes such as judicial review. The dominance of party in government is made possible in part by the availability of civil service help and advice to the government of the day, thus giving it an enormous advantage over the opposition. The dominance of party and bureaucracy over parliament is reflected most accurately in the role ascribed to the TD by the electorate. Not only is the TD required to vote unquestioningly as directed by his leaders, he is also required by his constituents not so much to legislate for the nation as to mediate between them and the bureaucracy; party loyalty and service to local and individual interests are the main duties of the TD as enforced by the electorate.[9] The general underdevelopment of Irish parliamentary institutions contrasts with the highly developed civil service and semi-state body machine, in large part a legacy of the colonial period. It also contrasts with the strength, discipline and ideological malleability of the Fianna Fáil party organisation; parliamentary government, when transplanted to Ireland, was being transplanted into somewhat alien soil and has mutated into something which, if not always rich, is sometimes rather strange.

PARTY AND THE PHYSICAL FORCE TRADITION

Since the 1870s, the political party, as a central institution of Irish political life, has had to cope with aspects of its own historical origins which do not always assist in the task of constitutional government. Party has had to synthesise the constitutional tradition with other traditions which were often, at least initially, unconstitutional or at least non-parliamentary. The Catholic Church had highly ambiguous attitudes toward liberal democracy and has been induced to accept it in large part because liberal democracy benefited its flock rather than because of any prior philosophical leanings toward the individualist and liberal assumptions behind parliamentary democratic theory. However, the major non-liberal tradition which the political party has had to cope with in Ireland has not been the restrained illiberalism of the Church but the physical force tradition, one which is far older than the political party in Ireland and in which the latter has some of its roots. An early example of the difficulties with which nationalist party leaders had to cope is afforded by the assassinations of the new Chief Secretary for Ireland, Lord Frederick Cavendish, and his Under-Secretary, T.H. Burke, in the Phoenix Park, Dublin in 1882. The murders were perpetrated by a breakaway Fenian group known as the Invincibles. These murders could have wrecked the Parnellite movement, but Parnell took advantage of the revulsion they caused to drive the entire movement far closer to constitutionalism than it had been previously. The murders were, however, highly embarrassing, as they tended to highlight the links that existed between the Parnellite movement and the *emigré* Fenian organisations in the United States. The important point here is not that Parnell was a covert physical force man, which he was not, but rather that he was believed to be by a considerable number of people: his condemnations of violence were often taken with a grain of salt by some of his followers and were even admired as demonstrating his preternatural political cunning. Rather like Ribbon leaders claiming that the local priests were secret sympathisers, violent men could claim the Parnellite leadership to be their tacit allies. The Parnellite leaders' extravagant and often militant political rhetoric often sounded

little different from Fenianism: to compete with violence, constitutionalism often had to wrap itself in a very green flag indeed. It
was claimed afterwards that violent men sometimes rationalised
their actions by claiming that they were acting in accordance with
the constitutional leadership's unspoken wishes. The father of
Joseph Brady, one of the murderers of Cavendish and Burke,
insisted that the demagoguery of the leaders of the Parnellite party
had encouraged the assassins: 'It was they who misled my brave
boy. Joe had as good a right to kill Cavendish as others to kill Lord
Mountmorres. And Parnell knew well what was being done,
though all the bridges were cut that might lead up to him.'[10] Parnell
was not, of course, privy to the plans of the Invincibles, but many,
and not all of them his political opponents, thought that he might
be, or that he covertly approved. Irish constitutional leaders were
often prisoners of an older, more violent, tradition.

The slow, painful and not particularly graceful process by which
de Valera and his party extricated themselves from the violent
tradition between 1923 and 1936 reflects a similar problem of the
overlap between the civic and the guerrilla traditions in Irish
politics. De Valera's position was more difficult than Parnell's in
that he had, after all, commenced his public career in the Irish
Volunteers, had commanded during Easter Week and had been
President of the Dáil during the War of Independence. His
transition to constitutional politics was therefore far more difficult, and was also complicated by the split in the constitutional
tradition itself that the nationalist revolution had created. He
appeared to regard the new Free State as the apparatus of a
foreign-controlled clique and as the product of a British-instigated
swindle backed up by force. He questioned the right of the Free
State government to repress the IRA: as late as 1931, he questioned
a Cabinet condemnation of illegal organisations when there were
'gentlemen in that front bench that went around this country
organising secret societies [before 1921] . . .'[11] However, de Valera's
solution was to focus his complaints on the symbols of the state;
by making symbolic aspects of the Free State such as the Governor-
General or the oath of allegiance central to its legitimacy, he made
that legitimacy easier to achieve afterward by the relatively simple

and inexpensive method of changing the objectionable symbols to more acceptable ones. De Valera appears to have been more worried about the legitimacy of the Free State in the eyes of those who continued to adhere to the physical force tradition than about its legitimacy in the eyes of the general population; he expressed himself as accepting majority rule 'for the time being' in November 1927.[12] He was, however, worried about the allegiance of the young men. The Free State did not, he insisted, satisfy 'the aspirations of our people' and it could only be used as 'something on the road to a greater freedom', echoing a phrase of Michael Collins, perhaps intentionally. Unfortunately, if the Free State was an interim stage rather than an end result of the Irish national campaign, a 'section of people . . . particularly of the younger people who will be close in touch with the national tradition' would claim the right 'to strive for that greater freedom which is denied them at present . . .'[13] Fianna Fáil's solution was to build a new version of the old united movement, and to give people a sense, however faint, of unity of purpose. Lemass urged in late 1927 that the dissensions of the Civil War should be forgotten and that a new consensual unity should be built.[14] When in office, however, Fianna Fáil still oscillated between nationalist intransigence and constitutionalism. In particular, it continued to regard the pro-Treaty group as lacking in national piety and had a guarded sympathy with the emotions, if not the means, of the IRA. The IRA, however, while it co-operated with Fianna Fáil governments for a period after 1932, was not, as a body, won over to the state, and de Valera reached no concordat with it. In late 1933, Joseph McGarrity, an important Irish-American leader, wrote to de Valera, by this time head of the government for over a year. He urged de Valera to come to an agreement with the IRA, on the interesting and very traditional grounds that the IRA could 'do the things you will not care to do or cannot do in the face of public criticism . . .' De Valera's answer was, interestingly, not a critique of the ethics of McGarrity's proposal, but a short essay in the applied sociology of legitimate government and of nationalist solidarity:

You talk about Fianna Fáil's coming to an understanding with the IRA. You talk of the influence it would have both here and abroad. You talk as if we were fools and didn't realise all this. My God! Do you not know that ever since 1921 the main purpose in everything I have done has been to try to secure a basis for national unity. How can you imagine for one minute that I don't realise what division in the Republican ranks means at a time like this? But is this need and desire for unity to be used as a means of trying to blackmail us into adopting a policy which we know could only lead our people to disaster. It has taken us ten long years of patient effort to get the Irish nation on the march again after a devastating Civil War. Are we to abandon all this in order to satisfy a group who have not given the slightest evidence of any ability to lead our people anywhere except back into the morass?[15]

De Valera's curious synthesis of constitutionalism, revolutionism and national solidarity endured. The 1937 Constitution eliminated the remaining symbols of the imperial link and also withdrew full recognition of the state of Northern Ireland. For practical reasons, it stopped short of declaring a republic, but it used Gaelic, Catholic and nationalist symbols generously, and was intended to complete the legitimation of the state. Structurally, it was not all that much more than a restatement of the Free State's Constitution which had been, in turn, a version of the Westminster model of parliamentary cabinet government. It also echoed in its phraseology a draft constitution of the Republic of Ireland produced by the rump Sinn Féin party between 1929 and 1933. The Sinn Féin document was heavily Catholic in tone and also heavily Gaelic, anti-British and anti-'Free Stater'. De Valera's 1937 Constitution was, by comparison, a liberal document, but the similarities in phraseology indicate who, or what tradition, it was that de Valera was trying to pacify.[16]

Fianna Fáil soon broke decisively with the IRA and introduced non-jury courts analogous to those which the previous government had used. During World War II, the de Valera government was quite willing to intern or jail IRA members and showed an inflexible determination not to concede 'political' status to IRA prisoners. This reflected in large part the government's sensitivity to the IRA challenge to its political legitimacy, which was similar to that de Valera himself had issued to Cumann na nGaedheal governments in the 1920s. The IRA/Fianna Fáil split quickly became final and the IRA came off worst. However, the violent tradition lived on in Fianna Fáil in the form of 'constitutional republicanism' and a curious ideological affinity—and antipathy —persisted for a long time between Fianna Fáil and the hodge-podge of radical, fundamentalist and socialist groups collectively referred to as the 'republican movement'. Fianna Fáil's perceptible ambiguity toward the republican movement was somewhat similar in psychological quality to the relationship between Gaullism and the *Algérie Française* movement of the late 1950s or to that between the British Conservative Party and militant Ulster unionism after 1884. This historical link between Fianna Fáil and the IRA should not, perhaps, be over-emphasised: after all, the pro-Treaty group had included Michael Collins and Richard Mulcahy, architects of the 1919–21 campaign, and had only exorcised its rebel past by the extensive use of execution without trial. Civil war saved Fine Gael from being haunted by its republican past; Fianna Fáil's IRA past dogged it through the 1950s and 1960s. During the 1950s' IRA campaign, Fianna Fáil representatives, in defiance of the national leadership, expressed sympathy with the young men of the IRA, regarding them as being in the same tradition as the men of 1919–21.[17] During the 1969–70 crisis in Ulster, of course, the party's past showed itself spectacularly, when some Fianna Fáil ministers called for militant action on Ulster and were accused in court of conspiring to smuggle arms for the IRA into Ulster.[18] This reversion to type reflected the absence of a dominant de Valera or Lemass figure in the Cabinet and the consequent factional jockeying among the leaders of the party. The reversion was, however, partial, opportunistic and confused; it ran against the general evolution of Fianna Fáil into a voter-directed party over the previous decades. By 1970, Fianna Fáil was in its second elite generation; the younger men did not share the memories or passions of the older men, nor did they have the same popular authority or revolutionary charisma as the old men.

The older men themselves had acquiesced in de Valera's constitutional or 'dictionary' republicanism for far too long. In 1976, one veteran Fianna Fáil TD who had been an IRA leader in Cork during the 1919–21 period summed up his own mentality and that of many of his generation:

> At times I hate politicians. Part of me had a strong dislike for politics. I was a soldier basically and the whole business of politics was too slow . . . The funny thing is, I always believed the old boy would reunite Ireland . . . I was always convinced he had a plan . . . I followed him for most of my life. And I'd do it again. He even changed my mind a bit about politics.[19]

THE EVOLUTION OF THE IRISH STATE

Apart from the political party, the central lay political institution in independent Ireland was the apparatus of the state, and the relationships between party and state are important in attempting to understand the dynamics of the political process in the Irish Republic. Unlike the political party, the state in Ireland was not a native invention. In the medieval period, the Dublin state could scarcely enforce its rulings on the small territory in the east which was under its direct rule, let alone rule the Anglo-Irish marcher lordships or the Gaelic chieftaincies which covered the rest of the island. Even after the laboriously achieved suppression of the Gaelic and Old English chieftains of Munster and Ulster in the sixteenth and seventeenth centuries, settled administration was rendered difficult, if not impossible, by political instability and war. It was only with the imposition of Protestant Ascendancy rule after 1690 that ordered and relatively centralised rule became possible. Eighteenth-century Ireland was ruled by a system which might be described as aristocratic devolution: an essentially subordinate, if occasionally fractious, parliament sat in Dublin, representing the landed Anglican Ascendancy. Anglo-Irish gentry formed the backbone of the local administration and where, as in parts of the west and north-west, there were few such gentry, local administration went by default. This tiny landed governing caste was isolated in a sea of Irish-speaking, Catholic peasantry who, even when they had affection and 'feudal' feelings of loyalty for their new lords, had no religious links with them and were culturally remote from them. The administrative penetration of the state was limited, and local government tended to be carried on with great independence of the centre. Whiteboy insurrections, for example, were usually put down by volunteer militias under local command, and sometimes such militias were heavily Catholic in their membership, despite the prohibition on Catholics bearing arms.

In the west and south, smuggling was a way of life for entire communities and illegal communication with the continent was a routine occurrence. Early agrarian crime was directly connected with the land system and may have been influenced by memories of Jacobite grudges and clan feuds, but it also prospered in great part because the repressive apparatus of the state was almost non-existent by later standards.[20]

The Dublin parliament theoretically shared the government of the country with the king's executive government, headed by an English lord lieutenant. The Westminster parliament claimed the right, as it had done since medieval times, to legislate for Ireland, and it became the usual thing for the executive to buy majorities in the Irish parliament to ensure co-operation with the wishes of London.[21] However, the Dublin parliamentarians had to be relied upon to tax the country and to police and defend it; they therefore had some bargaining power of their own. As in the American colonies, the executive tended to become identified with the 'London interest' and a 'patriot party' in parliament became identified with the 'local interests'.[22] The executive was mainly Anglo-Irish in origin and tended to reflect a particularly rabid tendency in Anglo-Irish opinion. The Ascendancy was vulnerable internally as well and even open to public pressure at times; popular demonstrations to pressurise parliament were quite common in eighteenth-century Dublin.[23]

Despite the immense amount of patronage available to the lord lieutenant and his executive, Anglo-Irish nationalism forced London to concede the partial independence of 1782 and to remove mercantilist restrictions on trade. The American and French wars encouraged the habit of relying on the Anglo-Irish to defend

Ireland. However, most of the armed forces available consisted of
territorial militias, raised locally and led by local gentry. These
militias were eminently accessible to political activists of various
stripes, and frankly political volunteering in the 1780s ensured that
the official militias of the 1790s would be, in effect, party militias.
In a sense, it was not the ruthlessness of the Irish government that
brought on 1798, but its chronic underdevelopment: because of its
lack of independent resources, it was unable to come between
Catholic and Protestant or to raise forces not susceptible to
partisan influence. Unable to guarantee to both sects their physical
preservation, it was forced to join one against the other. The
political bankruptcy of the Ascendancy was marked by the union,
although the Ascendancy regime died a lingering death in the
nineteenth century. The Act of Union also reflected the British
government's overriding interest in Ireland, which was security.

The early nineteenth century saw a very impressive overhaul of the
Irish state apparatus under Westminster auspices. The Ascendancy
regime continued, but in somewhat attenuated form, and after
1829 some penetration of positions of influence was achieved by
Catholics; admittedly, it was not until the twentieth century that
the numbers of Catholics in government began to approximate
their numbers in the general population, and it was not until after
independence that Irish Catholics actually dominated senior
posts. However, a start was made very early in the nineteenth
century, and, characteristically, one of the first major areas of
reform was in the judiciary and police. The old, ineffective local
systems were replaced by an efficient, bureaucratically organised
and centralised armed force, the Irish Constabulary, renamed the
Royal Irish Constabulary (RIC) after the Fenian Rising. From 1836
onward, recruitment to the constabulary was mainly non-
sectarian and meritocratic. The RIC is the direct ancestor of the
Royal Ulster Constabulary of Northern Ireland and is a structural
ancestor of the Garda, which inherited much of its administrative
framework, its centralisation and such practices as the prohibition
on any policeman serving in his own county so as to ensure that
he would be unlikely to become entangled in local feuds or
political affairs.[24] In the early 1820s, salaried magistrates were

introduced to supplement the old gentry-dominated magistracy. Both systems continued together in one form or another for the remainder of the period of the union, but the stipendiary magistrates ('resident magistrates') gradually became more important and also acted as representatives of state power in outlying areas.

Another example of advanced reform by the standards of the period was the founding of the primary education system in the 1830s. Originally the system was intended to be non-denominational and state aided, but the mutual distrust and dislike of the churches led to the enforcement of de facto religious segregation in the schools by the 1860s. Secondary- and third-level reforms generated similar tensions as well as enormous controversy, the Catholics fearing proselytism and the Protestants fearing clerical domination of education. Large-scale university education for Irish Catholics was delayed for a generation and, when instituted, bore clear marks of the *Kulturkampf* of the nineteenth century.

A series of commissions of inquiry into Irish affairs analysed Irish land, communications, education, economic and governmental problems, and Westminster displayed an increasing willingness to bypass the Ascendancy. Ireland, like India, and for analogous reasons, became a laboratory for administrative experimentation and, again like India, the diagnoses which led to reforms were not always local in origin; even when local expertise was used, it was often the opinions of the Ascendancy, of the Catholic clergy, of civil servants or, occasionally, of the better class of Catholic layman which were solicited. Irish government in the nineteenth century was modernised from outside and in accordance with an outsider's view of what reforms were needed, often in opposition to the wishes of the leaders of both religious communities. The eighteenth-century system of 'indirect rule' through Anglo-Irish Ascendancy institutions gradually gave way to centralised, 'rational-bureaucratic' executive-centred government. By 1900, British government intervention had made Ireland the most administered part of the United Kingdom and had involved a 'degree of government action and administrative penetration unknown in Britain'.[25] Local government was a particular target of the reformers. The municipal corporations were in the hands of unpopular Anglo-

Irish cliques up to the 1830s. Franchise reform brought Catholics into control of many municipal corporations long after the Famine.[26] However, as there were far too few Protestants in many parts of the country and as Catholic politicians were politically difficult, English-style amateur local government could not survive. By 1840, the Irish local councils had lost much of their power and key local officials were being subjected to central appointment, co-ordination and supervision.[27] Even before mid-century, urban government was directed from Dublin Castle 'in an authoritarian fashion scarcely imaginable in early Victorian Whitehall, whence the new bureaucracy in England sallied, generally in vain, to overcome local resistance to positive innovation'.[28]

By the end of the nineteenth century, then, Ireland had one of the most advanced, centralised and rationalised administrative machines in Europe. This machine owed both its pervasiveness and its high level of development to two factors: the under-developed character of Irish society and the external support of Whitehall. The contrast between Irish administrative development on the one hand and Irish social and economic development on the other was stark; government was, over most of the island, the only large modern organisation that existed, and the civil, police, military and educational bureaucracies were the main sources of skilled non-agricultural employment for the better-educated sections of the population. This situation echoed India and was, of course, also similar to that in many underdeveloped colonial territories which became independent after 1945. Political scientists have begun to point to the penetration of the state apparatus into the local political scene as being itself a major source of general politicisation: as the government gets involved in local affairs, it bypasses the cellular structures of local authority and weakens the local gentry and clergy by divesting them of functions which were previously theirs. Local groups see the state machine as threatening their position or else as a source of political and social opportunity. In Britain, some politicisation of this kind did indeed occur up to the 1870s but, because of weaknesses in the central apparatus and because of successful local resistance, a new equilibrium was achieved between central and local forces.[29] In

Ireland, for obvious reasons, the equivalent balance was found, in so far as it was ever found, far later and was of a different nature: the state apparatus was stronger and civil society proportionately weaker, resulting in a far greater degree of direct governmental regulation of social life. This development, so unlike Britain's and so similar to that of many post-revolutionary states, was to leave a permanent imprint on the new state's administrative structures after 1921.

Even in its recruitment policy, the Irish Victorian state was able to counteract the traditional caste-bound system and permit large numbers of Catholics to gain middle-level and senior-level experience in bureaucracy long before independence. As already noted, the police instituted even-handed recruitment quite early and had eliminated its grossest sectarian biases by the 1840s. By 1911, as the era of the union was ending, even senior-level recruitment had become reasonably fair. With the significant exception of the army and, to some extent, the senior civil service, recruitment to the state machine had become fairly well balanced.

The composition of the judiciary had always been a major political issue, as the system continued to be dominated by the Ascendancy up to quite a late date. In 1887, only one-quarter of unpaid magistrates and one-third of stipendiary magistrates were Catholics. After 1898, a concerted effort was made to balance the proportions, and 60 per cent of unpaid magistrates appointed between April 1906 and May 1908 were Catholics. However, the imbalance persisted among the stipendiary magistrates and, by 1907, the proportion of Catholics in this group was one-third, or the same as twenty years previously. Furthermore, at senior levels, the imbalance was even greater: Catholics were in a very small minority on the High Court of Justice and were only a large minority among the county court judges and recorders as late as 1908.[30] The courts and the army consituted the entrenched citadels of the Castle system, and in nineteenth-century Ireland the courts and the army could only too easily be represented as two aspects of the same garrison. Reform was occurring, but the old rhetoric could still sound convincing.

PARTY AND GOVERNMENT IN INDEPENDENT IRELAND

Despite these imbalances, the new state inherited a fairly large group of civil servants who were willing to throw in their lot with it. New judicial and military hierarchies were, of course, instituted, but the central civil service remained much as it had been under the last viceroys. In the politics of underdeveloped or newly independent states, the state machine is often, as it was in Ireland, an island of relative modernity in a society which is somewhat less than modern. In such a country, if democratic or populist politics persist, the state apparatus tends to come under siege. Politicians often owe their power to popular forces and organisations which are less than wedded to the idea that government should be 'rational-bureaucratic', impersonal, even handed or tolerant. Typically, the politicians are themselves nationalist or socialist modernisers in their personal inclinations, but they must take account of their constituents, who may be less modern minded, and also of those who shape public opinion, whether they be religious leaders, journalists, party activists, local notables or trade union leaders. They are also constrained by the views of financial backers, foreign allies or patrons and, perhaps, by the views of the armed forces. Because of these kinds of pressures and constraints, even well-intentioned politicians are tempted to permit, or even encourage, the conversion of the bureaucratic system to a spoils system of recruitment and promotion and to let the bureaucracy be penetrated by party cliques and special interests. If the politicians are less than well intentioned or are simply incompetent, the willingness to suborn the bureaucratic machine will, presumably, be even greater. Classically, the bureaucracy fails to retain the autonomy and freedom from political pressure prescribed by the Victorian 'Whitehall model' of government. Patronage, distortion of the administrative process to favour certain groups and individuals, privileged access to the machine, discrimination and nepotism are common dangers. The prototype of the process was perhaps the penetration of the New York city government in the early nineteenth century by the political machine of Tammany Hall. These developments are held to be particularly likely where one party has a monopoly or near-monopoly of executive power.[31]

In extreme cases, the bureaucracy acts in collusion with the dominant party, merit recruitment is replaced by or heavily tempered by, political appointment, and impersonal and fair administration becomes subordinated to the demands made by clients or partisan groups on local political leaders.

This picture of a corrupt, clientelist 'party-state', characteristic of many countries which received their independence since 1918 is unlike the usual picture drawn of the Irish civil service and its relationship with political parties. This picture is of an austere and rather conservative rational-bureaucratic machine, liable to keep its own counsel, unresponsive to outside pressures, staffed by recruitment systems immune to political intervention, ruled by seniority and generally protected from party appointment with the exceptions of senior posts and an undergrowth of petty patronage at local and subordinate levels.[32] The Irish system inherited both the centralisation and the pervasiveness of its British predecessor. It also inherited the primacy of the Department of Finance of the Dáil government of 1919–21 and benefited from the 1919–20 overhauls of the British and Irish administrative systems.[33] The centralisation of local government was intensified after independence, partly by the development of a county manager system which increased the authority of the Department of Local Government at the expense of the local representative councils; the manager became a somewhat prefectorial figure in Irish local government.[34] Local authorities' taxing powers have been whittled away and they have become increasingly dependent on central funding.

Significantly, this continuing centralised concentration of power does not correspond to the term of office of any particular government: it commenced under the Cumann na nGaedheal governments of the 1920s, whom one might expect to be enthusiastic centralisers because of the relative strength of the republicans in peripheral areas, but it continued and, if anything, intensified under the Fianna Fáil governments of the 1930s. This combination of Fianna Fáil rule and centralisation of local government appears odd when contrasted with the party's support base and general policy line, which emphasised decentralisation and economy in government.

On the face of it, there was no great urgency to centralise local government from the point of view of Fianna Fáil, as there was no great bloc of Fine Gael councils opposing the new government outside the towns, and Fianna Fáil dominated the councils in the more rural western half of the country.[35] However, centralisation on Dublin and the bypassing of the elective councils reached its peak during the terms of office of the electorally sensitive and populistically inclined Fianna Fáil party. The reasons for this are complex, involving a mixture of bureaucratic and party-political considerations.

Parties like Fianna Fáil tend to have debts to pay, if only in the form of rewards for the loyal services of large numbers of activists. Many of these activists and small contributors to the party in its early years received no recompense beyond the standard thank-you note from the leader himself, signed personally. After the election victory of 1932, the pressure to use government as a source of favours and patronage must have been immense, as it usually is in poor countries. One veteran civil servant recalled that after that election, the Department of Local Government suffered an 'inundation' of grievance letters, often citing private promises given by Lemass and other Fianna Fáil leaders.[36] De Valera resisted pressure to withdraw pensions from 'Free State' personnel, but instead extended pensions to those who had fought on the republican side in the Civil War, thus ensuring that the community ended up paying off both sides. Fianna Fáil was welfarist by the standards of the period, and used state enterprise to create employment as a substitute for private enterprise and to ensure greater national self-sufficiency. In creating jobs, the government appears to have been able to strike a balance between the demands of local influentials and the requirements of orderly and coherent administration.

Two local studies carried out in the late 1960s addressed themselves to the triangular relationship between the citizen, the party and the civil service. These were the anthropological studies of Paul Sacks and Mart Bax, carried out in north Donegal and in Munster.[37] Both authors described a political culture which had apparently changed very little since the 1930s: it was intensely localist and was deeply cynical about government because of 'a general ambivalence toward authority arising from the colonial past.'[38] This culture tended to require politicians to act as grievance men and as intermediaries between local society and central government, as I have described earlier. The two studies disagreed, however, on one crucial point: Sacks suggested that the politician was essentially a broker or communicator of individual grievances and that the amount of real patronage at his disposal was very limited, the bureaucracy being essentially honest and inaccessible to local political manipulations. Bax, however, portrayed the local bureaucracy as penetrated and manipulated by local political bosses in the style characteristic of clientelistic political systems in underdeveloped countries. According to Bax, the merit system of appointment through the Civil Service Commission and Local Appointments Commission had been 'turned' by local politicians either on their own or with the help of politicians at national level. These power-holders, Bax claimed, succeeded in getting their clients appointed to local bureaucratic posts by means of ingenious manipulations.[39] His evidence was less than conclusive, however, and he occasionally appeared to be unable to distinguish clearly between what had occurred and what local people liked to say had occurred. Evidently, it is difficult, if not impossible, to assess exactly the nature and level of corrupt practices in a society like Ireland, where libel laws are very strict and where story-telling is a national occupation. There is, for what it is worth, a rich folklore concerning petty patronage and also, at a slightly more serious level, concerning irregular allocations of public housing and planning permissions. It is difficult, however, to be able to clearly distinguish between patronage and bona fide meritocratic practice in many cases.

What is clear, however, is that many Irish people are deeply pessimistic about the possibility of government being honest and impersonal. The particularism of the culture ensures that government will also be seen as particularistic and the idea of government as a machine that operates impersonally and fairly is somewhat less than universally entertained. The problem is to decide to what extent this public scepticism is justified, and what the exact relationships between party and bureaucracy, between politics and administration, really are. Survey evidence, at any rate, has confirmed that many Irish people have low levels of political self-confidence, are not overly impressed by the probity of civil servants and feel that they need the politician as inter-mediary and as someone who will 'use influence' on their behalf. There is also a strong tendency to think of political action in individualistic terms; rather than form a group to pursue common goals, the typical reaction to a political problem or a problem with the bureaucracy is to go and contact the local TD to gain redress. This pattern of individualistic responses to political problems is far more pronounced in Ireland than in other Western liberal democracies.[40] It was presumably even more pronounced forty years ago. What is almost surprising is the apparently relative absence of favouritism and corruption on a large scale, given the poverty and culture of the society; what is odd in Ireland is that the majority of civil service posts are filled by merit recruitment, by impersonal, if perhaps imperfect, processes of examination and interview. There has been relatively little development of a spoils system such as that of Jacksonian America, and the core of bureau-cracy has retained a considerable independence of party politics. An explanation of this outcome involves a general consideration of the character of the nationalist political elite that took over power in Ireland after 1921 and of the civil service machine which it inherited from the British.

The pre-1922 Sinn Féin nationalist leaders saw themselves as the creators of a movement of national regeneration, and they saw the politics of patronage from a puritanical and idealistic viewpoint. Corruption was associated with the despised 'Castle Catholics', with the 'Tammany' politics of the Irish Party and with the British administration. A taker of patronage was, in their lexicon, only slightly higher than the felon-setters and informers in the pay of the Castle. An American political scientist observed of the Irish politicians whom he encountered in the 1920s that they had a puritan attitude toward favour-doing.[41] Even before the Truce of 1921, Collins was worrying about patronage and probity in government.[42] Ernest Barker was struck by Sinn Féin's intense clean-up-the-corruption mood.[43] Like revolutionary elites else-where, Sinn Féin's leaders were middle class, urban, educated and young: in 1918, one-third of Sinn Féin MPs were under thirty-five and three-quarters were under forty-five. Some had had a little political experience, but mainly at local level, and most had a background of rather idealistic Gaelic League training, Volunteer experience and the internment camps as a preparation for political leadership. Most of them were outsiders in the constituencies which elected them. The most influential among them displayed that curious mixture of self-righteousness and lack of self-consciousness that revolutionary politicians often display. They were puritanical, idealistic and austere and were adherents of the politics of national redemption rather than of the politics of compromise, bargaining and pay-offs. Even the more hard-headed of them tended to adhere to this image of themselves.[44] The obverse side of such intense and self-confident idealism is, perhaps, an abnormal ability to justify one's own actions and, perhaps, to condemn the actions of one's political opponents as being evilly intended. Relativism, rather than truth, is the first casualty of war. Crane Brinton's generalisations about the kinds of men who come to lead revolutions are apposite:

It is probable that, especially in their crisis periods, our revolutions threw up into positions of prominence and even of responsibility men of the kind who would in stable societies not attain similar positions. Notably, great revolutions would appear to put extreme idealists during the crisis periods in possession of power they do not ordinarily have. They would also seem also to give scope for special talents, such as Marat had, for yellow journalism and muckraking of a very lively sort. They certainly create a number of empty places to fill, and give an opportunity to clever young men who may also be unscrupulous. They probably ensure a bit more public attention, for a while at least, to the chronic rebel and complainer, as well as to the lunatic fringe of peddlers of social and political nostrums ... There is no question that in the turmoil of revolutions a good many scoundrels rise to the top ... But the level of ability ... to handle men and to administer a complex social system ... is certainly very high.[45]

In the Irish case, the revolutionaries needed an executive machine, and were short of professional expertise. They were also perhaps unusually conscious that Belfast and London were predicting political decay for their new state and were keen to confute those predictions. The central civil service was exactly what they needed; it was a modern institution and contained a number of experienced, well-trained and intelligent senior officers. Sinn Féin had few such people in its ranks and had also the usual complement of cranks, fanatics and opportunists. Joseph Brennan, a senior official in the Castle administration and later first head of the Irish civil service, was almost openly contemptuous of Sinn Féin's 'experts' on economic and financial affairs. Quite irregularly, and with considerable political acumen, Brennan gave Collins advice on matters of government finance during the period of the Truce.[46] During the 1920s and 1930s, new officials were recruited, but the senior civil service remained dominated by men whose careers had commenced under the British regime together with a carry-over contingent from the Dáil underground civil service, itself set up on the British model. The key to the continued dominance of these officials lay in the fact that the new politicians were often desperately dependent on their technical expertise and corporate morale, so much so that they could scarcely afford to damage either by imposing party nominees on them or by interfering too violently with the process of self-perpetuating recruitment, which is what meritocratic recruitment procedures often amounted to.[47]

The relationship that evolved between the party politician and the permanent official can be examined best, perhaps, by examining it in the light of a particular issue. Land reform was a traditional political touchstone in Ireland, and land reform and redistribution were, of course, issues of great symbolic and practical importance to people of Sinn Féin background. Land redistribution was the cause of one of the most ill tempered of the debates during the 1921–22 period.[48] An extraordinarily emotional exchange between the leaders of the two factions of Sinn Féin occurred, in which each denounced party politics and denied practising such politics himself; they were, of course, to become the founding fathers of a major party each.[49] Fianna Fáil's activists continually pressed for land reform and land grants for IRA veterans at the *ard fheiseanna* of the 1920s and 1930s. Some response to these pressures occurred, and after 1932 Fianna Fáil did engage in some land distribution, although not on the scale of the pre-independence land distributions. After 1935, the Fianna Fáil land reform programme came to a halt.[50] In 1934–35, over 100,000 acres were divided, but by 1941–42, only 22,000 acres were divided, and this decline dated back about five years.[51] The decline in land division was accompanied by a Parkinsonian increase in the staff numbers in the Land Commission.[52] This contrasted with Fianna Fáil's anti-grazier rhetoric of 1932, with its ambitious plans to break up the large estates even outside the western Congested Districts and with its promises to encourage a general pattern of the middle-sized 'family farm' on which a family could be reared 'in decency and comfort.'[53] Eventually, Joseph Connolly, the Minister for Lands and Fisheries, had words with de Valera over the issue of land distribution:

> In the course of one of these *tête-à-tête* conferences de Valera referred to a number of problems that were causing him concern and adverted to the question of land division and the Land Commission. I smiled at this and asked him if he were serious. He seemed irritated and he asked me what I meant and said of course he was serious. I said it was difficult to realise that; that we had discussed the position frequently . . . nothing had been done. I said I could only conclude that he had changed his policy. This remark sparked off a minor fireworks display. He denied that there was any change of policy and I retorted that looking at the position, how was one to think otherwise?[54]

The basic reason behind the tacit refusal to extend land division to the areas outside Connacht may or may not have been a general realisation that it was less than totally desirable on practical economic grounds. However, two sets of political relationships might be found to contribute to an explanation for the policy shift: those between Fianna Fáil ministers and their party and the electorate, and those between the Cabinet and the civil service.

Fianna Fáil's electoral base began to shift in 1937, and the party went through a major realignment between 1938 and 1943. Eventually, it succeeded in alienating much of its Congested Districts support. Gallagher reports that between 1933 and 1937 'Fianna Fáil lost votes heavily in the most agricultural areas of the country', and the Economic War hit farmers hard.[55] The electoral pressure to appease the farming community must have been enormous, particularly in view of the party's waning popularity during this period, a waning due in large part to its nationalist and economic adventurism. The other set of relationships, those between the Cabinet and the civil servants, is also important. As a policy-formulating body, the Cabinet had at least two great weaknesses: firstly, it was dependent on voters for its continuance in office, and secondly, it had committed itself to various policies before it had experienced government at first hand and was, to a great extent, a prisoner of its own rhetoric. Unlike the old Irish Party, it actually had to deliver on its noisily made promises, and unlike the Irish Party, Fianna Fáil had to compete electorally. Presumably, almost any policy change was perceived as preferable to a Fine Gael government. The officials of the Department of Finance were hostile to further land division. Their arguments mainly concerned the large financial outlay involved, but also emphasised the distortion of the land market and the weaker economic viability of smallholders as contrasted with large farmers.[56] The Department's representative on the Land Commission was Michael Deegan, and he was suspected of representing a 'Finance attitude' toward land division. Deegan himself assessed the situation in a minute of 1942: the egalitarian family farm pattern had already been achieved or even over-achieved in Connacht. Consequently, further land division was only possible in areas outside the western Congested Districts, that is, in areas such as Meath where the grazier/labourer pattern of land usage persisted and where the agricultural tradition was essentially one of stock-rearing. Logically, western landless men should be given eastern land. However, local party politics hindered such a programme. Deegan minuted, 'Experience shows that local approval for land division work can only be secured in many cases only by the allocation of some holdings to suitable landless applicants.' He also felt that the local landless men made bad small farmers because of their stockman tradition. The landless men had sympathy in the cumainn, however, and Fianna Fáil, having already annoyed the big farmers, could scarcely afford to alienate local landless men and smallholders in the east and south. The programme sometimes became grotesquely distorted because of grass-roots political considerations; in Meath, '. . . there was local opposition to the settlement of colonies from the Gaeltacht . . . and in order to placate the local landless claimants, they distributed among them 4,000 acres for the 600 they gave the migrants.' The technical and financial objections put forward by the officials, combined with the electoral embarrassment it threatened, paralysed the land distribution programme.[57]

The case history is not necessarily typical, but it is one example of the sometimes difficult transition from the politics of protest to the politics of government by Fianna Fáil. What is interesting is that the old rhetoric of protest continued as a cloak for an increasingly pragmatic and cautious style of government in a small and increasingly isolated state in the 1930s and 1940s.

Naturally, the relationship between minister and party and minister and official varied enormously from period to period and from department to department, not to mention the importance of the personalities involved. The abilities and ambitions of a particular minister, for example, could change that relationship radically. However, certain weaknesses in the politician's institutional role encouraged the growth of the civil service's contributions to policy formation until, by the mid-1950s, the senior civil service officials were able to effect a major reversal in economic policy. Politicians were not administrators or policy-creators by role: they were moved from department to department, their tenure was conditional and often insecure, their energies were distracted from policy-making by Dáil duties and by the demands of an electorate rendered almost tyrannical by culture and by the magnification of the voter's power effected by PR-STV. Under PR-STV there are no safe seats, and it is not possible for the party headquarters to guarantee seats even to party leaders. Furthermore, a popular TD, even if his own seat were secure, would be under pressure to cultivate his constituency energetically so as to earn his party another seat in the constituency through a 'coat-tails' effect. The voters were apparently less concerned with general policy-making than with personal service; once the original generation of ex-revolutionaries had retired in the 1950s and 1960s, successful politicians were increasingly likely to be trusted and popular local men rather than national figures, ideologues or technocrats. Whereas the first generation of politicians was able to rely on its 'national record' in the 'Troubles', the second generation was not. Many of the older men could count on their 'name' to get them elected and could even dispense with formal organisation. On the Fine Gael side in particular, voters appear to have tolerated extended absences from the constituency on the part of their TDs: Cosgrave, Mulcahy and Dillon were each elected for constituencies widely distant from their places of residence. This toleration does not seem to have been extended to the second generation and, interestingly, Fianna Fáil's first generation exploited such toleration relatively little.[58]

Since the 1950s, the vast bulk of TDs have lived in, or near, their constituencies.[59] The pressure on politicians to pacify voters ensures that they have little time or energy left to deal with administrative and policy issues on anything approaching a full-time basis. This appears to be particularly true of Fianna Fáil.

In 1932, the new Fianna Fáil government found itself dealing with officials chosen under British and Cumann na nGaedheal dispensations. Subsequently, the public service expanded enormously, as did the 'semi-state' sector. The party has been in power since 1932, with three brief interruptions totalling about eleven years. The party and the permanent officials have, to put it mildly, become accustomed to each other, the former valuing the latter's expertise in government and the latter appreciating the former's ability to pacify the electorate and to create the political conditions within which orderly administration became possible. Changes in recruitment policy also tended to make the civil service generally sympathetic to Fianna Fáil. Few graduates were hired, which ensured that the civil service would not be overstocked with the alumni of either of the Dublin universities, neither of which could be described as being Fianna Fáil strongholds. Civil servants were required to have a good command of the Irish language, an intellectual achievement which tends to be associated with general political sympathy for Fianna Fáil, as we have seen. Proficiency in traditional culture and probable sympathy with nationalist and even nativist ideological assumptions ensured a patriotic civil service which was at least not hostile to Fianna Fáil. Certainly, one member of the 1973–77 coalition government occasionally felt during his tenure as minister that he was an interloper at a Fianna Fáil *comhairle ceanntair* in perpetual session.[60] He was probably overstating the case. Party influence in the appointment of judges and senior executives in state boards is considerable, but little detailed research has been done in this area. The important general point that should be made is that the penetration of Fianna Fáil into the bureaucracy appears to be very great, and is due mainly to the fact that the party has had a near-monopoly on public office for almost fifty years and has, by its own success, generated social categories created in its own image. Sartori has urged us not to think of political parties as dependent variables or as mere 'projections' of social forces more 'real' in some sense than they are, but as independent, or partially independent, political actors in their own right capable of modifying their own political environment. Fianna Fáil's dominance of the Irish political system is a classic example of such a feedback process.[61]

The bureaucracy, however, became a central political institution in independent Ireland, profiting from the extensive modernisation and streamlining carried out by successive British governments during the century before independence. The enormous impor- tance of the civil service and semi-state bureaucracies was also heightened by the dominance of the public sector in the rather underdeveloped economy of the post-independence period. Because there was so little rivalry from the private sector and because underemployment was chronic, the public service seems also to have been able to recruit a large group of highly able men. Because of its political indispensability, the civil service was able to retain its corporate integrity and identity and resist all except the more subtle pressures toward politicisation. The result of this situation was the creation of an informal system of demarcation of areas in which merit recruitment was to operate from areas in which patronage considerations were to be paramount; an 'executive redoubt', independent of the party machine, survived and even prospered, relying on its own indispensability and on its own very considerable sense of corporate responsibility and self-interest. However, ultimately even the civil service has to bow to party in Ireland. Whether it does depends on whether the party really wishes it to do so.

12 | SOME COMPARATIVE PERSPECTIVES

LIBERAL DEMOCRACY

Despite an unpromising beginning in civil war, liberal democratic politics have become deeply rooted in Ireland and have come out of crises such as that of the 1920s or that of the Ulster civil war since 1969 with increased legitimacy. The fact that liberal democracy survived in Ireland is itself of some interest when seen in the light of the well-known general correlation between political stability and high levels of economic development. In an influential study published in 1960, Seymour Martin Lipset presented comparative evidence which suggested that high levels of economic development, education and urbanisation were closely associated with stable liberal democracy.[1] Lipset also suggested that Catholicism was not totally compatible with liberal democracy because of the ethical relativism inherent in some liberal-democratic systems of ideas.[2] Subsequent studies have elaborated on Lipset's basic argument and have concluded that economic development is important, but not in quite the way Lipset thought.[3] Communications systems, mass literacy, education and ethnic or religious homogeneity, all essentially cultural factors, are of great importance as well. There is no simple relationship between liberal democratic government and economic development: 'Certain levels of "basic" socio-economic development appear to be necessary to elevate countries to a level at which they can begin to support complex, nation-wide patterns of political interaction, one of which may be democracy.'[4]

Poor countries are never materially egalitarian or well integrated politically; richer countries may be.

Ireland has been regarded as an exception to this general set of relationships.[5] It has been, since independence, the poorest liberal democracy in the North Atlantic area and its offshoots, and has also been one of the most stable of these democracies, with extremely low levels of political violence, a very low crime rate and little support for anti-system movements. Despite progress in recent decades, the country was still considerably poorer than any of the other Western democracies. The Irish case looks slightly less odd, however, if the totality of liberal-democratic states in the world is considered as the universe of reference and if a wider range of socio-economic variables is looked at. Of twenty liberal democracies extant in the early 1960s and stable since 1945, Ireland ranked seventeenth in GNP per capita and fourteenth in terms of urbanisation, confirming the usual 'poor and rural' characterisation of the country in its first generation of independence.[6] However, it ranked eighth in terms of the proportion of the population under nineteen still in school, seventh in terms of egalitarian land-holding patterns and fourth (behind Japan, German Federal Republic and Italy) in terms of ethnic homogeneity. The country is one of the most ethnically homogeneous nation-states in the world, regardless of whether language, race or religion is taken as the appropriate ethnic marker. Another demographic peculiarity of Ireland until the 1960s was the country's extraordinary emigration history; between 1890 and 1960, despite a very high birth rate, the country's population remained static, partly due to high levels of celibacy but also because of the siphoning off of much of the population to the rest of the English-speaking world.

This general picture suggests that the advanced administrative and mass educational system set up in the nineteenth century and the co-operation of British political leaders with Irish nationalists in bringing about a revolution in land tenure amounted to achievements which if attained elsewhere were attained only by means of prolonged turmoil and political revolution. Similarly, the secession of Northern Ireland from Ireland in 1922 'solved' or rather 'contained' a chronic ethnic problem on the other side of an international frontier. It is not clear that an unpartitioned Ireland would have been capable of bearing the load of Ulster's historical problems. Lastly, emigration functioned as a means of 'exporting' possible social problems and perhaps enabled Irish governments to evade demands made on governments elsewhere for social and economic reforms. Because Ireland's economic performance has improved greatly in recent years, and has improved particularly in relation to that of the United Kingdom, Irish politics seems to be in the process of becoming more 'normal', and the emphasis on economic and social management as political issues has increased.

The most peculiar feature of Ireland's nineteenth-century political development was the fact that though the country was ruled directly from London and was represented directly at Westminster, the country was, in all other respects, essentially colonial, with the typical cultural and economic dependencies and native/settler antagonisms characteristic of colonial countries. Many of these antagonisms were resolved *within* the framework of the old two-island United Kingdom prior to secession; the present-day Irish Republic itself is an end result of the United Kingdom's inability to solve these part-colonial and part-religious antagonisms by any means short of secession.[7]

THE PARTY SYSTEM IN COMPARATIVE PERSPECTIVE
A central argument of this study has been the thesis that the decolonisation model is of considerable use in interpreting the Irish political system. However, at a somewhat lower level of generality, it does not give us an adequate idea of the analogies between the Irish party system and other liberal democratic party systems. It gives only very general answers, for example, to such questions as where to fit Irish parties on a 'left-right' spectrum, a 'secularist-clericalist' spectrum or any other set of standard ideo-logical labels. The most comprehensive comparative framework for the study of mass movements in electoral politics is that of Stein Rokkan.[8] His framework focused on party rather than on state structures, limited itself to liberal democracies and to the culture-area of Western Europe. Any attempt to extend it to Ireland is, in a sense, an attempt to extend it beyond Europe; as

already suggested, although Ireland is geographically and culturally European, in some important ways the country is politically rather non-European, or could be said to be closer to Eastern than to Western Europe in some of its political patterns.

Rokkan offers a comparative framework for the analysis of partisan cleavages within contemporary nation-states. As has been pointed out by several critics, the framework has a certain teleological quality: it takes a nation-building perspective for granted and tends to take frontiers as being more or less fixed.[9] However, it is provocative, despite its limitations. It posits two main dimensions of political cleavage in societies in which the state-building process is occurring, the 'territorial-cultural' or centre-periphery dimension and the 'functional' dimension. The former dimension involves, at the periphery of the incipient or developing territorial state, local territorially or culturally based oppositions to the encroachments of the state-building elites or their bureaucratic, military, commercial or ecclesiastical allies: 'the typical reactions of peripheral regions, linguistic minorities, and culturally threatened populations to the pressures of the centralising, standardising, and "rationalizing" machinery of the nation-state.' At the centre of the developing nation-state, this dimension would involve conflicts within the national elite over power and strategies for the national unit as a whole.[10] The second, or 'functional', dimension is non-territorial and concerns socio-economic cleavages. Such polarisations unite people of similar economic circumstances ('classes') regardless of their territorial position or ethno-linguistic background; the obvious examples are conflicts between tenants and owners or between employers and workers. The 'conflict-space' of the nation-state contains cleavage systems which generate party systems and which can, in Lipset and Rokkan's view, be interpreted in the light of these two territorial and functional dimensions, given a certain minimum level of territorial consolidation and state-formation.[11]

Cleavage structures in contemporary European nation-states derive, then, from historical experiences of state-formation and the outcomes of political conflicts which the process of state-formation involved. These conflicts can be summarised in terms of those conflicts emanating from the *national revolution*, or the setting up of the nation-state, and those involved in the *industrial revolution*. In most of Western Europe, these conflicts took place over a long period, and are now over, but elsewhere in the world they are still occurring, and at an accelerated pace and in a 'telescoped' pattern. In Europe, the old conflicts left a permanent residue, in the shape of cleavage lines and political organisations which have become institutionalised.[12] Four main cleavages are generated by the two revolutions: the national revolution involved conflict between the 'nation-building' centre and unincorporated peripheries and also conflicts between Church and state, while the industrial revolution generated oppositions between political forces based on the primary and secondary economies and between bourgeoisie and workers.[13] This admittedly very general scheme, which I have reproduced in severely abbreviated form, has the great merit of being sensitive to the evident importance of spatial, cultural and other essentially non-economic sources of political allegiance in Western societies, and attempts to give a general account of the interaction of these factors with the more generally understood economic and 'class' factors.

The Church-state conflict is, of course, best symbolised by the Reformation. The Reformation divided Europe into political systems in which the Church's position varied widely. In systems where the Church remained Catholic and in easy or uneasy alliance with the state, Church-state relations remained permanently unresolved, as in France, Italy or Spain. In those northern systems where the Church was reformed, a common outcome was the subordination of the 'national' Church to the state, as in Sweden or England. A third set of 'mixed' states, of which Germany and the Netherlands are the primary examples, also emerged.[14]

The centre-periphery conflicts, of course, took the form of territorially based movements of resistance to central attempts to standardise the laws, languages and religions of the country. Since the early nineteenth century, such movements have often been regionalist, as in the case of the Norwegian Venstre party, or outright secessionist-nationalist, as in the case of the late Irish nationalist movement within the United Kingdom or as in the case of Norway as a unit within the Sweden-Norway union.

The primary economy versus secondary economy oppositions which arose after the growth of the cities often had a marked effect on the subsequent party systems, the classic case being the entrepreneurs', artisans' and urban workers' support for urban liberalism in Britain against the landed interests of the Conservative Party up to the 1880s. Usually, these oppositions softened and reconciliation occurred, although conflicts over issues such as tariffs often divided town from country very deeply. In the *Kaiserreich*, a weak liberalism did not ally with the workers, but effected an early reconciliation with landed conservatism in the marriage of Iron and Rye.

Finally, the worker-employer cleavages which have dominated European political thought, if not always European political behaviour, since the time of Marx were far more uniformly divisive.[15] However, the way in which the workers became organised for political action and the extent to which they became integrated into the national political system were heavily affected by the structure of the cleavage system which existed prior to the rise of the urban working classes. In particular, the character of labour movements was profoundly affected by the political position of the Church. If there existed a prior tacit alliance between the landed aristocracy and the Church (as in most Catholic countries), counter-alliances between urban bourgeois anti-clerical 'radicals' and sections of an anti-clerical working class could develop, and the labour movement was likely to become anti-clerical and communist. If, on the other hand, the Church had been weakened, an anti-clerical note was far less likely to appear in the workers' movements, and they were far more likely to evolve along 'labourist' and pragmatic lines. The workers also became profoundly affected by prior centre-periphery regionalist or nationalist cleavages, Ireland affording several spectacular examples. Where older cleavages reinforced each other, as in Bavaria versus *Kaiserreich* Germany (religion, region), as in Britain-Ireland (religion, region, primary/secondary economy) or as in Finland-Russia (language, religion, region, economy) the workers were likely to be incorporated in local nationalist or even religious movements.

Another general insight offered by Rokkan is the conditioning effect of the timing of suffrage extensions. With the achievement of full suffrage and the completion of the process of popular mobilisation, this nation-building process is, he argues, complete: whatever the political goals of the various classes and other groups may be, they take place within a generally accepted territorial-national arena. Universal suffrage marks the point where the party structures and mass folio wings freeze or crystallise. The party systems become permanent: 'the party alternatives, and in remarkably many cases the party organisations, are older than the majorities of the national electorates.'[16] Movements which arise after the attainment of full suffrage tend to be ephemeral, as their support is stolen from them by the older and better established parties, good examples being the *Poujadiste* movement in France, third-party movements in the United States or Clann na Talmhan or Clann na Poblachta in Ireland. Nazism was, in a sense, the exception that proves the rule, as it appears to have profited from the weakness of the prior party organisations, and also appears to have peaked in 1932 in the classic fashion of protest parties. As already suggested, the timing of suffrage extension can also affect the political prospects for popular socialism, early suffrage extension weakening those prospects, as in Ireland or the United States.

Can Ireland be fitted into this general scheme? My answer is that although Ireland is not an example of any of the classic patterns of cleavage listed by Rokkan for Europe, his ideas on the analysis of cleavage systems are eminently useful in deciphering the Irish system. The first problem is a revealing one: the problem of the unit of analysis. It is not entirely clear whether Irish parties should be considered essentially within the 'conflict-space' bounded by the frontiers of the *Klein-Irland* of the present-day Republic of Ireland, the *Gross-Irland* of the entire island or even within the historical context of the political union of Ireland and Britain that existed in one form or another from 1690 to 1922. The Irish case has this element of double- or even triple-vision inherent in it because the boundaries of the state are not stable and have themselves been one of the issues in Anglo-Irish conflicts and in the superimposed Irish domestic conflicts.[17] To put one aspect of this problem in Rokkan's terms, was nineteenth-century Ireland a periphery of the United Kingdom, or was it a colony of Britain? The answer of this essay has been that it was a colony, with its own acknowledged corporate identity up to 1800, which London attempted to convert into periphery in the nineteenth century by means of bureaucratic modernisation policies. London almost succeeded, but in succeeding in the linguistic and economic assimilation of Ireland to Britain, political equality also had to be accorded, thus reviving or unleashing unsolved religious, regional and class animosities deriving from the *English* national revolution of Tudor and Jacobean times. Thus, within the *United Kingdom* context, Irish nationalism was a classic example of a movement of peripheral protest, reinforced by religious differences, economic contrasts and, of course, both agrarian and urban labour/employer tensions, often entangled in the traditional religion-based caste distinctions.[18]

The subordination of the urban and rural working classes to nationalism becomes quite comprehensible in view of the fact that the cleavage lines of the combined British-Irish political system overlapped and reinforced each other, giving rise to the peculiarly irreconcilable nature of the opposition. Separatist nationalism based on resistance to the encroachment of the British state, economic protectionism due to the pressure on outmoded craft industries from the British factories, religious differences and anti-city sentiment together formed an 'ideological package' composed of elements which in other countries might be thought to be unconnected or even opposed; as we have seen, Irish socialists, clericalists, anti-clericals, conservatives, liberals and even landlords could be persuaded to see something in the package for themselves. For some, it was the protection of Irish culture, for some, Catholic triumphalism and for others, the establishment of a modernising nation-state under capitalist or socialist principles. Nationalism had such a wide-ranging appeal that nationalists genuinely found unionism incomprehensible, and have rarely grasped the depth of Ulster resistance to separatism. The intensity of the nationalist campaign, together with its longevity, had the result of institutionalising nationalism, or rather the odd-looking blended ideology of separatism, majoritarianism and Catholicism as a permanent and pervasive belief system in Irish popular political culture.[19] Like other belief systems, the Irish 'package' is composed of elements which might be queried on logical grounds as being in conflict with each other, but which do not owe their presence there to logical thought, but to social-psychological processes of cultural inheritance.[20]

The fact that this belief system was already in existence and had very deep and old roots in the traditional culture had enormous consequences for the form which political life was to take after secession. As mentioned earlier, the new party system was a second-generation one, and was inevitably heavily conditioned by the party system of the pre-1922 period. This earlier system was based on religious communal identity and, in the Catholic areas, it tended to be non-competitive, single party and factional, rather like the American Solid South. Sinn Féin and its successor parties inevitably inherited these characteristics; what distinguished Fianna Fáil and Fine Gael was the different sets of characteristics they inherited, the former building, in its early years, on the same agrarian traditions as the old Leagues of Parnell and O'Brien, while Fine Gael built more on the more respectable traditions of the later, 'deagrarianised' UIL and the AOH.

The new state's sovereignty was in doubt, and it remained, for economic purposes, a part of the United Kingdom for much of its early years; in the 1920s, well over nine-tenths of the Irish Free State's trade was with Britain, and even today, the Irish Republic does rather more than half its total trade with the United Kingdom. The attempt to dismantle symbolic and substantive forms of sub-ordination generated social tensions within the new state itself. There was considerable labour/owner trouble, and in principle there was no reason why Catholic/Protestant, Gaelic/English, urban/rural and centre/periphery tensions should not have found separate expression in the party system. Rokkan has in fact noted that something of this sort did occur and that, despite Catholicism being the national religion, Iceland's domestic politics centre around territorial and cultural oppositions 'typical of the Protestant secession state'. The tacit parallel here is with Norway or Finland.[21] There are indeed parallels, but also at least one enormous difference. Irish Catholicism differs from much continental European Catholicism and resembles Protestantism's more nonconformist varieties in being mainly popular as distinct from aristocratic in its recent historical experience. However, unlike popular Protestantism, and like continental Catholicism, Irish Catholicism is intensely bureaucratic and centralised, being very much a reformed Catholicism of the Counter-Reformation. It thus combined the strengths of popularity and centralisation. This combination is oddly and ironically reminiscent of the communist movements of France or Italy and is, in a sense, an independently invented form of 'democratic centralism'.

Thus, although the Irish Free State did develop political forces vaguely reminiscent of those of the Scandinavian states, these forces had to work in the context of a society traditionally integrated by a very united and authoritarian clerical bureaucracy with a long tradition of political leadership. Furthermore, the effect of the ecclesiastical and military models on the development of Irish party organisations in the nineteenth century may have been to encourage the emulation of ecclesiastical organisational styles. These styles included pragmatism, internal unity, authoritarianism and social omnivorousness. These centralising and unifying influences were further heightened by the tradition of militant secret organisation; 'within the Lodge' as an expression meaning confidentiality or 'between ourselves' applies to the style of politics in the Republic at least as much as it does to that of Northern Ireland. These centralising and unifying influences were further intensified by the existence of a highly centralised state apparatus, by the already old tradition of single-party politics and by the extremely well-developed communications system which had put all of Ireland within a few hours reach of Dublin by the 1880s. Thus, the interest-group and cultural/territorial politics 'typical of the Protestant secession state' occurred only in a curiously muffled form, a muffling which was increased by the low levels of economic performance of the new state and the consequent lack of a large and self-confident middle class.

Protestant communities did operate as distinct political groups in the new state, and farmers' and other interests did get some distinct representation. Peripheral protest against the centralisation of power in Dublin received its classic expression in Clann na Talmhan but, more typically, cultural, territorial and religious differences were aggregated within the catch-all parties descended from Sinn Féin and the UIL. Clann na Talmhan was absorbed into Fine Gael. No clerical or 'Christian Democrat' party emerged to cater for the very considerable number of people who espoused integration of Church and state because both Fine Gael and Fianna Fáil, in interestingly different ways, accommodated themselves to clericalism. No 'Gaeltacht Party' emerged, partly because the Irish-speaking communities had little concept of themselves as a linguistic group with a separate political identity; linguistic politics has usually been a speciality of the English-speaking, urban-bred nationalist ideologue rather than of the rather pragmatic, Irish-speaking farmers of the west. Fianna Fáil captured both the Gaeltacht vote and the revivalist vote, two quite distinct groups. These developments were possible because, after 1922, habits of political action left over from pre-independence times persisted; the politics of Ireland as a protesting periphery of the United Kingdom continued in the form of the international politics of Ireland as a peripheral state to the United Kingdom, and the old traditions of peripheralist solidarity worked to the advantage of the cross-class and cross-territorial party organisations of Fianna Fáil and Fine Gael.

Fianna Fáil's early development is worth considering again at this point. Up to World War II, the party was strongly western and peasant in its electoral support. The party gradually exchanged that base for one spread more evenly across the country, and succeeded in completing this exchange at a time when international tension between Ireland and the United Kingdom was greater than at any time since independence; whatever the secret understandings between de Valera and the British government, the population saw neutrality as a dangerous and necessary defiance of British power, and many expected an invasion. Essentially, Fianna Fáil took advantage of two historical peripheries, one superimposed on the other: the western periphery of the Irish state, and the status of nationalist Ireland as a periphery of the pre-1922 United Kingdom. It created a core support of rural, nationalist and poor people who were relatively close to the Gaelic tradition and added a more general constituency of groups interested in protectionist industrialisation, cultural defence and religious fundamentalism. Because of its immense electoral appeal, it was able to further augment its popularity, as Mair has suggested, by representing itself as the only party likely to command a big enough majority to be able to govern alone and therefore as the only party capable of giving the country unified and coherent government. Lastly, the party thrived by re-enacting, in the international arena, the 'stand-up-to-Britain' politics that had made the careers of so many Irish politicians in the nineteenth century. The double-periphery effect submerged urban 'class' politics, favouring a political party which was, from the point of view of the 'old' centre, London, 'hyper-peripheralist' in ethos and support but which was so even from the point of view of Dublin. To strain Rokkan's language only slightly, Ireland was a case of a 'periphery-dominated centre', where the concerns, style and support of a rural society came to dominate the politics even of the state's only true urban centre for a generation.[22] There are signs that the Fianna Fáil tide is ebbing in Dublin, nearly sixty years after independence. It is, however, doing so very slowly, and there is no reason in principle why it should erode.

To return to the Lipset/Rokkan framework, this analysis suggests that Ireland is not so much a deviant case as an extreme one, and that the real problem is the 'unit of analysis' problem, as Coakley has pointed out: the Republic versus 'All-Ireland' versus the British Isles or, as I have suggested, all three units of analysis simultaneously. One of the great but necessary fictions of comparative politics is the bland assumption that states are independent of each other and have domestic political patterns which are unaffected by the outside world. The Irish case makes that assumption look rather unrealistic.[23]

NOTES

Abbreviations

AD UCD   Archives Department, University College, Dublin
LTCD   Library, Trinity College, Dublin
NLI   National Library of Ireland
PROD   Public Record Office, Dublin
PROL   Public Record Office, London
SPO   State Paper Office, Dublin

Chapter 1. Irish Parties and Irish Politics (PAGES 1–15)

1. Leon Epstein, *Political Parties in Western Democracies*, New York 1967, 138; D. Urwin and K. Eliassen, 'In Search of a Continent: The Quest of Comparative European Politics', *European Journal of Political Research*, 11 (1974), 85–113.
2. Cf. S. Rokkan, *Citizens, Elections, Parties*, Oslo 1970, 125–6.
3. Louis Hartz, *The Founding of New Societies*, New York 1964, *passim*. But see J.G.A. Pocock, 'The Limits and Divisions of British History', Glasgow 1979.
4. Cf. M. McDunphy, *The President of Ireland*, Dublin 1945, 3–4.
5. S.P. Huntington, *Political Order in Changing Societies*, New Haven 1968, 75. The standard study of Ireland as a colony of England is still E. Strauss, *Irish Nationalism and British Democracy*, London 1951.
6. Huntington, 78.
7. Cf. M. Marriott, 'Cultural Policy in the New States', in C. Geertz (ed.), *Old Societies and New States*, New York 1963, 27–56.
8. A.D. Smith, 'Introduction: the Formation of Nationalist Movements', in his *Nationalist Movements*, London 1976, 1–30, at 19–20.
9. G. Almond and G.B. Powell, *Comparative Politics*, Boston 1969, 23. See also G. Almond and S. Verba, *The Civic Culture*, Princeton 1963.
10. B. Chubb, *The Government and Politics of Ireland*, London 1969, 43–60. Cf. J. Raven, Christopher Whelan *et al.*, *Political Culture in Ireland*, Dublin 1976.
11. D. Schmitt, *The Irony of Irish Democracy*, Lexington 1973.
12. House of Commons, *Reports . . . on the State of Ireland, 1825*, 76. On the distinctiveness of Ulster, M. Heslinga, *The Irish Border as a Cultural Divide*, Assen (Netherlands) 1963.
13. E. Rumpf and A. Hepburn, *Nationalism and Socialism in Twentieth-Century Ireland*, Liverpool 1977, 38–57.

14. Rumpf and Hepburn, 3.

15. Cf. Heslinga, *passim* as well as the British and Irish Communist Organisation's lively analysis conceding the 'modernising' role of the Catholic Church in its anonymous pamphlet, 'Against Ulster Nationalism', Belfast 1975.

16. For some interesting insights into the later stages of this modernisation process, Joseph Lee, *The Modernisation of Irish Society, 1848–1918*, Dublin 1974, and Brian Farrell, *The Founding of Dáil Éireann*, Dublin 1971, ix–xx.

17. J.T. Gilbert, *Documents Relating to Ireland, 1795–1804*, Shannon 1970 (first published Dublin 1893, a reprint of parliamentary committee reports from the 1790s), 167. The ideas and images of the French Revolution penetrated into even the agrarian/sectarian peasant organisation of the Defenders, the purveyors often being schoolmasters (see Chapter 2). In 1793 Meath Defenders were ordering assassinations and intimidation in the name of their 'sekrit comitti' or very Jacobin-sounding 'Comitti of Public Safety'; cf. S. Ó Loinsigh, 'The Rebellion of 1798 in Meath', *Riocht na Midhe* IV, 33–40. The political awareness of the ordinary people contrasted oddly with the almost medieval cultural ethos.

Chapter 2. The Origins of Irish Popular Politics (PAGES 16–37)

1. R. Kee, *The Green Flag*, London 1972, differs. On the 1641 rebels, M. Hickson, *Ireland in the Seventeenth Century*, London, two vols, 1884. Quotes from vol. I, 169–70 and 325. On the Gaelic poets, Cecile O'Rahilly, *Five Seventeenth-Century Political Poems*, Dublin 1952. On primordial political identity in Ireland, D. Ó Corráin, 'Nationality and Kingship in Pre-Norman Ireland' in T.W. Moody, *Nationality and the Pursuit of Independence*, Belfast 1978, 1–36. For a fascinating account of the early use of political prophecy to encourage national resistance to the English in both Ireland and Wales, K. Thomas, *Religion and the Decline of Magic*, Harmondsworth 1978, 472–3. Many later Irish nationalist prophecies were descended from religious prophecies fortelling the fall of Protestantism. Such prophecies were popular in England as well, and persisted in some areas for centuries after the Reformation. Thomas remarks (op. cit., 493) '. . . political prophecies tended to be invoked at a time of crisis, usually to demonstrate that some drastic change, either desired or already accomplished, had been foreseen by the sages of the past. In this way prophecies were felt to provide a sanction both for resistance to established authority and for the consolidation of a new regime.' cf. P. O'Farrell, 'Millenialism, Messianism and Utopianism in Irish History', *Anglo-Irish Studies*, II (1976), 45–68.

2. Richard Bagwell, *Ireland Under the Stuarts* II, London 1909, 154–5.

3. Charles O'Kelly, *The Destruction of Cyprus*, Dublin 1850, 15, 23–6.

4. John Gilbert (ed.), *A Jacobite Narrative of the War in Ireland, 1688–1691*, Shannon 1971, viii and *passim*.

5. G.D. Zimmermann, *Irish Political Street Ballads and Rebel Songs, 1780–1900*, Geneva 1966, 90–91; T.N. Brown, 'Nationalism and the Irish Peasant, 1800–1848' in *Review of Politics*, XV (October 1953), 403–45, at 423–4.

6. As cited in L.M. Cullen, 'The Hidden Ireland: Reassessment of a Concept', *Studia Hibernica*, IX (1969), 7–47, at 25.

7. Alan Buford, *Gaelic Folk-Tales and Medieval Romances*, Dublin 1969, 55.

8. Crofton Croker, *Researches in the South of Ireland*, Shannon 1969, 328. Schoolmasters with 'levelling', nationalist or blended ideologies were of some importance during the 1790s; cf. J. Brady, 'Lawrence O'Connor— A Meath Schoolmaster', *Irish Ecclesiastical Record*, 5th series, XLIX (March 1937), 281–7; S. Ó Coindealbháin, 'The United Irishmen in Cork County', *Cork Archaeological and Historical Society Journal*, 2nd series, LIII (1948), 115–29, on Micheál Óg Ó Longáin, ex-Whiteboy, Gaelic scholar, schoolmaster and United Irish organiser in Cork. His committee consisted mainly of 'opulent farmers'.

9. Croker, 328–9; William Carleton, *The Party Fight and Funeral*, Cork 1973, 119–25. 'Poetry' from Lady Gregory (ed.), *Mr Gregory's Letter-Box, 1813–1830*, London 1898, 26.

10. A. Ó Suilleabháin, *Cinnlae*, Dublin 1936–7, four vols, vol. I, entries for 9 October 1827 and 5 January 1828; vol. II, entry for 25 June 1830; vol. IV, 109–15.

11. On Raftery, D. de hÍde, *Abhráin agus Dánta an Reachtabhraigh*, Dublin 1974, 18–19, 124–9.

12. D. O'Donovan Rossa, *Recollections*, Shannon 1972, 332–3; Cullen, 20–25; cf. D. Corkery, *The Hidden Ireland*, Dublin 1967.

13. J. Scott, 'Hegemony and the Peasantry', *Politics and Society*, VII (1977), 267–96, at 283–4.

14. D. Sabean, 'The Communal Basis of Pre-1800 Peasant Uprisings in Western Europe', *Comparative Politics*, VIII (1976), 355–64.

15. M. O'Connell, 'Class Conflict in a Pre-Industrial Society: Dublin in 1780', *Irish Ecclesiastical Record*, CIII (1965), 93–106, at 96–9.

16. O'Connell, 98, 102.

17. W. Lecky, *History of Ireland in the Eighteenth Century* II, London 1892, 392–3.

18. D.A. Chart (ed.), *Drennan Letters*, Belfast 1931, 51.

19. T.W. Tone, *Autobiography*, Dublin n.d., two vols, vol. I, 26. Cf. T.W. Moody, 'The Political Ideas of the United Irishmen', *Ireland Today*, III, 1 (January 1938), 15–38.

20. Tone, vol. I, 73; Kee, 41–62.

21. Chart, 54.

22. Source for Table 1, R.B. McDowell, 'The Personnel of the Dublin Society of United Irishmen, 1791–4', *Irish Historical Studies*, II (1940–41), 12–20. Cf. the very similar backgrounds of English Jacobin activists in the 1790s in E.P. Thompson, *The Making of the English Working Class*, Harmondsworth 1977, 111–203. The British and Irish activists were in friendly communication. By 1798, all seemed to have agreed on Irish republican independence (Thompson, 187). Cf. W.B. Kennedy, 'The Irish Jacobins', *Studia Hibernica*, XVI (1976), 109–21.

23. 'Memoir . . . of the Origin and Progress of the Irish Union', in J. Gilbert, *Documents Relating to Ireland, 1795–1804*, Shannon 1970, 147–62, at 153–4.

24. Cf. F. Gross, *The Revolutionary Party*, Westport 1974, xiv–xv and 122–4.

25. Cf. English agrarian movements of the early nineteenth century as described in E.J. Hobsbawm and G. Rudé, *Captain Swing*, London 1969. See also F. Braudel's survey of early modern Mediterranean banditry and its blend of economic and political motivation in his *The Mediterranean and the Mediterranean World in the Age of Philip II*, London 1975, two vols, 734–56. He remarks (751), 'Banditry . . . was a latent form of the *jacquerie*, or peasant revolt, the product of poverty and overpopulation; a revival of old traditions, often of brigandage in its "pure" state of savage conflict between man and man. But we should beware of reducing it merely to this last aspect, the one most stressed by the rich and powerful . . .' cf. also E.J. Hobsbawm, *Bandits*, Harmondsworth 1972.

26. G.C. Lewis, *On Local Disturbances in Ireland*, London 1836, 3–4.

27. A. Young, *A Tour in Ireland*, Shannon 1970, 153.

28. As cited in Lewis, 12.

29. Young, 429.

30. J. Rush, *Hibernia Curiosa*, London 1782, 136.

31. R. Musgrave, *Memoirs of the . . . Rebellions in Ireland*, Dublin 1801, 534. House of Commons, *Report . . . on Orange Lodges*, London 1835, 33.

32. W.H. Crawford and B. Trainor, *Aspects of Irish Social History, 1750–1800*, Belfast 1969, 171–5.

33. Tone, I, 98.

34. Crawford and Trainor, 181–2.

35. Musgrave, 534.

36. Musgrave, appendix IX, 20–23.

37. F. Plowden, *Historical Review of the State of Ireland* II, London 1803, 460.

38. Musgrave, 57–9; Lecky, III, 390–92; but see Brady. The Irish House of Lords commented in 1793 that the Defenders' measures 'appear to have been concerted and conducted with the utmost secrecy and a degree of regularity and system not usual in people in such mean condition, and as if directed by men of a superior rank'. *Report from the Secret Committee of the House of Commons*, Dublin 1798, 37–41. Cf. my 'Defenders, Ribbonmen and Others', University College, Dublin, mimeo, 1980.

39. Cf. *Report . . . on Orange Lodges*, 4; *Memoir of Jemmy Hope*, Belfast 1972, 16.
40. Pakenham, *Year of Liberty*, 228.
41. 'Memoir . . . of the Irish Union', 149.
42. Crofton Croker, *Memoirs of Holt* I, London 1838, 210–21, quote from 210.
43. E. Hay, *History of the Insurrection of the County Wexford*, Dublin 1803, 88 and Appendix V, xxv–xxvi.
44. Musgrave, 42–4.
45. Musgrave, 42–7.
46. C. Dickson, *Life of Michael Dwyer*, Dublin 1944, 25–7; M.V. Ronan (ed.), *Insurgent Wicklow*, Dublin 1948.
47. 'Memoir . . . of the Irish Union', 150.
48. J. Beresford, *Correspondence* II, London 1854, 128.
49. R. McHugh (ed.), *Carlow in '98*, 64–75.
50. As cited by Castlereagh, *Memoirs and Correspondence* I, London 1848, 354.
51. Gilbert, *Documents*, 115.
52. R. Madden, *United Irishmen*, second series, Dublin 1858, 396; M. Byrne, *Memoirs of Myles Byrne*, Shannon 1972, 55–6.
53. For the already classic account of the Rising, Pakenham, *Year of Liberty*.
54. C. Ross (ed.), *Cornwallis Correspondence* II, London 1859, 355–8 and 404.
55. Ross, III, 306–7.

Chapter 3. The Development of Nationalist Popular Politics, 1800–48
(PAGES 38–59)

1. Lewis, *Local Disturbances*; J.S. Donnelly, 'The Whiteboy Movement, 1761–5', *Irish Historical Studies*, XXI, No. 81, 20–54; D. Trant, *Considerations on the Present Disturbances in the Province of Munster*, Dublin 1787; R. Kernan, *The Trial of the Caravats and Shanavests*, Dublin 1811 and Maureen Wall's pioneering 'The Whiteboys' in T.D. Williams (ed.), *Secret Societies in Ireland*, Dublin 1973, 13–25. Donnelly reports that the Whiteboys were often led by artisans, sometimes Protestant by religion, and used a mixture of Jacobite and *Aisling*-style symbols. Their cry was 'Long Live George the 3rd and Queen Sive', Sive being an old woman who symbolised Ireland; these two monarchs were not yet regarded as irreconcilable.
2. E.D. Steele, *Irish Land and British Politics*, Cambridge 1974, 7.
3. Wall, *passim*.
4. B.L. Solow, *The Land Question and the Irish Economy*, Cambridge 1971, 196–201.
5. House of Commons, *Reports . . . on the State of Ireland, 1825*, 70.
6. Wellington, *Civil Correspondence and Memoranda: Ireland*, London 1860, 139–41.
7. Wellington, 331–3; Kernan suggests the factions were actually sporting and local, with agrarian and non-political undertones. Sport can carry

political freight, as Glasgow football teams demonstrate. Six Shanavests and two Caravats were sent to Kilkenny jail in 1834. One Caravat was a *spailpín* (labourer), the other a Protestant weaver. Of the Shanavests, one was a *spailpín*, one a farmer's son, one a shoemaker and two were 'prosperous persons' (Ó Suilleabháin, *Cinnlae*, IV, entry for 1 August 1834).

8. S. Ó Muireadaigh, '*Buachaillí na Carraige*', *Galvia*, IX (1962), 4–13.

9. House of Commons, *Report on the State of Ireland*, 1831–2, 123.

10. *Report . . . on the State of Ireland, 1825*, 85.

11. Ibid., 397.

12. Ibid., 401–2.

13. Lewis, 124.

14. *Report . . . on the State of Ireland, 1831–32*, 139.

15. R.L. Sheil, *Legal and Political Sketches* I, London 1832, 258–66 and 287–316; House of Commons, *Poor Inquiry (Ireland)*, Appendix H, II, London 1836, 37.

16. On Ribbonism, Garvin, 'Defenders, Ribbonmen and Others'. On Swatragh, PROL CO 904 7, Hines to Drummond, 25 July 1839.

17. Gregory, *Letter-Box*, Gregory to Peel, 4 May 1816. Cf. generally LTCD 869/1, Sirr Papers.

18. S. Ó Muireadaigh, 'Na Fir Ribín', *Galvia* X (1964–5), 18–32, at 28.

19. PROL CO 904 7, Kelly, 6 December 1837; Anonymous, *Report of the Trial of Michael Keenan*, Dublin 1822.

20. PROL CO 904 8, statement of M. McGarry, September 1841. On police rumours on Jones, F. Porter, *Gleanings and Reminiscences*, Dublin 1875, 198.

21. PROL CO 904 8, 'Ribbonism'.

22. *Report . . . on the State of Ireland, 1825*, 125–6; *Report on the State of Ireland in Respect of Crime, 1839*, London 1839, 191–9; PROL CO 904 7, statement of Kelly, 6 December 1837. Some of the phraseology is identical to that of Defender oaths of the previous century, cf. W. Carleton, *Autobiography*, London 1968, 76–84.

23. House of Lords, *Report . . . on the State of Ireland . . . 1839*, 405, 422–3.

24. Ibid., 426–7.

25. W.J. FitzPatrick, *Correspondence of Daniel O'Connell*, London 1888, 113; PROL CO 904 7.

26. *Report . . . on the State of Ireland . . . 1839*, 369; on Armstrong incident, W.J. FitzPatrick, *The Secret Service under Pitt*, London 1892, 333.

27. House of Lords, *Summary Digest . . . of Evidence taken before the 'Select Committee . . . on the State of Ireland . . .*, London 1839, xvii–xx.

28. *Report . . . 1839*, 413, 1125–6.

29. Houses of Parliament, *Report . . . on Bribery at Elections, 1836*, Shannon 1968, 364.

30. PROL CO 904 7, Kelly.
31. PROL CO 904 8, McGarry. Cf. Lewis, 225. The Dublin Ribbonmen remonstrated with their Ulster rivals about their exploitation of the people; cf. M.J. Martyn, *An Authentic Report of the Trial of Richard Jones*, Dublin 1840, 149–50. The Dubliners may have been 'shopped' by the Ulstermen in 1839.
32. A.M. Sullivan, *New Ireland*, London 1877, 36–45; *The Times*, 2 July 1840; *Irish Law Reports*, IV, 264–8; Martyn, *passim*.
33. PROL CO 904 8, *passim* and statement of CD; PROL CO 904 9, Hogan, O'Brien, February 1842; Martyn, 150.
34. *Dublin University Magazine*, X (1837), 628; XI (1838), 129.
35. PROL CO 904 8, Hogan.
36. M. Doheny, *The Felon's Track*, Dublin 1951, 289–96.
37. *Evidence Taken . . . in respect to the Occupation of Land in Ireland* (Devon Commission) II, Dublin 1845, 660.
38. D. Lerner, *The Passing of Traditional Society*, Glencoe 1958; K. Deutsch, 'Social Mobilisation and Political Development', *American Political Science Review*, LV (September 1961), 493–514.
39. S. Lipset and S. Rokkan, 'Party Systems and Voter Alignments: An Introduction', in their *Party Systems and Voter Alignments*, Toronto 1967, 1–64.
40. *Report . . . on the State of Ireland, 1825*, 143–4, 269, 323; C. Gavan Duffy, *Young Ireland*, New York 1973, 72–8.
41. *Report . . . 1825*, 270.
42. Ó Muireadaigh, 'Na Fir Ribín', 19; LTCD 869/1, Sirr Papers.
43. T. McCullagh, *Sheil's Memoirs* I, London 1855, 187.
44. On O'Connell's career, K.B. Nowlan, *The Politics of Repeal*, London 1973.
45. The Volunteer symbols were borrowed again in the twentieth century by unionist and separatist forces alike.
46. Emancipation's quid pro quo was a severe narrowing of the franchise. On the Liberator's electioneering, G.J. Lyne, 'Daniel O'Connell, Intimidation and the Kerry Elections of 1835', *Journal of the Kerry Archaeological Society*, IV (1971), 74–97.
47. G. Broeker, *Rural Disorder and Police Reform in Ireland, 1812–1836*, 190–92.
48. Nor was he over-enthusiastic about mobilising the masses, at times. See FitzPatrick, *Correspondence*, I, 112.
49. O. MacDonagh, *Ireland*, London 1977, 53–4; D. Bowen, *The Protestant Crusade in Ireland, 1800–70*, Dublin 1978.
50. McCullagh, I, 288–9.
51. House of Lords, *Report . . . 1839*, 838.
52. Ibid., 837; Sheil, II, 137.
53. House of Commons, *Report . . . 1832*, 123.

54. Ibid., 85.

55. FitzPatrick, I, 265–6, 72.

56. Zimmermann, 46.

57. FitzPatrick, II, 291–2.

58. W.J. O'Neill Daunt, *Ireland and her Agitators*, Dublin 1845, 239–40.

59. F. D'Arcy, *Dublin Artisan Activity, Opinion and Organisation, 1820–50*, M.A. thesis, 1968, University College, Dublin, i and 14.

60. F. D'Arcy, 'The Artisans of Dublin and Daniel O'Connell, 1830–47: An Unquiet Liaison', *Irish Historical Studies*, XVII (1970–71), 221–43.

61. FitzPatrick, I, 272.

62. Ibid., 278–9, 300.

63. D'Arcy, *Artisan Activity . . .*, 54–6.

64. A.D. MacIntyre, *The Liberator*, London 1965, Appendix III.

65. J.H. Whyte, 'Daniel O'Connell and the Repeal Party', *Irish Historical Studies*, XI (1958–9), 297–315, at 314.

66. C. Gavan Duffy, *My Life in Two Hemispheres* I, London 1898, 175.

67. Ibid., 184–8; D'Arcy, *Artisan Activity . . .* 72–3.

68. D'Arcy, 76.

69. Duffy, I, 209.

70. PROL CO 904 9, 'Reports . . . on the State of the Recently Disturbed Districts', January 1849.

Chapter 4. Secret Societies and Party Politics after the Famine (PAGES 60–76)

1. For example, *State of Ireland . . . 1825*, 13; *Poor Inquiry*, Appendix H, II, 1836, 17; T.C. Foster, *Letters on the Condition of the People of Ireland*, London 1846, 331–3.

2. Lewis, 320.

3. Foster, 349–50.

4. E. McKenna, 'Age, Region and Marriage in Post-Famine Ireland: An Empirical Examination', *Economic History Review*, second series, XXXI, 2 (May 1978), 238–56.

5. W. Lecky, *Leaders of Public Opinion in Ireland*, London 1871, xiii.

6. G. Ó Tuathaigh, *Ireland Before the Famine*, Dublin 1972, 47.

7. See, for example, T. Ó Fiach, 'The Clergy and Fenianism, 1860–70', *Irish Ecclesiastical Record*, fifth series, CIX (February 1968), 81–103.

8. Ó Tuathaigh, 57.

9. E. Larkin, 'The Devotional Revolution in Ireland, 1850–75', *American Historical Review*, LXXVII, 3 (June 1972), 625–52. Cf. K. Connell, 'Catholicism and Marriage in the Century after the Famine', in his *Irish Peasant Society*, London 1968, 113–62.

10. Larkin, 648–9.

11. P. Gibbon, *The Origins of Ulster Unionism*, Manchester 1975, *passim*.

12. D. Miller, 'Irish Catholicism and the Great Famine', *Journal of Social History*, IX, 1 (1977), 81–98.

13. *Report of the Royal Commission on the Land Law (Ireland) Act, 1881 and the Purchase of Land (Ireland) Act, 1885* (Cowper Commission), London 1887, *passim* and 568, 976. Cf. P. Bew, *Land and the National Question in Ireland 1858–82*, Dublin 1978, 7–33; cf. generally, S. Clarke, 'The Political Mobilisation of Irish Farmers', *Canadian Review of Anthropology and Sociology*, XII (Part 2), 1975, 483–99.

14. J.H. Whyte, *The Independent Irish Party, 1850–9*, London 1958, 12.

15. Ibid., 158–61.

16. Ibid., 11–12, 56–62.

17. Ibid., 80.

18. House of Commons, *Report from the Select Committee on Parliamentary Elections*, London 1869, xviii, 293–6, 337.

19. Ibid., 289.

20. Ibid., 478.

21. Ibid., 174.

22. Ibid., 176–7, 207, 215–16. Cf. K.T. Hoppen, 'Landlords, Society and Electoral Politics in Mid-Nineteenth-Century Ireland', *Past and Present*, No. 75 (May 1977), 62–93.

23. Hoppen, 78–81.

24. Nassau William Senior, *Journals* II, 1868, 56–7.

25. G. Shaw Lefevre, *Combination and Coercion*, London 1980, 65–70.

26. *Report . . . on Elections, 1869*, 29–30.

27. J. O'Leary, *Recollections of Fenians and Fenianism*, I, London 1896, 50.

28. NLI MS 7722, Larcom Papers, clippings from *Evening Packet*, 10, 11 December 1858; *Daily Express*, 14 December 1858; *Freeman's Journal*, 15 December 1858.

29. J. Devoy, *Recollections of an Irish Rebel*, New York: 1929, 21. Cf. NLI MS 331–3, Luby Papers.

30. D. Ryan, *The Fenian Chief*, Dublin 1967, 93–100.

31. M. Ryan, *Fenian Memories*, Dublin 1945, 66.

32. Ibid., 49–51.

33. Anon., *The Repeal of the Union Conspiracy*, London 1886, 9–10.

34. 'Cato' [John Devoy], 'The Fenian Organisation in Ireland', NLI MS 15378, Devoy Papers.

35. Devoy, *Recollections*, 26. On the social status of Limerick Fenians, B. Mac Giolla Choille, 'Mourning the Martyrs', *North Munster Antiquarian Journal* X (1966–7), 173–205. There were few farmers, many shopkeepers and artisans, and procession leaders and those of the 'worst Fenian character' were bakers, tailors and other artisans, cf. also NLI MS 915,

describing Fenianism in 1863 as a town movement but as also beginning to inherit well-established Ribbon traditions in the Midlands and south Ulster.

36. O'Leary, II, 238–9; L. Ó Broin, *Revolutionary Underground*, Dublin 1976, 21.
37. SPO FP Carton 1, 'Return to Special Commission, April 1867, Prisoners Arrested and Committed'.
38. Ibid.
39. SPO A Files, A124.
40. W. Bence Jones, *A Life's Work in Ireland*, London 1880, 62.
41. Ibid., 67.
42. L. Ó Broin, *Fenian Fever*, London 1971, 163–4; M. Tierney, *Croke of Cashel*, Dublin 1976, 93–4.
43. M. Ryan, 32–7.
44. Ibid., 42.
45. *Report . . . on Elections, 1869*, 208–10.
46. Ibid., 209.
47. T.D. Sullivan, *A.M. Sullivan*, Dublin 1885, 121–2.
48. Figures for 1878, NLI MS 18025, Devoy Papers.
49. J. Rutherford, *The Fenian Conspiracy* I, London 1977, 86–8. Cf. NLI MS 915.
50. NLI MS 331–3, Luby Papers.
51. O'Leary, I, 111.
52. Ibid., I, 132.
53. SPO CBS 126/S and attachments; GAA, *Sixty Glorious Years of the GAA*, Dublin 1947, 22–6; W.F. Mandle, 'The IRB and the Beginnings of the Gaelic Athletic Association', *Irish Historical Studies*, XX, No. 80 (September 1977), 418–38 and E. De Blaghd, 'Cold War in the Dublin GAA, 1887', *Dublin Historical Record*, XXII (1968), 252–62. Cf. M. Bourke, 'The Early GAA in South Ulster', *Clogher Record* VII (1967), 5–26.
54. SPO CBS 126/S and attachments.
55. Ibid.
56. SPO CBS 2452/S; SPO CBS 4467/S.
57. SPO CBS 2786/S.
58. SPO CBS DICS carton no. 3, May 1888.

Chapter 5. Aggrarianism, Nationalism and Party Politics, 1874–95 (PAGES 77–98)

1. D. Thornley, *Isaac Butt and Home Rule*, London 1964, 125.
2. Ibid., 138–9.
3. Ibid., 207; F.S.L. Lyons, *The Irish Parliamentary Party, 1890–1910*, London 1951, 169.
4. H. Staehle, 'Statistical Notes on the Economic History of Irish Agriculture, 1847–1913', *Journal of the Social and Statistical Society of*

Ireland, XVIII (1950–51), 444–51; quote from T. Barrington, 'A Review of Irish Agricultural Prices', ibid., XV (1927), 249–80, at 255.

5. Cf. K. Deutsch, *Nationalism and Social Communication*, Cambridge 1956, 123–30.

6. Solow, 145–6.

7. Cf. Deutsch; Clarke, 'Social Mobilisation'; J.C. Davies, 'Toward a Theory of Revolution', *American Sociological Review*, XXVII (1962), 5–19.

8. W.H. Hurlbert, *Ireland Under Coercion* II, Edinburgh 1888, 193–4.

9. W. Bence Jones, 18–19, 139–40.

10. F. MacRugh, 'Who Killed the "Bad Earl" of Leitrim?', *The Irish Times*, 27 May 1978.

11. NLI MS 13502, Gill Papers.

12. *Proceedings of the Dublin Mansion House Relief Committee*, Dublin 1881, 11 and *passim*.

13. W.L. Féingold, 'The Tenants' Movement to Capture the Irish Poor Law Boards, 1877–86', *Albion*, VII (1975), 216–31.

14. Cf. for example, Sir Charles Russell, *The Parnell Commission: The Opening Speech for the Defence*, London 1889, 336–7.

15. E. Rumpf and A. Hepburn, *Nationalism and Socialism in Twentieth-Century Ireland*, Liverpool 1977, 52. It should be remembered that much of the 1880s violence took place outside Ireland and much of it was perpetrated by the Irish-Americans, cf. K.R.M. Short, *The Dynamite War*, Dublin 1979; H. Le Caron, *Twenty-five Years in the Secret Service*, London 1892.

16. For example, Liberal Unionist Association, *Parnell Commission Report*, London 1890; Hurlbert, *passim*; H.B. Pollard, *The Secret Societies of Ireland*, London 1922, 80–95.

17. Source for Table 2: *Return of Outrages Reported to the Constabulary Office, 1846–1860* and ibid., for 1861–1880, London 1861 and 1881. Eviction figures from PP 1881 (185) LXXVII.

18. *Freeman's Journal*, 20 September 1880.

19. As cited in T.P. O'Connor, *The Parnell Movement*, London 1886, 348.

20. W. O'Brien and D. Ryan, *Devoy's Post Bag* II, Dublin 1948 and 1953, 21–5.

21. SPO ILL/INL, carton 7.

22. Data on INL branches for 1880s, ibid., and carton 10.

23. Rumpf and Hepburn, 52.

24. SPO ILL/INL, cartons 7 and 10.

25. D.S. Jones, *Agrarian Capitalism and Rural Social Development in Ireland*, Ph.D. thesis, Queen's University, Belfast 1977, 35.

26. SPO ILL/INL, carton 6.

27. C.C. O'Brien, *Parnell and His Party*, Oxford 1957, 125, 132 and *passim*.

28. NLI MS 8933 and 9484.

29. NLI MS 8933.

30. SPO CBS DICS, carton 4, January 1889.

31. D.D. Sheehan, *Ireland Since Parnell*, London 1921, 168.

32. S. Clarke, 'The Social Composition of the Land League', *Irish Historical Studies*, XVII, No. 68 (1971), 447–69.

33. F.H. O'Donnell, *A History of the Irish Parliamentary Party* I, London 1910, 369.

34. F.S.L. Lyons, *Ireland Since the Famine*, London 1973, 195–6.

35. T.P. O'Connor, 315.

36. C.C. O'Brien, 326–34.

37. M. Davitt, *The Fall of Feudalism in Ireland*, London and New York 1904, 643.

38. J. Horgan, *Parnell to Pearse*, Dublin 1948, 58–9.

39. *Freeman's Journal*, 15 July 1892.

40. As cited in J.V. O'Brien, *William O'Brien and the Course of Irish Politics, 1881–1918*, Berkeley, n.d., 92.

41. LTCD, Davitt Papers, 3761–869.

42. As quoted in P.H. Bagenal, *The Priest in Politics*, London 1893, 112.

43. Ibid., 85–6, 92.

44. SPO CBS 4467/S, 7828/S 2831/S and 2701/S. Quote from 2701/S.

45. SPO CBS 4467/S, 7828/S.

46. SPO CBS 7828/S, 2828/S.

47. SPO CBS 2828/S.

48. SPO CBS 11921/S.

49. O'Donnell, II, 342.

50. SPO CBS DICS, carton 1, July 1889.

51. SPO CBS DICS, carton 1, January 1888.

52. SPO CBS DICS, carton 2, April 1889.

53. SPO CBS DICS, carton 2, August 1890.

54. SPO CBS DICS, carton 4, January 1890.

55. Paul Bew, in his *Land and the National Question in Ireland*, urges us not to read the sectarianism of the 1970s into the struggles of the 1880s (217–19). It is valid, however, to read the sectarianism of the late eighteenth century into the politics of the late nineteenth century; in that sense, the fall of Parnell marked a return to normal.

Chapter 6. The Reconstruction of Nationalist Politics, 1891–1910 (PAGES 99–110)

1. O'Brien, *William O'Brien*, 98–100.

2. Lyons, *Irish Parliamentary Party*, 41–5, and his 'The Machinery of the Irish Parliamentary Party in the General Election of 1895', *Irish Historical Studies*, VIII (1952–53), 115–39.

3. Lyons, 'Machinery', 122–3 and *passim*.

4. Lyons, *Parliamentary Party*, 131–2.

5. C.C. O'Brien, '1891–1916', in his *Writers and Politics*, London 1976, 121–31. Source for Table 6, SPO CBS 2828/S and 26268/S.

6. For O'Brien's own view, see his *An Olive Branch in Ireland and its History*, London 1910, 97.

7. *Olive Branch*, 106.

8. SPO CBS 17425A/S.

9. D.S. Jones, *Agrarian Capitalism, passim*.

10. SPO CBS 25435/S.

11. SPO CBS21933/S.

12. LTCD, Davitt Papers, 3761–9, Featley to O'Brien, 22 July 1898.

13. Ibid., O'Brien to Davitt, 30 November 1898.

14. Ibid., and 4677–734.

15. SPO CBS 17425 A/S.

16. J.V. O'Brien, 132–3; SPO CBS 26449/S.

17. SPO CBS 26449/S; 27478/S.

18. SPO CBS, *Inspector-General's Reports*, December 1899, July, August 1900.

19. Ibid., August 1900.

20. Ibid., June, August 1900; *The Irish Times*, 10 September 1907.

21. C.B. Shannon, *Local Government in Ireland, the Politics of Administration*, M.A. thesis, University College, Dublin 1963, *passim*.

22. SPO CBS, *Inspector-General's Reports*, January 1899.

23. Ibid., March, April 1899.

24. O'Donnell, II, 475.

25. SPO CBS 114/S. On the AOH, M.T. Foy's pioneering M.A. thesis, *The Ancient Order of Hibernians*, Queen's University, Belfast (1976), *passim*.

26. J.J. Bergin, *History of the Ancient Order of Hibernians*, Dublin 1910, 12–35; Pollard, 3–4, 37–8, 110–15; the best account of the AOH in this period is A.C. Hepburn's 'The Ancient Order of Hibernians in Irish Politics, 1905–14', *Cithara* X, 2 (1971), 5–18. Cf. Bourke, 'Early GAA' on AOH–GAA relations in south Ulster.

27. On Hibernianism between 1887 and 1891, SPO DBS DICS, carton 1, June 1889; carton 4, January, March 1890, January, February 1891.

28. SPO CBS, *Inspector-General's Reports*, August 1906; SPO CBS 26268/S.

29. SPO CBS, *Inspector-General's Reports*, August 1909, 1909 *passim* and 1912 *passim*; Hepburn, 10.

30. Hepburn, 6–7.

31. NLI MS 15181, Redmond Papers, Devlin to Redmond, 22 June 1907.

32. Hepburn, 7.

33. O'Brien, *Olive Branch* . . ., 435–40; Hepburn, 12–13.

34. As cited in Irish Unionist Alliance, *Ireland and the Union*, Dublin 1914, 53.

35. O'Donnell, II, 388.

36. Hepburn, 14; PROL CO 903 19.

37. PROL CO 904 89, CO 904 120.

38. AD UCD, P7a/209, Mulcahy Papers, M. O Muirthile, *Memoir*, 113.

39. Liam Deasy, *Toward Ireland Free*, Cork 1973, 36.

40. Foy, 150.

41. Ibid., 155.

42. Maurice Manning, in his *The Blueshirts*, Dublin 1972, argues cogently for the *sui generis* character of this movement.

Chapter 7. The New Nationalism and Military Conspiracy, 1900–16 (PAGES 111–125)

1. Martin J. Waters, 'Peasants and Emigrants: Consideration of the Gaelic League as a Social Movement', in D.J. Casey and R.E. Rhodes (eds.), *Views of the Irish Peasantry*, Hamdon 1977, 160–217.

2. NLI MS 11127; A.S. Cohan, *The Irish Political Elite*, Dublin 1972, 26–7.

3. A.S. Cohan, *Revolutionary and Non-Revolutionary Elites: The Irish Political Elite in Transition, 1919–1969*, Ph.D. dissertation, University of Georgia, 1970, 140 and 162.

4. M. Brown, *The Politics of Irish Literature*, London 1972, 354.

5. As cited in Lyons, *Ireland Since the Famine*, 226.

6. In general, D.P. Moran, *Philosophy of Irish Ireland*, Dublin 1905.

7. A.D. Smith (ed.), *Nationalist Movements*, London 1976, 16.

8. Cf. J. Newsinger, '"I Bring not Peace but a Sword": The Religious *Motif* in the Irish War of Independence', *Journal of Contemporary History*, XIII (July 1978), 609–28.

9. Cf. H. Tudor, *Political Myth*, London 1972.

10. Ibid., 138.

11. Cf. F. Hearn, 'Remembrance and Critique: The Use of the Past for Discrediting the Present and Anticipating the Future', *Politics and Society*, V (1975), 201–27; D. McCartney, 'The Political Use of History in the Work of Arthur Griffith', *Journal of Contemporary History*, VIII (1973), 3–20.

12. SPO CBS *Inspector-General's Reports*, September 1903.

13. M.A. Laffan, *The Development of Sinn Féin, 1916–1917*, M.A. thesis, University College, Dublin 1968, *passim*.

14. D. Lynch, *The IRB and the 1916 Insurrection*, Cork 1957, 24 and 150. See in general L. Ó Broin's *Revolutionary Underground*, Dublin 1976.

15. NLI MS 11127, 25.

16. NLI MS 13170, Hobson Papers.

17. SPO CBS 26268/S.

18. NLI MS 11127, 26–32.

19. Ibid., 24.

20. AD UCD P7/D/14, Mulcahy Papers; PROL CO 904 118, August 1908.

21. PROL CO 904 118, May 1909.

22. As cited in W. Thompson, *The Imagination of an Insurrection*, New York 1967, 81.

23. NLI MS 13171, Hobson Papers.

24. M. Denieffe, 'The Men of the West who Knew Pearse', *Sunday Independent*, 4 March 1979; D. FitzGerald, *Memoirs*, London 1968, 43.

25. J.T. Gilbert, *Documents Relating to Ireland*, 99.

26. PROL CO 904 120.

27. As cited in Dáil Éireann, *The National Police and the Courts of Justice*, Dublin 1921, 11; emigration figures from W.E. Vaughan and A.J. Fitzpatrick, *Irish Historical Statistics: Population, 1821–1971*, Dublin: 1978, 264–5.

28. A. Hirschman, *Exit, Voice and Loyalty*, Cambridge 1970, *passim*.

29. NLI MS 13168, Hobson Papers, J.J. O'Connell memoir, 4–6.

30. AD UCD, P7/D/14, Mulcahy Papers, taped interview with Denis McCullough.

31. NLI MS 13,168, Hobson Papers, O'Connell typescript, 4.

32. Ibid.

33. Ibid., 8.

34. AD UCD, P7/D/14, 6.

35. Ibid., 7.

Chapter 8. Elections, Revolution and Civil War, 1916–23 (PAGES 126–147)

1. W. O'Brien, *Forth the Banners Go*, Dublin 1969, 1–8; E. Erikson, *Childhood and Society*, London 1972; see also M. Gallagher, 'Socialism and the Nationalist Tradition in Ireland, 1798–1918', *Éire-Ireland*, XII, 2 (Summer 1977), 63–102.

2. O'Brien, 123–40, 142, 144–6.

3. House of Commons, *Minutes of Evidence of the Royal Commission on the Rebellion in Ireland*, London 1916, 20.

4. Ibid., 22.

5. PROL CO 903 19, PROL CO 904 120.

6. M. Laffan, 'The Unification of Sinn Féin in 1917', *Irish Historical Studies*, XVII (1970–71), 353–79, at 374–8.

7. R. Davis, *Arthur Griffith and Non-violent Sinn Féin*, Dublin 1974, 83; PROL CO 904 20 2. By-election results from B.M. Walker (ed.), *Parliamentary Election Results in Ireland, 1801–1922*, Dublin 1978, 184–5.

8. Lyons, *Ireland Since the Famine*, 392.

9. PROL CO 903 19, 1918.

10. Ibid. PROL CO 904 107, 1918.

11. R. Brennan, *Allegiance*, Dublin 1950, 167–8.

12. P.S. O'Hegarty, *The Victory of Sinn Féin*, Dublin 1924, 74–6.

13. AD UCD P7/D/16, Mulcahy Papers.

14. AD UCD P7a/109.

15. D. Hogan, *The Four Glorious Years*, Dublin 1950, 44.

16. PROL CO 904 107, December 1918; *Irish Independent*, 3 January 1919.

17. On the result, see Lyons, *Ireland Since the Famine*, 398–9.

18. Anon., *The Voice of Ireland*, Dublin n.d. (1919), 4; cf. Hogan, 44–53; *Irish Independent*, 28 December 1918.

19. B. Farrell, *The Founding of Dáil Eireann*, Dublin 1971, 49.

20. Farrell, 45–50; *Voice*, 7–10.

21. Farrell, 45–50.

22. Lyons, *John Dillon*, 451.

23. Rumpf and Hepburn, 56.

24. But cf. Hogan, 53.

25. Farrell, 29–49; P. Mair, 'Labour and the Irish Party System Revisited: Party Competition in the 1920s', *Economic and Social Review*, IX (October 1977).

26. W. O'Brien, 160–61.

27. D. Fitzpatrick, 'The Geography of Irish Nationalism, 1910–1921', *Past and Present*, 78 (February 1978), 113–44, at 131.

28. On post-independence electoral participation, see Chapter 9.

29. Source for Tables 8 and 9: *Voice, passim; Census, 1911, passim*. PROD 2B 82 118, 20; Hogan, 54.

30. Rumpf and Hepburn, 50; Anon., *The Last Post*, Dublin 1976.

31. Rumpf and Hepburn, 41–2.

32. Rumpf and Hepburn, 48.

33. Sources for Tables 10 and 11: as Note 30 and Census, 1881, 1911 and 1926, *passim*.

34. S. Ó Maoileóin, *B'Fhiú an Braon Fola*, Dublin 1958, 145–50.

35. NLI MS 5848, Bourke Papers.

36. AD UCD P7/A/38, Mulcahy Papers.

37. Ibid.

38. Ibid.

39. Ibid.

40. F. O'Donoghue, *No Other Law*, Dublin 1954, 72.

41. AD UCD P7/A/38, Mulcahy Papers.

42. PROL CO 904 109.

43. SPO DE 2/175.

44. Joseph Connolly, TS Memoir, 233–4.

45. Dáil Éireann, *The National Police*, 6; J. Gaughan, *Austin Stack*, Dublin 1977, 293–4.

46. PROL CO 904 117, 1920.

47. *National Police*, 12.

48. Gaughan, 293–4; *National Police*, 8.

49. *National Police*, 22–3.

50. O'Hegarty, 70.

51. Ó Broin, *Revolutionary Underground*, 191–2.

52. Ó Broin, 191–2 and AD UCD P7/C/30, Mulcahy Papers.

53. PROL CO 903 19.

54. S. Cronin, *The McGarrity Papers*, Tralee 1972, 112.

55. Cronin, 110.

56. Cronin, 110–11.

57. Ó Broin, 191–2; AD UCD P7a/109, 167; Ó Maoileóin, 160; E. D'Alton, Interview, RTÉ TV, 22 August 1978; Tom Barry, *Guerrilla Days in Ireland*, 1955, 189–91, for assessments of IRA's poor armament in 1921.

58. AD UCD P7a/109, 175.

59. Cronin, 112.

60. Ó Broin, 181.

61. Cumann na mBan, *Report of Convention*, October 1921, mimeo, 1921; *The Irish Times*, 27 June 1979, letter of R. Mulcahy.

62. Notes of P. O'Keefe in private possession.

63. SPO DE 2/486.

64. Ibid.

65. Ibid.

66. M. Laffan, 'The Sinn Féin Party, 1916–1921', *Capuchin Annual*, 1970, 227–37, at 234.

67. PROL CO 903 19; PROL CO 904 115.

68. PROD2B 82 116.

69. *Freeman's Journal*, 16 March 1922.

70. NLI MS 17436, McGarrity Papers, Collins to McGarrity, 5 April 1922.

71. O'Donoghue, 334; Rumpf and Hepburn, 58.

72. O'Donoghue, 334.

73. *Freeman's Journal*, 1 June 1922; 1922 election results in B. Walker, *Dáil Éireann Election Results, 1922–1944*, Dublin mimeo, 1974.

Chapter 9. The Origins of the Party System in Independent Ireland
(PAGES 148–174)

1. R. Rose and D. Urwin, *Regional Differentiation and Political Unity in Western Nations*, London and Beverly Hills 1975; ibid., 'Persistence and Change in Western Party Systems since 1945', *Political Studies*, XVIII (September 1970), 287; Arend Lijphart, 'Class Voting and Religious Voting in European Democracies', *Acta Politico*, VI (1971), 158–71.

2. The key reference is A. Campbell *et al.*, *The American Voter*, New York 1960; see also S.M. Lipset and S. Rokkan, 'Cleavage Structures, Party Systems and Voter Alignments: An Introduction', and E. Allardt and P. Pesonen, 'Cleavages in Finnish Politics', both in Lipset and Rokkan, *Party Systems and Voter Alignments*, New York 1967, 1–61 and 325–66.

3. Lipset and Rokkan, 'Cleavage Structures', 50.

4. D. Fitzpatrick, *Politics and Irish Life, 1913–21*, Dublin 1977, 133–4.

5. PROL CO 903 19.

6. Sources for Table 12: SPO CBS 2828/S, SPO CBS 26268/S; SPO ILL/INL cartons 7, 10; PROL CO 903 19.

7. W. Moss, *Political Parties in the Irish Free State*, New York 1933, 64.

8. SPO DE 2/147.

9. AD UCD P7/C/99.

10. Ibid.

11. Ibid.

12. Ibid.

13. AD UCD P7/A/11 (d), Notebook 3, No. 2, 73, O'Malley Papers.

14. P.L.R. Horn, 'The National Agricultural Labourers' Movement in Ireland, 1873–79', *Irish Historical Studies*, XVII (March 1971), 340–52; D.D. Sheehan, *Ireland Since Parnell*, London 1921, 168–86; SPO ILL/INL, carton 6; S. Daly, *Cork: a City in Crisis* I, Cork 1978, 109–38.

15. Clarke, 'Social Composition', 452.

16. Sheehan, *passim*.

17. William O'Brien, *Forth the Banners Go*, Dublin 1969, 110–13.

18. *Report of the Registrar of Friendly Societies*, Dublin 1927, 34–46.

19. This suggestion is Peter Mair's.

20. Cf. P. Pyne, 'The Third Sinn Féin Party, 1923–1926', *Economic and Social Review*, I, (1969–70), 29–50 and 229–57 and his 'The Politics of Parliamentary Abstentionism: Ireland's Four Sinn Féin Parties, 1905–26', *Journal of Commonwealth and Comparative Politics*, XII (July 1974), 2, 206–27.

21. PROD 2B 82 116, *Judgement*, 37.

22. S. Ó Faoláin, 'The Admirer and the Disillusioned', *The Irish Times*, 21 April 1976; Connolly memoir, 335–6.

23. PROD 2B 116, *Judgement*, 37.

24. C. Brady, *Police and Government in the Irish Free State, 1922–1933*, M.A. thesis, Department of Politics, University College, Dublin 1977, 36.

25. Pyne, 'Third Sinn Féin Party', 232.

26. PROD 2B 82 119, part I, 46.

27. Ibid., part III, 1–8.

28. *An Phoblacht*, 9 October 1925.

29. Ibid., 16 October 1925.

30. Ibid., 13 November 1925; Sinn Féin, *Clár: Ard Fheis 1925*, 13.

31. Pyne, 43.

32. Pyne, 45.

33. Pyne, 46.

34. Pyne, 48.

35. PROD2B 82 118, 39.

36. PROD 2B 82 116, 6 *et seq.*

37. M. McInerney, 'The Name and the Game', *The Irish Times*, 19 May 1976.
38. M. McInerney, 'From Sinn Féin to Fianna Fáil', *The Irish Times*, 23 July 1974.
39. M. McInerney, 'The Making of a National Party', *The Irish Times*, 16 February 1974.
40. G. McKenna, '"Mind the Organisation", Said Dev', *Irish Press*, 26 May 1976.
41. James Hogan, *Could Ireland Go Communist?*, Dublin 1934.
42. O.D. Edwards, 'Frank Talking in the Era of the Provisional Government', *The Irish Times*, 21 April 1976.
43. NLI MS 17441, McGarrity Papers.
44. NLILO PIII.
45. *Irish Press*, 16 September 1931.
46. Ibid., 17 September 1931.
47. Ibid., 28 September 1931.

Chapter 10. An Analysis of Electoral Politics, 1923–48 (PAGES 175–194)

1. R. Sinnott, 'The Electorate', in H.R. Penniman, *Ireland at the Polls*, Washington 1978, 35–68, at 37–8; cf. V.O. Key, 'A Theory of Critical Elections', *Journal of Politics*, XVII (1955), 3–18.
2. M. Gallagher, *Electoral Support for Irish Political Parties, 1927–73*, London and Beverly Hills 1976, 69.
3. Table 13 reproduces, with revisions, material first presented in my 'Nationalist Elites, Irish Voters and Irish Political Development: A Comparative Perspective', *Economic and Social Review*, VIII (April 1977), 161–86. Election statistics from Walker, *Dáil Éireann Results*. The subsequent analysis also uses some material in a rather heavily reworked form from that article. The argument is also informed by my 'The Destiny of the Soldiers: Tradition and Modernity in the Politics of de Valera's Ireland', *Political Studies*, XXVI (September 1978), 328–47. Figures in Table 13 are percentages subject to rounding error. Labour includes National Labour; section g includes Sinn Féin IV, Clann Éireann, Independent Republicans, National League, communists and Independent Protestants.
4. 'Destiny', 341.
5. 'Third Sinn Féin', 243–4.
6. P. Gibbon and C. Curtin, 'The Stem Family in Ireland', *Comparative Studies in History and Society*, XX (July 1978), 429–53.
7. Mair, 'Labour and the Irish Party System', *passim*.
8. In 1923, a Fianna Fáil catch-cry in Longford was 'We took the Lad down from the counter', the 'Lad' being the cured US bacon which competed with the local product even in farming areas in the unprotected economy of the 1920s.
9. Rumpf and Hepburn, 76–81.

10. Gallagher, *Electoral Support*, 66.

11. Andrew Orridge, personal communication.

12. NLI MS 18376, Gallagher Papers.

13. B. Farrell, 'Labour and the Irish Political Party System: A Suggested Approach to Analysis', *Economic and Social Review*, I, (1969), 477–501.

14. Mair, 62.

15. Labour Party, 'Official Statement Relating to the Disaffiliation from the Labour Party of the ITGWU', Dublin 1944.

16. J. Meenan, *The Irish Economy Since 1922*, Liverpool 1970, 92–107. On the collapse of western smallholder society after 1940, D. Hannan, *Class, Kinship and Social Change in Irish Rural Communities*, Dublin 1979.

17. *Connacht Tribune*, 16 January 1943.

18. Ibid., 29 May 1943.

19. On the 1945 election, 'Destiny', *passim*; on MacBride, MacBride interview, RTÉ TV, 15 March 1972.

20. J. Bowyer Bell, *The Secret Army*, London 1972, 288–9; *The Irish Times*, 31 January 1948.

21. *Irish Press*, 23 January 1948.

22. Gallagher, 57.

23. 'Destiny', 345–6; J. H. Whyte, 'Ireland: Politics Without Social Bases', in R. Rose, *Comparative Electoral Behavior*, 619–52; Gallagher; all *passim*.

24. Government of Ireland, *Report of the Committee on Irish Language Attitudes Research*, Dublin 1975, 29. Cf. *The Irish Times*, 3 and 4 June 1980.

Chapter 11. The Roots of Party and Government in Independent Ireland
(PAGES 195–225)

1. I. McAllister, *The Northern Ireland Social Democratic and Labour Party*, London 1977, 13–17.

2. Cf. for an example of lay and lower clergy alliance against a bishop with ethnarchic ambitions, *Northern Star*, 8 April 1905; *Freeman's Journal*, 8 March 1905.

3. A. Gramsci, *Selections from the Prison Notebooks*, London 1971, 151, on primacy of the political party.

4. B. Farrell (ed.), *The Irish Parliamentary Tradition*, Dublin 1973, 13–25.

5. Farrell, 13–20.

6. Farrell, 224–5, where Lyons argues somewhat similarly.

7. T.W. Moody and L. Ó Broin, 'Selected Documents: XXXII, the IRB Supreme Council, 1868–78', *Irish Historical Studies*, XIX, No. 75 (March 1975), 286–332, at 298.

8. A.J. Ward, 'Parliamentary Procedures and the Machinery of Government in Ireland', *Irish University Review*, IV, No. 2 (Autumn 1974), 222–43; T. Garvin, *The Irish Senate*, Dublin 1969.

9. B. Chubb, 'Going About Persecuting Civil Servants: The Role of the Irish Parliamentary Representative', *Political Studies*, XI, No. 3 (1963), 272–86.

10. F.H. O'Donnell, *A History of the Irish Parliamentary Party*, II, 131.

11. *Dáil Debates*, 14 October 1931, 51.

12. *Dáil Debates*, 10 November 1927, 1271.

13. *Dáil Debates*, 23 November 1927, 1796–7.

14. *Dáil Debates*, 11 October 1927, 54.

15. NLI MS 17441, McGarrity Papers.

16. Cf. PROD 2B 82 119, Part III, 61.

17. S. Edmonds, *The Gun, the Law and the Irish People*, Tralee 1971, 198.

18. J. Kelly, *Orders for the Captain?*, Dublin 1971, *passim*.

19. *Irish Press*, 26 May 1976. In 1972, Fianna Fáil was still bedevilled by a 'swing' group in its electoral base which made its support at the polls contingent on a more aggressive posture on the Northern issue by the Fianna Fáil leadership; of loyal FF voters, 14 per cent wanted a 'harder line' on the North, but of occasional FF voters, 28 per cent wanted a tougher stance. The figure for the electorate as a whole was 18 per cent. (Information courtesy of William Beamish, Politics Department, UCD, derived from a reanalysis of the Larsen/Raven survey of 1972.)

20. Lecky, I, 357–67.

21. F.G. *James, Ireland and the Empire, 1688–1770*, Cambridge 1973, 51–82.

22. Ibid., 138. Cf. R.B. *MacDowell, Irish Public Opinion, 1750–1800*, London 1944, 9–26.

23. James, 260.

24. Brady, *Police and Government*; Broeker, *Rural Disorder*, both *passim*.

25. J. Bulpitt, 'The Politicisation of the Periphery: United Kingdom Politics, 1870–1930', paper presented to the European Consortium for Political Research Workshop on Nationalism and Regional Movements in Western Europe, University of Strathclyde, January 1978, 9.

26. R.M. Martin, *Ireland Before and After the Union*, London 1848, 274.

27. O. MacDonagh, *Ireland*, 34.

28. MacDonagh, 35.

29. Bulpitt, 6.

30. *Census, 1911*, General Report, 9–15; R. B. O'Brien, *Dublin Castle and the Irish People*, Dublin 1909, 78–9, 164–8, 199–200; R.B. MacDowell, *The Irish Administration, 1801–1914*, London 1964, 46–7.

31. Cf. for example M.S. Grindle, *Bureaucrats, Politicians and Peasants in Mexico*, Berkeley 1977, 177; on Tammany, G. Myers, *The History of Tammany Hall*, New York 1971.

32. B. Chubb, *The Government and Politics of Ireland*, Stanford 1969, 218–46 and 295–312.

33. R. Fanning, *The Irish Department of Finance 1922–1958*, Dublin 1978, 1–29.

34. Chubb, 269–94.

35. *The Irish Times*, 30 June 1934.

36. John Garvin, interview, RTÉ Radio, 12 August 1975.

37. P. Sacks, *The Donegal Mafia*, New Haven 1976; M. Bax, *Harpstrings and Confessions*, Assen 1976.

38. Sacks, 209.

39. Bax, *passim* and 73–7.

40. J. Raven and C. Whelan, *Political Culture in Ireland*, Dublin 1976, 25–32.

41. A. Malone, 'Party Government in the Irish Free State', *Political Science Quarterly*, XLIV (1929), 363–78, at 363.

42. SPO DE 2/443.

43. E. Barker, *Ireland in the Last Fifty Years*, Oxford 1919, 122.

44. Cf. R. Fanning, 'Leadership and Transition from the Politics of Revolution to the Politics of Party: The Example of Ireland 1914–1939', paper given at the Fourteenth International Congress of the Historical Sciences, San Francisco, 1975.

45. C. Brinton, *Anatomy of Revolution*, New York 1965, 119–20.

46. L. Ó Broin, 'Joseph Brennan, Civil Servant Extraordinary', *Studies*, LXVI (Spring 1977), 25–37.

47. Fanning, *Finance*, 178–86.

48. *Dáil Debates*, 1 March 1922, 158.

49. Ibid., 161.

50. SPO CAB S.6490; Connolly memoir, 497.

51. Connolly, 497.

52. Ibid., 497–8.

53. Ibid., 499.

54. Ibid., 573.

55. Gallagher, *Electoral Support for Irish Political Parties*, 21.

56. Fanning, *Finance*, 270–71.

57. SPO CAB S.6490.

58. A.S. Cohan, *Irish Political Elite*, Dublin 1972, *passim*.

59. T. Garvin, 'Continuity and Change in Irish Electoral Politics, 1923–1969', *Economic and Social Review*, III (April 1972), 359–72.

60. Private source.

61. G. Sartori, 'From the Sociology of Politics to Political Sociology', in S.M. Lipset (ed.), *Politics and the Social Sciences*, London 1969, 65–100.

Chapter 12. Some Comparative Perspectives (PAGES 226–237)

1. S.M. Lipset, *Political Man*, New York 1963, 27–63.

2. Lipset, 70–3.

3. P. Cutright, 'National Political Development: Measurement and Analysis', *American Sociological Review*, XXVII (1963), 253–64; D.E. Neubauer,

'Some Conditions of Democracy', *American Political Science Review*, LXI (1967), 1002–9; R. Dahl, *Polyarchy*, New Haven 1971; R.W. Jackman, *Politics and Social Inequality*, New York 1975.

4. Neubauer, 1007.

5. F. Munger, *The Legitimacy of Opposition*, Beverly Hills and London 1976, 11–12. Due, no doubt, to bad visibility conditions in the Celtic twilight, Lipset includes Ireland in some of his tables and omits it from others.

6. B. Russett *et al.*, *World Handbook of Political and Social Indicators*, New Haven 1964, 51–3, 108–10, 155–7, 219–20 and 239–40; C.L. Taylor *et al.*, *World Handbook . . .*, second edition, New Haven 1972, 271–4.

7. Cf. Whyte, 'Ireland: Politics Without Social Bases', *passim.*

8. Lipset and Rokkan, 'Cleavage Structures', *passim.*

9. Cf. in particular R. Alford and R. Friedland, 'Nations, Parties and Participation: A Critique of Political Sociology', *Theory and Society*, 1 (1974), 307–28.

10. Lipset and Rokkan, 9.

11. Ibid., 13.

12. Ibid., 14.

13. Ibid., 14.

14. Ibid., 15.

15. Ibid., 21.

16. Ibid., 50.

17. John Coakley, 'Irish Political Parties and the Irish Party Systems', National Institute for Higher Education, Limerick mimeo, n.d. (1976).

18. A. Orridge, 'Explanations of Irish Nationalism: A Review and Some Suggestions', *Journal of the Conflict Research Society*, I, 1 (August 1977), 29–57, at 49. James Scott makes the related point that the evolution of peasant radicalism does not consist of substituting new ideas for old but of adding new ideas to older ones; see his 'Revolution in the Revolution: Peasants and Commissars', *Theory and Society*, VII, Nos. 1 and 2 (January–March 1979), 97–134.

19. The 'blended ideology' phrase is Dahl's; see *Polyarchy*, 43.

20. On belief systems, P. Converse, 'The Nature of Belief Systems in Mass Publics', in D. Apter (ed.), *Ideology and Discontent*, Glencoe 1964, 206–61.

21. S. Rokkan, *Citizens, Elections, Parties*, Oslo 1970, 126.

22. T. Garvin, 'Political Cleavages, Party Politics and Urbanisation in Ireland: The Case of the Periphery-Dominated Centre', *European Journal of Political Research*, II (1974), 307–27.

23. Coakley, 'Irish Political Parties'; for a sophisticated analysis of the interactions between the nations of the islands of Britain and Ireland and those of the colonies descended from British and Irish settlers, see J.G.A. Pocock, 'The Limits and Divisions of British History', Glasgow; University of Strathclyde, Center for the Study of Public Policy, 1979.

INDEX